PROPORTIONALIT
CONSTITUTIONAL Cl

Although the most important constitutional doctrine worldwide, a thorough cultural and historical examination of proportionality has not taken place until now. This comparison of proportionality with its counterpart in American constitutional law – balancing – shows how culture and history can create deep differences in seemingly similar doctrines. Owing to its historical origin in Germany, proportionality carries to this day a pro-rights association, while the opposite is the case for balancing. In addition, European legal and political culture has shaped proportionality as intrinsic to the state's role in realizing shared values, while in the USA a suspicion-based legal and political culture has shaped balancing in more pragmatic and instrumental terms. Although many argue that the USA should converge on proportionality, the book shows that a complex web of cultural associations make it an unlikely prospect.

MOSHE COHEN-ELIYA is Dean of the Law School of the Academic Center of Law and Business, Israel.

IDDO PORAT is a senior lecturer at the Law School of the Academic Center of Law and Business, Israel.

CAMBRIDGE STUDIES IN CONSTITUTIONAL LAW

The aim of this series is to produce leading monographs in constitutional law. All areas of constitutional law and public law fall within the ambit of the series, including human rights and civil liberties law, administrative law, as well as constitutional theory and the history of constitutional law. A wide variety of scholarly approaches is encouraged, with the governing criterion being simply that the work is of interest to an international audience. Thus, works concerned with only one jurisdiction will be included in the series as appropriate while, at the same time, the series will include works which are explicitly comparative or theoretical – or both. The series editors likewise welcome proposals that work at the intersection of constitutional and international law, or that seek to bridge the gaps between civil law systems, the US, and the common law jurisdictions of the Commonwealth.

PROPORTIONALITY AND CONSTITUTIONAL CULTURE

MOSHE COHEN-ELIYA

and

IDDO PORAT

CAMBRIDGE
UNIVERSITY PRESS

CAMBRIDGE UNIVERSITY PRESS
Cambridge, New York, Melbourne, Madrid, Cape Town,
Singapore, São Paulo, Delhi, Mexico City

Cambridge University Press
The Edinburgh Building, Cambridge CB2 8RU, UK

Published in the United States of America by Cambridge University Press, New York

www.cambridge.org
Information on this title: www.cambridge.org/9781107021860

First published 2013

Printed and bound in the United Kingdom by the MPG Books Group

A catalogue record for this publication is available from the British Library

Library of Congress Cataloging-in-Publication Data
Cohen-Eliya, Moshe.
Proportionality and constitutional culture / Moshe Cohen-Eliya and Iddo Porat.
pages cm. – (Cambridge studies in constitutional law)
ISBN 978-1-107-02186-0 (Hardback) – ISBN 978-1-107-60571-8 (Paperback)
1. Constitutional law. 2. Proportionality in law. I. Porat, Iddo. II. Title.
K3165.C54 2013
342.001–dc23
2013001250

ISBN 978-1-107-02186-0 Hardback
ISBN 978-1-107-60571-8 Paperback

To our beloved parents:
Nissim and Rachel Cohen
Yehuda and Dina Porat

CONTENTS

ACKNOWLEDGMENTS

It is a happy task to thank the people and institutions who helped us along the way.

Parts of the book were written during our sabbatical years: for Moshe Cohen-Eliya, as a Fellow at the Edmond J. Safra Center for Ethics at Harvard University, 2009–10, and for Iddo Porat, as Visiting Professor at San Diego Law School, 2008–9. We wish to thank these institutions for the scholarly environment and generous funds they provided for the research. We wish to thank the Academic Center for Law and Business, our home institution, for providing each of us with generous sabbatical and research funds. The Max Planck Institute for Comparative Public Law and International Law at Heidelberg and the Canadian Government Faculty Research Program also provided financial support for earlier stages of this research.

Different parts of the book and the articles on which it is based were presented at the following faculty seminars and colloquia, and we are grateful to the participants for their helpful comments and suggestions: the Harvard–Stanford International Junior Faculty Forum at Stanford University, 2008; the University of California, Los Angeles, Faculty Seminar, 2009; the Annual Conference of the Israeli Association for Law and Society, the Hebrew University, 2009; the international workshop on Rights, Balancing, and Proportionality, Tel Aviv, January 2009; the Faculty Seminar, University of San Diego School of Law, 2009 and 2010; Faculty Fellows' Seminar, Edmond J. Safra Center for Ethics, Harvard University, 2010; the Law Faculty Colloquium, Stellenbosch University, South Africa, 2011; and the Jerusalem Political Philosophy Forum, the Hebrew University in Jerusalem, 2012.

Our special thanks go to those who read earlier versions of the chapters of this book or of the articles on which they are based and provided us with invaluable comments: Lawrence Alexander, Robert Alexy, William Alford, Aharon Barak, Daphne Barak-Erez, David Beatty, Eric Beerbohm, Yishai Blank, Tino Celluar, Hanoch Dagan, David

Dyzenhaus, Nir Eyal, Richard Fallon, Lawrence Friedman, Stephen Gardbaum, Thomas Grey, Dieter Grimm, Alon Harel, Ran Hirschl, Duncan Kennedy, Mattias Kumm, Bert Lazerow, Pierre Legrand, Lawrence Lessig, Sergio López Ayllón, Jonathan Marks, Barak Medina, Georg Nolte, Geo Quinot, Mike Ramsey, Tommie Shelby, Alec Stone Sweet, Mark Tushnet, and Daniel Viehoff.

For a wonderful editing job we wish to thank Dana Meshulam and, for footnote editing, Michele Manspeizer. To Stefan Kus our thanks for excellent research assistance on German public law. Above all, we thank our families, the anchors in our lives and the sources of our pride and joy, for their support and patience during this long process and for being who they are: Iris Eliya-Cohen, Naomi, Uriya, Eitan, and Assaf, and Natalie Steinberg-Porat, Yoav, Yael, Uri, and Itay.

In this book we draw on several of our prior writings. Chapter 1 draws in a small part on "American balancing and German proportionality: the historical origins" (2010) 8 Inst. J. of Const. L. 263. Chapter 2 draws heavily on the same article. Chapter 3 relies heavily on "The hidden foreign law debate in Heller: proportionality approach in American constitutional law" (2009) 46 San Diego Law Review 367. Chapter 5 draws on segments of our "Judicial minimalism and the double effect of rules and principles" (2012) 26 Canadian Journal of Law and Jurisprudence 283, and Chapter 6 draws heavily on "Proportionality and the culture of justification" (2011) 59 American Journal of Comparative Law 463. We thank the publishers for their permission to draw liberally from these pieces.

~

Introduction

American constitutional lawyers have been asking themselves in recent years more and more whether US constitutional law is as relevant and influential in the global scene as before.[1] They are worried at what some term the waning influence of American constitutional law, and the apparent rise in influence of other legal systems – in particular Germany, Canada and the European Union – as the focal point for inspiration and emulation by emerging constitutional systems.[2] This question is related to two other questions that have preoccupied American constitutional law in the past decade or so – whether American constitutional law is exceptional in being fundamentally different than other constitutional systems,[3] and whether American constitutional lawyers and judges should look at foreign law when interpreting and applying the American Constitution.[4]

---

[1] See, e.g., Adam Liptak, "US court is now guiding fewer nations" (2008) *New York Times*, September 18, 2008 (quoting Princeton Professor Anne-Marie Slaughter: "[O]ne of our great exports used to be constitutional law. We are losing one of the greatest bully pulpits we have ever had.").

[2] David Law, "The declining influence of the United States Constitution" (2012) 87 N.Y.U.L. Rev. 762.

[3] Such resistance is often termed "American exceptionalism," a coinage that can be traced back to Alexis De Tocqueville, *Democracy in America* (J.P. Mayer ed., George Lawrence trans., New York: Anchor Books, 1969) 455–6 (1835). The literature on American exceptionalism is vast. See, e.g., Steven G. Calabresi, "'A shining city on a hill': American exceptionalism and the Supreme Court's practice of relying on foreign law" (2006) 86 B.U. L. Rev. 1335; Harold Hongju Koh, "On American exceptionalism" (2003) 55 Stan. L. Rev. 1479, 1483; Michael Ignatieff (ed.), *American Exceptionalism and Human Rights* (Princeton, NJ: Princeton University Press, 2005); Georg Nolte (ed.), *European and US Constitutionalism* (Cambridge: Cambridge University Press, 2005) 49.

[4] Compare Anne-Marie Slaughter, "A global community of courts" (2003) 44 Harv. Int'l L.J. 191, 201–2; Jeremy Waldron, "Foreign law and the modern ius gentium" (2005) 119 Harv. L. Rev. 129 with Richard Posner, "No thanks, we already have our own laws" (July–August 2004) Legal Aff. 40; Charles Fried, "Scholars and judges: reason and power" (2000) 23 Harv. J.L. & Pub. Pol'y 807, 819.

While these questions seem to preoccupy recent American constitutional literature, an entirely different set of questions dominates European constitutional literature. European constitutional lawyers are concerned predominantly with one thing – proportionality! Whether you are a German constitutional lawyer, an Italian, a French or an English one, you will invariably have been debating and talking about the proportionality doctrine as part of your work. Indeed not only if you are a European scholar. This would probably be true if you were a Canadian, Australian, Indian, Israeli, or a Chinese lawyer. Almost every discussion of constitutional law in these countries seems to touch at some point on proportionality, and the academic literature on proportionality has by now spawned a plethora of articles and books.[5]

Proportionality is a German-bred doctrine that structures the way judges decide conflicts between rights and other rights or interests, basically requiring that any interference with rights be justified by not being disproportionate. It consists of four (or three, depending on your perspective) stages: whenever the government infringes upon a constitutionally protected right, the proportionality principle requires that the government show, first, that its objective is legitimate and important; second, that the means chosen were rationally connected to achieve that objective (suitability); third, that no less drastic means were available (necessity); and fourth, that the benefit from realizing the objective exceeds the harm to the right (proportionality in the strict sense). In addition to its simplicity, two important features of proportionality also stand out: it is standard-based rather than categorical, and it is results-oriented rather than being a formal and conceptual doctrine.

Due in part to these characteristics, proportionality has spread dramatically into national legal systems far and wide and is considered to be one of the most prominent instances of the successful migration of constitutional ideas. As we will show in Chapter 1, within a few decades, it traveled from its original birthplace in Germany, through the

---

[5] To mention just a few: Robert Alexy, *A Theory of Constitutional Rights* (Oxford: Oxford University Press, Julian Rivers trans., 2002) 66; Nicholas Emiliou, *The Principle of Proportionality in European Law; A Comparative Study* (London: Kluwer, 1996); David Beatty, *The Ultimate Rule of Law* (Oxford: Oxford University Press, 2004); Grégoire Webber, *The Negotiable Constitution: On the Limitation of Rights* (Cambridge: Cambridge University Press, 2009); Aharon Barak, *Proportionality: Constitutional Rights and their Limitations* (Cambridge: Cambridge University Press, 2012); Aaron Baker, *Proportionality under the UK Human Rights Act (Human Rights Law in Perspective)* (Oxford: Hart Publishing, 2012).

jurisprudence of the European Court of Human Rights (ECtHR), to all of Western Europe and Canada, followed by its widespread adoption in Eastern Europe, Latin America, and many legal systems elsewhere, such as South Africa, Israel, and India. In most of the adopting legal systems, moreover, proportionality has been incorporated as a central method of constitutional analysis. It is viewed as infusing coherence into the entire constitutional system, applicable to all types of rights and interests, and spreading sometimes even to other branches of the law.

The two constitutional discourses – the American and the European/ global one – seem therefore almost disconnected. The literature on proportionality usually does not draw on US experience and literature, as US law does not use the proportionality test, and the American discussion on foreign law and on its exceptionalism usually does not discuss proportionality and, instead, concentrates on differences between the USA and Europe in terms of specific rights and their interpretation. Indeed proportionality, despite its immense importance outside the USA, hardly appears as a central issue in American legal academic literature.[6]

This book is an attempt to bridge this gap and talk to both the European and American audiences. It does so by comparing proportionality to its counterpart in American constitutional law – balancing. While not as structured as its European counterpart, and consisting of only one stage the American balancing test which, as its name suggests, consists of balancing rights with other rights and interest, captures the same basic function as proportionality, and is identical with the most important stage of proportionality (proportionality in the strict sense).

The book attempts to do something that is missing in both American and European current literature. It seeks to provide a comprehensive and culturally sensitive comparison between these two pivotal doctrines, including a discussion of their analytical similarities, historical origins, and embeddedness within their respective political and philosophical culture – the US culture (for balancing) and the German culture (for proportionality).

This comparison reveals fascinating lessons on the influence of context, history, and culture on the understanding of these two central legal

---

[6] For rare such instances see Vicki C. Jackson, "Being proportional about proportionality" (2004) 21 Const. Commentary 803; Alec Stone Sweet and Jud Mathews, "Proportionality, balancing and global constitutionalism" (2008) 19 Colum. J. Transnat'l L.72, 162; Alec Stone Sweet and Jud Mathews, "All things in proportion? American rights doctrine and the problem of balancing" (2011) 60 Emory L.J. 101.

concepts and, conversely, also illuminates the differences between the two constitutional cultures as they are reflected through the differences between the two doctrines. Our conclusion would be that despite important analytical similarities, legal, political and philosophical culture in America and Germany, bring about quite a different understanding and role for balancing and proportionality within their respective cultures.

The comparison also reveals important lessons with regard to projects of universalization and convergence in constitutional law and with regard to the unresolved tension in constitutional law between universalism and particularism. Proportionality is the archetypical universal doctrine of human rights adjudication. Although obviously varying in different countries and settings, its main aspiration and leading characteristic is its ability to spread and its universal applicability and straightforward structure. Going back to the issues that preoccupy American constitutional lawyers, American exceptionalism, and the wariness that the USA is losing its constitutional dominance in the global arena, these issues are related to the American reluctance to adopt proportionality and join the global move towards convergence and coherence around this doctrine. The fact that the USA does not adopt proportionality could be one of the reasons for its waning influence on other constitutional systems, as they cannot communicate with American jurisprudence in the same constitutional language. Particularly owing to the fact that the USA does have a similar doctrine – balancing – universalists see this American reluctance as based on parochialism, isolationism, and the maintaining of unnecessary barriers for US global integration. Some early signs on the side of the judiciary may also attest to a willingness to see American law as already comprising proportionality, therefore making its adoption much easier. As US Supreme Court Justice Breyer wrote in 2008: "Contrary to the majority's unsupported suggestion that this sort of 'proportionality' approach is unprecedented, the Court has applied it in various constitutional contexts, including election-law cases, speech cases, and due process cases."[7]

Our analysis, however, stresses the embeddedness of both balancing and proportionality within their respective legal and political cultures and, therefore, can both provide reasons why the convergence has not occurred as of yet, and also information about the difficulties of such

---

[7] *District of Columbia* v. *Heller*, 554 US 570, 690 (2008) (Breyer, J., dissenting).

possible convergence, and the possible ramifications it might have for the adopting legal system.

Before moving on to discuss the content of the various chapters we wish to make some preliminary points about the structure of the book and some of the choices that we have made. Several chapters of this book are based on our joint studies on proportionality and balancing over the past few years. We realized at a certain point that what we have produced amounts to a coherent enough message so that we should make an effort to synthesize our work into a more comprehensive narrative. The book thus has the quality of a discussion in layers. Some of the chapters are interrelated and sometimes overlap rather than being hermetically separate, and each looks at the subject-matter from a different angle and adds another layer to the overall picture. Secondly, in constructing this account, we have chosen to concentrate on constitutional systems that best exemplify the inner logic of the two constitutional cultures that we investigate: the USA, on the one hand, and Germany in particular, on the other, but also the Canadian and Israeli legal systems, which strongly manifest the logic of the European-based system. We therefore, necessarily, disregard many of the different contexts in which proportionality is set and the important variances between them. Finally, we do not wish to deny the importance of other, more normative, types of arguments regarding the question of adopting proportionality and its advantages and disadvantages, such as those relying on democracy, judicial legitimacy, and the distinctiveness of rights and interests.[8] Our approach and its emphasis are simply different, in that we stress the crucial relevance of context and social and historical background in understanding the transplantation and migration of constitutional concepts and principles.

After describing in Chapter 1 the rapid spread of proportionality and showing it to be analytically similar to the American doctrine of balancing, we begin in Chapter 2 the process of contextualizing the two concepts by discussing the impact of their different historical origins. We examine the emergence of proportionality in nineteenth-century Prussian administrative law and balancing in early-twentieth-century

---

[8] Grégoire Webber, "Proportionality, balancing, and the cult of constitutional rights scholarship" (2010) 23 (1) Can. J.L. & Jur. 179–202; Stavros Tsakyrakis, "Proportionality: an assault on human rights?" (2010) 7 ICON 468; Aileen McHarg, "Reconciling human rights and the public interest" (1999) 62 MLR 671, 673; Mattias Kumm, "Political liberalism and the structures of rights," in George Pavlakos (ed.), *Law, Rights and Discourse: The Legal Philosophy of Robert Alexy* (Oxford: Hart Publishing, 2007) 141; Tor Inge Harbo, "The function of the proportionality principle in EU law" (2010) 16 E.L.J. 158, 166 ff.

US constitutional law, showing the widely diverging origins of the two concepts. Proportionality, for instance, originated as an administrative law principle and was only tangentially (if at all) related to private law; balancing, in contrast, developed as part of private law and only later extended into public law. Proportionality emerged as part of an attempt to protect individual rights, whereas balancing was developed to serve the exact opposite purpose: as a check on what was considered the Supreme Court's overzealous rights protection during the Lochner era. Moreover, proportionality evolved in the framework of the formalistic and doctrinal jurisprudence of the Prussian administrative courts and was not part of any anti-formalistic legal movement, unlike balancing, which was a prominent aspect of the Progressivists' anti-formalism revolution.

Chapter 3 deals with culture, setting balancing and proportionality in their political cultures in the USA and Germany, respectively. In contrast to the American atomized conception of the self, German political theory emphasizes the embeddedness of the person in a community that shares common values and expresses solidarity towards all members of that community. Furthermore, American political culture is based on the idea of state neutrality and a deep suspicion of governmental intervention, whereas German political culture assigns the state the far more ambitious purpose of realizing a set of comprehensive social values. Accordingly, the role of proportionality in German constitutionalism is far more central than the role of balancing in US law. Proportionality facilitates the promotion of shared social values and interests as the main mechanism for solving conflicts between values and interests. Yet public wariness of the judiciary and government has led to a far more minor and subsidiary role for balancing in American constitutionalism, where it is limited by a more categorical approach towards individual rights.

In Chapter 4, we discuss constitutional design. In line with several established accounts, we categorize German constitutional design as impact-based and American constitutional design as intent-based. An impact-based constitutional model focuses on assessing and optimizing the constitutional consequences of governmental action, whereas an intent-based model centers on classifying the intention or motive behind governmental action as either permissible or impermissible. Proportionality is a central and inherent mechanism of the impact-based model, since it directly addresses the impact of governmental action. The intent-based model, in contrast, is categorical in nature and, thus, is seemingly altogether incompatible with balancing. But, as we show in this chapter, the US intent-based system in fact allows for balancing to be used in certain contexts. We identify three forms of balancing in US constitutional law, beginning with balancing as a means of smoking-out illegitimate government intentions, moving to balancing as an exception to categorical rules, and then analyzing a third type of balancing that we identify: uncovering what we term indifference to the violation of a constitutional norm.

In Chapter 5, we discuss the correlation between balancing and epistemological skepticism and between proportionality and epistemological optimism. In the USA, balancing is often associated with skepticism about human rationality, and with minimalism and pragmatism. Several prominent American advocates of balancing, such as Sunstein, Posner, and, more recently, Chief Justice Roberts, support balancing on these grounds. They conceive it as a legal reasoning that is minimalist in the sense of being limited to the facts of the case at hand and avoiding grand theory, as opposed to sweeping theory and broad generalization, which are associated with judicial maximalism and judicial rules. Proportionality, in contrast, is associated in Europe with notions of expansive interpretation, optimism regarding human rationality and capabilities, and lofty theories such as substantive democracy and universal rights. These differing associations impact how balancing and proportionality are construed, as well as how they are developed in their respective legal cultures, ultimately shaping their meanings as well.

Advancing to a more global level, Chapter 6 argues that proportionality epitomizes the emerging global legal culture, which, following Étienne Mureinik's lead, we term a culture of justification.[9] American balancing, in contrast, is embedded in a political culture that we characterize as a culture of authority. A culture of justification is typical of European democracies – for example, Germany – and Commonwealth countries – such as the UK, Canada, New Zealand, and South Africa – as well as non-European countries, such as Israel. At its core, this culture requires that the government provide substantive justification for all of its actions, in that it must show the rationality and reasonableness of those actions and the tradeoffs they necessarily entail – in other words, the proportionality of its actions. We identify several characteristics of Western constitutional systems that have developed since the Second World War that foster a culture of justification. These include: a broad conception of rights; a constitutional interpretation approach that

---

[9] Étienne Mureinik, "A bridge to where? Introducing the Interim Bill of Rights" (1994) 10 S. Afr. J. Hum. Rts. 31.

emphasizes fundamental principles and values rather than text; few barriers to substantive review; and no legal "black holes" (areas and actions with respect to which the government is not required to provide justification). Most significant to our discussion is that this type of constitutionalism involves two-tiered judicial review. The first stage focuses on the identification of an infringement of a right, while the second, more crucial, stage of review assesses the government's justification of the infringement.

The culture of authority that is the setting for American balancing is grounded in the government's authority to exercise its power. In this culture, the legitimacy and legality of government action derive from the fact that the actor is authorized to act. Public law, under this conception, focuses on demarcating the borders of public action and ensuring that decisions are made by those authorized to make them. It is thus characterized by categories and bright-line rules and distinctions. Given this, the notion of balancing is in fact foreign to the culture of authority. Consequently, it has been marginalized in this culture and has evolved as a pragmatic doctrine which functions only as a "safety valve" – providing solutions to conflicts that a categorical system cannot adequately contend with.

The discussion in this chapter closes by framing the gradual shift towards proportionality and the culture of justification as a move towards an administrative model of constitutional law. We term this process the "administratization" of constitutional law.

Lastly, in Chapter 7, we consider three possible consequences that incorporating proportionality could have for the domestic constitutional law of the adopting legal systems, particularly in the American context. The first such effect could be the emergence of a "race to the top" in terms of the expansiveness of the judicial construction of rights protection. With constitutional judges increasingly regarding themselves as members of what Anne-Marie Slaughter calls "a global community of courts,"[10] they could tend to compete over who provides more expansive or advanced rights protection. Second, the proportionality doctrine may be accompanied by a certain amount of cultural baggage, "German baggage" to be precise, when it enters the adopting legal system. Examples from Canada and Israel are shown to substantiate this point. Third, proportionality might have an "imperialistic" effect, in that it may

---

[10] Anne-Marie Slaughter, "Judicial globalization" (2000) 40 Va. J. Int'l L. 1103.

set aside and replace local constitutional doctrines. We do not propose that the importation of proportionality will generate immediate change to the importing legal culture, nor that it will lead to an embracing of values associated with proportionality, at least not in their entirety. Nevertheless, it is possible to discern certain such effects in systems that have adopted proportionality, and the same could possibly apply to the USA were it to eventually adopt proportionality as well.

This book, although discussing doctrines, is more a book on political and legal cultures and their interaction with doctrine. Context and culture should not be overemphasized, for that could lead to conservatism and aversion to change. Yet in view of the sweeping and far-reaching movement towards universalism in modern constitutional law, this book represents a call to take context and culture into consideration and to inquire into their effects.

1

The global spread of proportionality and some analytical similarities with balancing

We begin this chapter by briefly describing the astonishing spread of proportionality across legal systems in the latter half of the twentieth century, which often occurred without much debate or even awareness in the adopting legal systems.[1] We then show how the USA has remained the exception to this trend, in resisting the adoption of proportionality. But the USA has a similar doctrine of its own: the doctrine of balancing. We argue that there are no substantial analytical differences between these two doctrines. Thus, any attempt to resist proportionality in American constitutional law cannot be grounded on claims of such divergence. This discussion paves the way for our cultural account of the differences between proportionality and balancing, which is the heart of this book.

The spread of proportionality

As Alec Stone Sweet has colorfully described, proportionality "exhibits a viral quality, spreading relatively quickly from one jurisdiction to another."[2] Proportionality first emerged as a doctrine in nineteenth-century Prussian administrative law, in the jurisprudence of the Prussian Supreme Administrative Court, which was later incorporated into German administrative law.[3] Only after the Second World War did the

---

[1] We do not seek to explain at this stage the reasons for this phenomenon. We leave this to Chapter 6, where we argue that the rapid spread of proportionality can be accounted for by the rise of a global constitutional culture, which we term, following Mureinik, a "culture of justification." See Étienne Mureinik, "A bridge to where? Introducing the Interim Bill of Rights" (1994) 10 S. Afr. J. Hum. Rts. 31.

[2] Alec Stone Sweet and Jud Mathews, "Proportionality, balancing and global constitutionalism" (2008) 19 Colum. J. Transnat'l L. 72, 162.

[3] See Chapter 2. See also *ibid.* 102 n.71 (noting that "administrative courts in the other German states soon began following Prussia's lead, striking down police measures" on the ground that they are disproportional).

doctrine begin to spread, but once it did the process quickly gathered steam. The first stage was the gradual internal migration of proportionality from German administrative law to German constitutional law, in the late 1950s and early 1960s, through several landmark Federal Constitutional Court decisions.[4] Soon thereafter, proportionality became the central doctrine in German constitutional law, applied in practically every leading case.[5]

The prominence of German constitutional jurisprudence within European Union law has been a central factor in the expansion of proportionality beyond Germany and its adoption, first, by the European Court of Justice (ECJ) in 1970[6] and, then, by the European Court of Human Rights (ECtHR) in 1976.[7] These were critical milestones in the migration of proportionality. The weighty status of ECJ and, especially, ECtHR jurisprudence in Europe led, in turn, to the spread of proportionality to practically every Western European jurisdiction during the 1980s and then, in the 1990s, to Eastern European states.[8] The rapid and sweeping adoption of proportionality in Western Europe was due to both a natural process of migration of ideas and rights jurisprudence as well as the particular authority accorded to ECtHR jurisprudence by the national constitutional courts. In the UK, for example, the initially strong resistance to proportionality was overcome with the enactment of the Human Rights Act (HCA) in 1998, which instructed UK courts to ensure the compatibility of legislation with the European Convention of Human Rights. This paved the way for proportionality to become an integral part of UK jurisprudence.[9]

---

[4] *Lüth*, BVerfGE 7, 198 (1958); the *Pharmacy Case* BVerfGE 7, 377 (1958).

[5] For a thorough review of cases exhibiting proportionality in German constitutional law, see Donald P. Kommers, *The Constitutional Jurisprudence of the Federal Republic of Germany* (Durham, NC: Duke University Press, 2nd edn., 1997) 33. See also our discussions of the use of proportionality in German law in Chapters 3 and 4.

[6] Internationale Handelsgesellschaft 11/70 [1970] ECR 1125.

[7] *Handyside* v. *The United Kingdom* (1976) 24 Eur. Ct. HR (Ser. A) 23 at para. 49.

[8] Several recent seminal works, most notably by Aharon Barak and Alec Stone Sweet, have documented the spread of proportionality across Western Europe to countries such as Belgium, France, Greece, Italy, Portugal, Spain, and Switzerland. See Aharon Barak, *Proportionality: Constitutional Rights and their Limitations* (Cambridge: Cambridge University Press, 2012) 181–208; Stone Sweet and Mathews, "Proportionality, balancing and global constitutionalism" 75.

[9] See Baker, *Proportionality under the UK Human Rights Act* (pre-released abstract: "Prior to the UK's adoption of the Human Rights Act 1998 (HRA), proportionality enjoyed only sparing patronage by UK courts, and then typically only when EU obligations required it.

In Eastern Europe, following the collapse of the Soviet Bloc, proportionality was quickly embraced, with some countries, such as Albania, Moldavia, and Romania, explicitly including the doctrine in the text of their newly adopted constitutions.[10] Moreover, German constitutional law and ECtHR jurisprudence also had an impact outside Europe and thus facilitated the spread of proportionality into Asia (for example, to Hong Kong, South Korea, and India) and to Latin America (for example, to Columbia, Peru, Brazil, and Mexico).[11]

Two other bodies of law that have contributed to the global diffusion of proportionality are international law and Canadian constitutional jurisprudence. Proportionality has evolved into a general principle in international law.[12] It has become a central doctrine in humanitarian law through the interpretation of the Additional Protocol of the Geneva Convention.[13] It has also been very prominent in the interpretation of the application of the International Covenant on Civil and Political Rights (ICCPR, 1966) and has recently emerged as a central element in

---

The HRA, however, by making the ECtHR enforceable in UK courts, has introduced proportionality into UK public law to a degree some have called irreversible. Recent empirical research has indicated that no other principle has been more important in resolving conflicts between the interests of security and human rights. Proportionality has been the deciding factor in cases involving derogations from the ECtHR based on a state of emergency, clashes between ECtHR rights, the treatment of immigrants, the wearing of religious apparel, and the rights of parents over frozen embryos."); Alan Brady, *Proportionality and Deference under the UK Human Rights Act: An Institutionally Sensitive Approach* (New York: Cambridge University Press, 2012); Aaron Baker, "Proportionality, not strict, scrutiny: against a US suspect classifications model under Article 14 ECtHR in the UK" (2008) 56(4) Am. J. Comp. L. 847; Aaron Baker, "Proportionality and employment discrimination in the UK" (2008) 37(4) Industrial L.J. 305. Also see Margit Cohn, "Legal transplant chronicles: the evolution of substantive judicial review of the administration in the United Kingdom" (2010) 58 Am. J. Com. L. 583.

[10] Sadurski has documented the entry of proportionality, *inter alia*, into the jurisprudence of Bulgaria, Croatia, Czech Republic, Estonia, Hungary, Lithuania, Poland, Romania, Slovakia, and Slovenia. See Wojciech Sadurski, *Rights before Courts: A Study of Constitutional Courts in The Post-Communist States of Central and Eastern Europe* (Dordrecht: Springer, 2005) 263. Also see Alec Stone Sweet, "Investor–state arbitration: proportionality's new frontier" (2010) 4(1) L. & Ethics Hum. Rts. 46.

[11] Aharon Barak, *Proportionality: Constitutional Rights and their Limitations* 199–202.

[12] Thomas M. Franck, "On proportionality and countermeasures in international law" (2008) 102(4) Am. J. Int'l L. 715; Thomas M. Franck, "Proportionality in international law" (2010) 4 L. & Ethics Hum. Rts. 229.

[13] See Geneva IV, AP I, Art. 51(5)(b), Art. 57(2)(b) (prohibiting attacks expected to cause incidental civilian losses "which would be excessive in relation to the concrete and direct military advantage anticipated"). See also Georg Nolte, "Thick or thin: the principle of proportionality in international humanitarian law" (2010) 4 L. & Ethics Hum. Rts. 243.

the jurisprudence of international commerce institutions, such as the judicial body of the World Trade Organization (WTO, 1995)[14] and the International Center for the Settlement of Investment Disputes (ICSID, 1966).[15]

The adoption of proportionality in Canadian constitutional law in 1986, following the enactment of the Charter of Rights and Freedoms, was also a driving force in the global spread of the doctrine. In the landmark *Oakes* decision, Chief Justice Dickson of the Canadian Supreme Court interpreted Section 1 of the Charter, the "limitations clause," as introducing a proportionality test into rights adjudication.[16] Canadian constitutional proportionality jurisprudence has been a factor in the adoption of proportionality in such Commonwealth countries as New Zealand, after the enactment of its Bill of Rights in 1990,[17] South Africa, in its new constitution,[18] and Australia, in a landmark 1998 decision.[19] Moreover, Canadian jurisprudence also played a pivotal role in the Israeli Supreme Court's adoption of proportionality in its interpretation of the limitations clauses in two 1992 basic laws pertaining to human rights.[20]

What we see, then, is three main axes or focal points to the rapid and comprehensive process by which proportionality spread – German constitutional law, the ECJ and ECtHR jurisprudence, and Canadian constitutional law. Indeed, each contributed to the participation of many other legal systems in this process. Another notable feature of the migration of proportionality has been the relative ease with which it has occurred and the lack of any notable resistance to the doctrine in the adopting legal systems. In fact, in some jurisdictions, proportionality was adopted without any citation of an authority, precedents, or text, as though it needed no particular introduction or justification, yet its adoption was not contested in any significant way.

This type of process was most apparent in the three jurisdictions that have had the greatest impact in the global spread of

---

[14] Axel Desmedt, "Proportionality in WTO law" (2001) 4(3) J. Int. Eco. L. 441.
[15] Stone Sweet, "Investor–state arbitration: proportionality's new frontier."
[16] *R. v. Oakes*, [1986] 1 SCR 103.
[17] *Ministry of Transp. v. Noort*, [1992] 3 NZLR 260, 282–5.
[18] *S. v. Zuma & Others*, 1995 (2) SA 642 (CC).
[19] *Kartinyeri v. Commonwealth* (1998) 152 ALR 540.
[20] CA 6821/93 *United Mizrahi Bank Ltd. v. Migdal Coop. Village* PD 49(4) 221.

proportionality: Germany, the ECJ, and Canada. In Germany, for example, the Federal Constitutional Court ruled in 1965 that the principle of proportionality "follows from the principle of the rule of law [guaranteed in Article 20], even more from the very essence of fundamental rights."[21] Thus, in the very first decisions to introduce proportionality into German constitutional law, no attempt was made to ground it on precedent or text, as the principle was deemed to be flowing naturally from the meaning of rights. Similarly, in the 1970s, the ECJ recognized the principle of proportionality without making reference to any source or authority, as was the case with the Canadian Supreme Court's introduction of proportionality into its constitutional jurisprudence in *Oakes*, where no mention was made of foreign law or any other source in its decision.[22]

We discuss some of the reasons for proportionality's unprecedented success as a migrating doctrine, in Chapters 5 and 7. Suffice it to say for now that this was due to the combination of proportionality's simple structure, the fact that it conforms with the emerging global constitutional culture that we describe in Chapter 5, and the effects of globalization and constitutional emulation, which lead countries to perceive converging over a common template as a benefit.

Resistance to proportionality

Despite its clear allure and formidable global success, one legal system remains unimpressed by proportionality: the American constitutional system. To date, US courts have made practically no use of this doctrine, not even as a comparative point of reference. The only exception, at least in US Supreme Court jurisprudence, are a few brief passages, all written by Justice Breyer, that make mention of proportionality but with no

---

[21] BVerfGE 19, 342, at 348 (1965) as translated by Dieter Grimm, "Proportionality in Canadian and German constitutional law jurisprudence" (2007) 57 U. Toronto L.J. 383, 385–6. According to Grimm, the Court has not "elaborated how this principle flows from the rule of law or the essence of fundamental rights. The reason for this taciturnity may have been that in Germany, as opposed to Canada, in the early years the Court was not aware of the prominent role proportionality would play in the future. When this became apparent, the principle had already been established, so that further reasoning seemed unnecessary." *Ibid.* 386.

[22] For evidence that ECtHR jurisprudence played an implicit role in shaping the influential Oakes test in Canada, see Robert J. Sharpe and Kent Roach, *Brian Dickson: A Judge's Journey* (Toronto: University of Toronto Press, 2003) 334.

attempt to elaborate on it or even draw attention to it.[23] This has apparently warranted no notice by other justices.[24]

The complete disregard of proportionality in the USA is striking, but should come as no surprise, given the traditional US lack of interest in, and even outright resistance to, foreign legal concepts and ideas in constitutional law. The use of foreign law has taken center stage in a heated debate being waged in both the Court and academia. Even in this context, though, there has been relatively little interest in proportionality, and until recently, the literature made only few references to the doctrine.[25]

One possible explanation is that American constitutional law already has a doctrine that is similar to proportionality: balancing. As we show in Chapter 2, balancing bears no relation to proportionality in terms of its genealogy. It has evolved as an internal development of American constitutional law, and to the extent that it received foreign influence, it came from continental private law schools of thought rather than public and administrative law where proportionality has developed. However, as we discuss below, balancing has a striking analytical resemblance to proportionality and has acquired an important position in US constitutional jurisprudence.

Central to the description of balancing in this book is the fact that almost from its first appearance in American constitutional law, up to this day, its explicit use has been met with resistance and objections from judges and law professors alike. The first main round of this struggle occurred in the 1950s and revolved around the application of balancing in First Amendment law, and the second was in the early 1990s, when it came under attack from conservative and formalist justices, such as Antonin Scalia.

---

[23] *District of Columbia* v. *Heller*, 554 US 690. See the discussion in the introduction, at 4. Also see *Nixon* v. *Shrink Mo. Gov't PAC*, 528 US 377, 402 (2000) ("Rather, [the Court] has balanced interests. And in practice that has meant asking whether the statute burdens any one such interest in a manner out of proportion to the statute's salutary effects upon the others."); *United States* v. *Playboy Entm't Group, Inc.*, 529 US 803, 846 (2000) (Breyer, J., dissenting) ("Consequently § 505's restriction, viewed in light of the proposed alternative, is proportionate to need. That is to say, it restricts speech no more than necessary to further that compelling need.").

[24] Note that Justice Scalia, writing the majority opinion in *Heller*, did not respond to Justice Breyer's contentions regarding proportionality and did not refer to the doctrine in his own opinion.

[25] See discussion, *supra*, at Chapter 3, p. 6.

This is not to imply, however, that the notion of balancing is completely alien to US constitutional law. Indeed, Professor Alexander Aleinikoff has shown that balancing, which first began to emerge at the beginning of the twentieth century, appears in several areas of constitutional law, including First and Fourteenth Amendment jurisprudence and commerce clause and search and seizure cases.[26] Balancing is nevertheless a considerably less central doctrine in American constitutional jurisprudence than proportionality is in Germany and some of the other legal systems that have adopted it. Yet it has been the focus of a relatively significant amount of attention in both academic literature as well as judicial decisions.

In the book we discuss the place of balancing within the general framework of American constitutional law and, in particular, the question of how central it is. But first, for the comparison with proportionality to be productive, it is important to address the question of whether there are any analytical similarities between the two doctrines. As described in the Introduction, Justice Breyer seemed to allude to the claim that balancing and proportionality were analytically similar in his *Heller* dissent: "Contrary to the majority's unsupported suggestion that this sort of 'proportionality' approach is unprecedented, the Court has applied it in various constitutional contexts, including election-law cases, speech cases, and due process cases."[27] But there are those who maintain that strong analytical distinctions exist between the two doctrines. Below, we consider the question of whether there is, indeed, an analytical similarity between the two doctrines.

Analytical similarities between balancing and proportionality

Balancing and proportionality share several obvious features. Both are the second stage in a similar two-tiered constitutional review process. The first stage of the review requires the claimant to establish that his or her right has been infringed by a governmental action. In the second stage, the government must show that the infringement is justified,

---

[26] T. Alexander Aleinikoff, "Constitutional law in the age of balancing" (1987) 96 Yale L.J. 943. See also Jud Mathews and Alec Stone Sweet, "All things in proportion? American rights doctrine and the problem of balancing" (2011) 60 Emory L.J. 101.

[27] *District of Columbia* v. *Heller*, 554 US 690. Moreover, Justice Breyer specifically referred to the proportionality approach in Stephen Breyer, *Active Liberty: Interpreting Our Democratic Constitution* (New York: Knopf, 2005) 48–9.

i.e. that it has pursued a legitimate end and has properly balanced the right and the governmental interest (in the case of balancing) or that the infringement on the right is proportional to the importance of the governmental interest (in the case of proportionality). In this respect, both balancing and proportionality stand in contrast to categorical conceptions of rights that usually entail one step only in rights adjudication: identifying an infringement of a right.

In the case of proportionality, once the government has demonstrated that it is pursuing a legitimate end, it must meet the following three subtests: first, the means adopted to realize the government's goal must be suited to furthering that end (suitability). Second, the means chosen must be those that least infringe on the individual's right (necessity). Third, the harm to the individual resulting from the infringement on his or her right must be proportional to the government's gain from furthering its goal (proportionality in the strict sense).

An illustrative example of the application of the subtests of proportionality is the Israeli Supreme Court's analysis in its 2008 *Horev* judgment.[28] In this case, the Court deliberated a road detour that had been imposed by the Jerusalem municipality to prevent cars from passing through an Ultra-Orthodox Jewish neighborhood during the Sabbath. The Court first identified an infringement of the right to free movement, on the one hand, and the legitimate governmental end of protecting religious feelings, on the other. It then turned to the three subtests of proportionality: (1) whether the means chosen (the detour) furthered the government's end (protecting religious feelings), i.e. the suitability test; (2) whether those means were the least restrictive possible, i.e. the necessity test; and (3) whether the harm to the right to free movement was proportional to the benefit from protecting religious feelings – i.e. proportionality in the strict sense. The outcomes of these three subtests led the Court to conclude that the detour could be imposed only during prayer times on the Sabbath.

With balancing, there is no such division of the second stage of the review into subtests but, rather, the comparison is made between the infringed right and the governmental interest in one step. However, like proportionality, the balancing process is triggered when a constitutional right or provision has been infringed; and, moreover, like

---

[28] HCJ 5016/96 *Horev* v. *Minister of Transportation* (an English translation of the court decision is available at http://elyon1.court.gov.il/files_eng/96/160/050/A01/96050160.a01. htm).

proportionality, balancing entails a comparison between the impairment of the right and the importance of the governmental interest.[29]

Exemplifying this is the US Supreme Court's decision in *Schneider* v. *New Jersey*,[30] the first to apply balancing in the context of free speech, which revolved around a municipal ban on the distribution of handbills. In this instance, the Court balanced the right of free speech against the municipal interest in clean streets and held that in the circumstances of the case, the benefit from furthering cleanliness was too trivial to justify such a heavy infringement on the right to free speech.

Despite the resemblance between proportionality and balancing described above, several independent arguments can be made for why the two doctrines are in fact analytically distinct. These arguments have been put forth by scholars usually in the context of discussing the normative advantages of proportionality over balancing.

The first and most straightforward argument is that balancing is in fact analogous only to the third subtest of proportionality, namely, proportionality *stricto sensu*. Thus, the argument goes, proportionality includes two additional subtests that are not in the balancing doctrine.

A number of counterarguments to this claim can be raised. First, a sufficiently broad construction of balancing, it can be argued, includes also the other two subtests of proportionality. Balancing, when thus construed – what we would term *balancing writ large* – makes a general comparison of benefits versus burdens, which entails the question of whether there is any benefit to be derived at all. The latter question can be understood as comprising the first two subtests of proportionality: suitability – i.e. whether there is any benefit at all – and necessity – i.e. whether the same benefit can be achieved through less harmful means. Thus, while proportionality and balancing might differ in how they articulate or distinguish between these separate questions, both tests seem to be included in the inherent idea of balancing.

Second, even if we regard balancing as proportionality *stricto sensu* only and detach it from the first two subtests of proportionality, there is still no substantial difference between the two doctrines. The reason is that the suitability and necessity subtests can never bear the full weight of

---

[29] For descriptions of balancing in American constitutional law, see Aleinikoff, "Constitutional law in the age of balancing." See also Iddo Porat, "The dual model of balancing" (2006) 27 Cardozo L. Rev. 1393.

[30] *Schneider* v. *New Jersey*, 308 US 147 (1939).

any important constitutional decision, but rather most of the real "work" is done in the third subtest – i.e. proportionality in the strict sense.

In fact, the first two subtests, when narrowly construed, require only a better fit between means and ends, so that less harm would be caused to the right. In this respect, suitability and necessity seem to function as tests of Pareto-optimality or as a win/no-lose solution, allowing both sides to the dispute – the government interest and the individual right – to be either better-off or not-worse-off than before.[31] Thus construed, the two tests are of relatively limited importance, since cases with a Pareto-optimal solution are a rarity. To put it differently, governmental actions rarely encumber a right for no reason at all and for no benefit to a government objective. It is usually the case, rather, that a government interest was better realized as a result of the infringement on a right. In the words of John Hart Ely:

> "[L]ess restrictive alternative" analysis is common in constitutional law generally and in first amendment cases in particular. But there is always a latent ambiguity in the analysis ... Weakly construed, it could require only that there be no less restrictive alternative capable of serving the state's interest *as efficiently as it is served by the regulation under attack*. But as I have noted elsewhere, in virtually every case involving real legislation, a more perfect fit involves some added cost. In effect, therefore, this weak formulation would reach only laws that engage in the gratuitous inhibition of [rights] ... Legislatures simply do not enact wholly useless provisions.[32]

A third counterargument is that American constitutional law applies tests that are very similar to the first and second proportionality subtests, albeit not at the balancing stage of constitutional review. For example, the important and the central least restrictive means test operates very similarly to the necessity subtest,[33] while the suitability subtest is inherent in each of the three tiers of judicial scrutiny – strict, intermediate, and rational basis review.[34]

---

[31] See also Donald H. Regan, "Judicial review of member-state regulation of trade within a federal or quasi-federal system: protectionism and balancing, da capo" (2001) 99 Mich. L. Rev. 1853, 1853 n. 1.

[32] John Hart Ely, "Flag desecration: a case study in the roles of categorization and balancing in First Amendment analysis,"(1975) 88 Harv. L. Rev. 1482, 1485 (emphasis added).

[33] Note, "Less drastic means and the first amendment" (1969) 78 Yale L.J. 464, 468; Guy M. Struve, "The less restrictive alternative principle and economic due process" (1967) 80 Harv. L. Rev. 1464.

[34] See generally Richard H. Fallon, Jr., "Strict judicial scrutiny" (2007) 54 UCLA L. Rev. 1267.

Three other arguments for an analytical distinction between proportionality and balancing turn out to be similarly uncompelling. The first argument is that proportionality is more objective, factual, scientific, and, therefore, more transparent and legitimate than balancing. Balancing, it is asserted, is more value-laden, subjective, and opaque than proportionality.[35]

In most cases, this line of argument rests on proportionality's first two subtests, placing a great deal of emphasis on their role in structuring proportionality and in framing issues as scientific questions of efficiency and factual differences. But, as we showed above, the suitability and necessity tests cannot bear the full weight of constitutional decisions and their actual application, as apart from balancing, are relatively rare.

A second argument differentiates between proportionality as a process that involves no comparison of values, especially incommensurable ones, and balancing, which, it is claimed, does. The example of a dog show illustrates this claim nicely.[36] Consider a dog show in which there are a number of different competitions: for the best bulldog, the best schnauzer, etc. However, there is also an overall competition for the best dog in the show. Comparing one schnauzer to another of course makes sense, but how can bulldogs be compared to schnauzers? Proportionality, the argument goes, offers a solution: we can examine the bulldog that took first place in the bulldog competition and the schnauzer that won the schnauzer show and consider how close each comes to the ideal dog of its species based on the standards of that species. Similarly in law, the proportionality test assesses each competing value on its own terms, without any need to compare incommensurable values, and then asks,

---

[35] Beatty, *The Ultimate Rule of Law* (Oxford: Oxford University Press, 2004) 166–9 (praising such proportionality virtues as value-neutrality, objectivity, and focus on facts rather on values); Julian Rivers, "Proportionality and variable intensity of review" (2006) Cambridge L.J. 174 (highlighting the structured character of proportionality); Barak, *Proportionality: Constitutional Rights and their Limitations* 460–5 (pointing to the transparent, structured, and dialogical character of proportionality); Paul Craig, *Administrative Law* (Oxford: Oxford University Press, 6th edn., 2008) 637 ("The proportionality test provides a *structured form of inquiry*. The three-part inquiry focuses the attention of both the agency being reviewed, and the court undertaking the review." (Emphasis added.)); Aharon Barak, "Proportionality and principled balancing" (2010) 4 L. & Ethics. Hum. Rts., 1 (from the abstract: "The advantages of proportionality *stricto sensu* with its three levels of abstraction are several. It stresses the need to always look for a justification of a limit on human rights; it structures the mind of the balancer; it is transparent; it creates a proper dialogue between the political branches and the judiciary; and it adds to the objectivity of judicial discretion.").

[36] Our thanks to Bruce Chapman for this example.

with respect to each one, to what extent the core of the value is infringed. Balancing, it is asserted, engages in a different process, in which comparison between different values is unavoidable.

David Beatty implies a similar distinction between proportionality and balancing in his analysis of the Israeli Supreme Court's decision in *Horev*, which did not include a comparison of incommensurable values, by his account. Indeed, according to Beatty, the Court did not balance freedom of movement against the need to protect religious feelings but, rather, examined the extent of the harm to each value *on its own terms*. It looked for a solution that would dramatically decrease the extent of harm to one value (religious feelings) while minimizing the harm to the other value (freedom of movement). Allowing the imposition of a detour for only a few minutes during prayer times was just such a solution. Beatty's account of this decision emphasizes the advantages of proportionality in that it focuses on the facts of the case rather than on value judgments and, hence, promotes judicial legitimacy and reduces the extent of judicial subjectivity.[37]

Our objection to this distinction between proportionality and balancing is two-fold. First, to the extent that this argument holds, it is equally true of balancing and proportionality. That is to say, if the courts can apply the third proportionality subtest without any need to compare incommensurable values, there is no reason that balancing cannot be applied in the same way. If in practice this has failed to be the case with regard to the application of balancing, it is not because of its analytical limitations but due to the inclinations of American judges.

But more significantly, the claim critically disregards the indispensability and inevitability of *normative* assessments in any kind of proportionality or balancing process. The relative weight of the conflicting rights and interests cannot be disregarded. Thus, in *Schneider*,[38] for example, the substantial injury to the valid government interest in clean streets was not weighty enough to override the less substantial harm to free speech, due to the greater relative importance of the latter in a democratic society.

---

[37] Beatty, *The Ultimate Rule of Law* 169. Beatty relies on David Luban, "Incommensurable values, rational choice and moral absolutes" (1990) 38 Clev. St. L. Rev. 65, 75, stating that the Court in HCJ 5016/96 *Horev* v. *Minister of Transportation* reached a commonsense conclusion based on a small–large tradeoff. See also Paul-Erik N. Veel, "Incommensurability, proportionality, and rational legal decision-making" (2010) 4 L. & Ethics Hum. Rts. 176.

[38] *Schneider* v. *State*, 308 US.

The third argument that is made for an analytical distinction between proportionality and balancing is the following: advocates of proportionality often claim balancing to be less protective of rights as compared to proportionality. Proportionality, they assert, turns on the idea that upholding rights is the norm, whereas infringing them is the exception that requires strict justification.[39]

This argument, however, is also unsuccessful since it is not grounded on an analytical distinction between the two doctrines but, rather, is premised on the notion of constitutional cultural differences that tip the balance in favor of rights protection in legal systems that have adopted proportionality. There is nothing inherent in balancing that precludes a similar outcome from emerging in the USA. For example, the strict scrutiny test, even in its most moderate form, has been termed by Fallon a "weighted balancing test" that is "distinguished from other balancing tests by its premise that the stakes on the rights side of the scale are unusually high and that the government's interest must therefore be weighty to overcome them."[40] In fact, even in the Canadian proportionality-based system, the overwhelming priority accorded to rights, which was established in *Oakes*,[41] has eroded over time.[42] It is therefore inaccurate to depict proportionality, in contrast to balancing, as a mechanism that is analytically (as opposed to culturally) pro-rights protection.

---

[39] Lorraine Weinrib, "The Supreme Court of Canada and Section 1 of the Charter" (1988) 10 Sup. Ct. Rev. 469; Lorraine Weinrib, "Constitutional conceptions and constitutional comparativism," in Vicki Jackson and Mark Tushnet (eds.), *Defining the Field of Comparative Constitutional Law* (New York: Foundation Press, 2002) (describing proportionality as a method of rights protection); David Beatty, *Constitutional Law in Theory and Practice* (Toronto: University of Toronto Press, 1995) (similarly defining proportionality).

[40] Fallon, "Strict judicial scrutiny" 1306.   [41] *R. v. Oakes*, [1986] 1 SCR 103.

[42] The strict *Oakes* test was eroded quite quickly in *R. v. Edward Books and Art* [1986] 2 SCR 713, 772, when the Court deferred to the government in applying the necessity subtest of proportionality. For an excellent reading of the erosion of the *Oakes* test, see Sujit Choudhry, "So what is the real legacy of Oakes? Two decades of proportionality analysis under the Canadian Charter's Section 1" (2006) 35 Sup. Ct. L. Rev (2d) 501. See also Christopher M. Dassios and Clifton P. Prophet, "Charter Section 1: The decline of the grand unified theory and the trend towards deference in the Supreme Court of Canada" (1993) 15 Advocates' Q. 289, 291; Robin Elliot, "The Supreme Court of Canada and Section 1 – the erosion of the common front" (1987) 12 Queen's L.J. 277, 281; Gerard La Forest, "The balancing of interests under the Charter" (1993) 2 N.J.C.L. 133; Ruth Colker, "Section 1, contextuality, and the anti-advantage principle" (1992) 42 U. Tor. L.J. 77.

Thus, it emerges from the discussion that analytical differences between proportionality and balancing seem not to be substantial, a conclusion that seems to support Justice Breyer's claim in his *Heller* dissent.[43] The purpose of the next five chapters is, however, to show that, while analytically close, these two doctrines are very much embedded in different historical, cultural, and socio-political contexts, which have shaped their diverging meanings, functions, and consequences within their respective legal systems.

---

[43] 554 US 690.

2

History

This chapter begins with a review of the historical origins of balancing and proportionality, examining the development of the latter in Germany and of balancing in the USA. This inquiry will reveal important divergences between the two doctrines, showing how their different backgrounds contributed to and shaped these variances.

The origins of proportionality in German administrative law

The concept of proportionality has existed in some form in all cultures and from the earliest of times.[1] It has also existed for many years in several legal fields such as the laws of war, criminal self-defense, taxation, and the theory of punishment. Yet only in the nineteenth century, in Prussian administrative law, did a coherent doctrine of proportionality emerge in public law.

---

[1] Traces of the concept of proportionality can be found in Ancient times: from the images of balancing in Egyptian tomb paintings (if the deceased had committed a heavy wrong, his access to the realm of the dead was denied) and the Talion principle (requiring punishment identical to the offense) in the Hammurabi Codex and the Old Testament ("an eye for an eye"). Versions of this principle also appear in Section 20 of the Magna Carta, which limits arbitrary use of governmental power, and Article 8 of the 1989 French Declaration of Rights of Man and of the Citizen, which prohibits disproportional punishment. See Gerhard Robbers, in *Bonner Kommentar zum Grundgesetz Loseblattsammlung Band 5* (Heidelberg: C.F. Müller Verlag, 2012) Art. 20 Abs. 1 Rn. 1890. Franz Wieacker points to three factors underlying rationales in the development of the principle of proportionality in Ancient Roman and Greek tradition: first, there was the need to restrict private revenge and punishment. The rationale behind the Talion Principle was not to satisfy the private need for revenge, but to ensure public order by allowing only moderate and proportional punishment for offenses. Second, the notion of doing justice in Greek and Roman philosophy required proportionality between wrongs and compensations and rights and burdens. Third, Greek and Roman philosophers viewed proportionality as an essential tool for achieving efficiency. Franz Wieacker, "Geschichtliche Wurzeln des Prinzips der verhältnismäßigen Rechtsanwendung," in *Festschrift für Fischer* (Berlin and New York: de Gruyter Verlag, 1979) 874–80.

Proportionality and Rechtsstaat

From the second half of the eighteenth century, Prussia gradually evolved from an authoritarian state, in which the King was the supreme and sole source of authority, into a state that was governed by law: a *Rechtsstaat*. At the time, under the rule of Friedrich the Great, Prussia was a great military and economic power. Well versed in the principles of enlightened absolutism and influenced by the first blossoming of liberal social contractarianism and rationalism (upon which the French and the American Revolutions were founded), Friedrich believed that a monarch's authority was not unlimited and conceived himself instead to be "the first servant of his state."[2] He therefore worked to ground Prussia's legal system in principles of rationalism, religious tolerance, and individual freedoms.

It was only under his successor, Friedrich Wilhelm II, however, that the codification of Prussian law was completed. Article 10(2) of the *Allgemeines Landrecht* (ALR) of 1794 authorized the government to exercise police powers to ensure public peace, but at the same time restricted those powers to measures that were essential solely for achieving that goal: "The police is to take the *necessary* measures for the maintenance of public peace, security and order."[3] This reference to "*necessary* measures" constituted the first textual pronouncement of a requirement of proportionality in Germany.[4]

Proportionality should be viewed in conjunction with the principle of *Rechtsstaat*. The *Rechtsstaat* principle was a reversal of the default rule, which had legitimized state action under German public law. Up until that point, state action had been held to be valid even when it was not explicitly permitted under the law; henceforth the validity of any such action became contingent on explicit textual authorization. This remains the essence of the *Rechtsstaat* principle in German public law to this day. And although the precise meaning and implications of the "*Rechtsstaat*" principle continue to be debated, it is clear that the role played by this principle in Germany was similar to the impact of the British "rule of law": by imposing limits on governmental actions, it

---

[2] Carlyle Thomas, *The History of Friedrich the Second: Called Friedrich the Great* (New York: Harper Brothers, 1863).

[3] Werner Frotscher and Bodo Pieroth, *Verfassungsgeschichte* (Munich: Verlag C.H. Beck, 2010) Rn. 153 (emphasis in original). See also Alec Stone Sweet and Jud Mathews, "Proportionality, balancing and global constitutionalism" (2008) 19 Colum. J. Transnat'l L. 19.

[4] Frotscher and Pieroth, *Verfassungsgeschichte* 9. Auflage (Munich: Verlag C.H. Beck, 2010) Rn. 158; Stern, *Staatsrecht* I, 2. Auflage 873.

provided citizens with a far greater degree of freedom than would have otherwise been available.[5] Article 10(2) of the ALR bolstered this freedom by introducing the notion of necessity of state action.

Functionally, the requirement of proportionality in the ALR – namely, that the use of police power must be proportional to the goals defined by the law – corresponded with the *Rechtsstaat* requirement, but also supplemented it. Both principles offer ways of coping with a system, such as the Prussian system, that sets few formal constraints on police power and has no entrenched constitutional Bill of Rights. The concept of the *Rechtsstaat* allowed the government to infringe on individual rights, but subject to explicit authorization in a law. The principle of proportionality placed a further restriction on this power, by allowing the government to take only the measures necessary for achieving its legitimate goals. In other words, the requirement for a clear legal basis for the exercise of police power and the requirement that this use be proportionate to the goals sought were both meant to maximize individual autonomy under a legal system lacking a formal constitutional Bill of Rights.

Judicial review and the development of the principle of proportionality

In order to implement the principles of *Rechtsstaat* and proportionality, an institutional mechanism had to be created. This was the foundation of the formation of the highly influential administrative courts in Prussia in the second half of the nineteenth century.

Because the Prussian parliament was a reactionary, subservient body and tended to cave in to government demands, it did not require ministerial accountability, which is an essential mechanism for preventing abuse of police power. Thus, in the mid nineteenth century, German

---

[5] The *Rechtsstaat* principle is not identical to the notion of the rule of law, despite the liberalizing effects of both. The Anglo-American conception of natural rights assumes that men and women have rights that precede the existence of the state, whereas the German conception of *Rechtsstaat* is more state-centered. Thus, Krieger, in his classic *The German Idea of Freedom* (Boston, MA: Beacon Press, 1957) 460, argued that the *Rechtsstaat* is not "defined in terms of a state which permitted the individual rights apart from the state. It became now simply the kind of state whose power was articulated in legal modes of action – that is, in measures which conformed to general rules." Krieger depicts a conservative and even authoritarian concept of the *Rechtsstaat*. See also Hans Rosenberg, "Politische Denkstromungen," in *Deutschen Vormärz* (Göttingen: Vandenhoeck & Ruprecht, 1972) (the state was conceived in Germany not only as an institutional safeguard for the protection of individual rights but also as a "fatherland").

liberals, who had lost all hope of instituting an effective parliamentary system, shifted their focus from ministerial accountability to *judicial* accountability: instead of calling on ministers and their subordinates to be accountable to parliament, they demanded that public officials be held accountable to the courts.[6] Regarding judges to be the best guardians of individual rights against administrative abuse,[7] these reformists argued for the establishment of a system of administrative courts that was separate and autonomous from the state administration. Indeed, two of the more prominent reformist legal theorists, Otto Bähr and Rudolf von Gneist, understood the *Rechtsstaat* principle to require the state and its administration to act within the boundaries of the law and to be subject to the supervision of an independent administrative court system.[8]

In the end, the reformists prevailed, and independent administrative courts were established, with the authority to review the state's use of police power.[9] Between 1882 and 1914, the Prussian Supreme Administrative Court (PSAC) made intensive use of proportionality to examine the legitimacy of government intervention in economic and social life. In a series of important decisions, but without explicitly pronouncing a new legal principle,[10] the PSAC held that any exercise of police power that infringes on political or economic rights must be proportional and its permitted scope narrowly construed.

Several prominent decisions restricting the use of police power to only those measures that are closely related to the maintence of public safety reflect the use of proportionality in the jurisprudence of the PSAC. One prominent example was the seminal 1882 *Kreuzberg* decision, where the Court struck down a Berlin ordinance banning the construction of buildings that blocked the view of a national monument in the city. It held that the government could only act thus to prevent danger to public

---

[6] Kenneth F. Ledford, "Formalizing the rule of law in Prussia: the Supreme Administrative Law Court (1876–1914)" (2004) 37 Cent. Eur. History, 203, 222.

[7] *Ibid.* 210.

[8] *See* Bähr, *Der Rechtsstaat* S. 15ff; *Bonner Kommentar zum Grundgesetz, Loseblattsammlung seit 1950* (Heidelberg: C.F. Müller Verlag) Band 5, Art. 20 Abs. 1, Rn. 1743; *Bonner Kommentar zum Grundgesetz, Loseblattsammlung seit 1950* (Heidelberg: C.F. Müller Verlag) Band 5, Art. 20 Abs. 1 Rn. 1744 ff.

[9] Section 127 of the 1883 State Administrative Act granted the Prussian Supreme Administrative Court the explicit authority to review any governmental order after all administrative appeals had been exhausted.

[10] Lothar Hirschberg, *Der Grundsatz der Verhältnismäßigkeit* (Göttingen: Schwartz, 1981) 3.

safety and could not impose its aesthetic judgment.[11] In another case the Court ruled that any restrictions on the right of Social Democrats to assemble and demonstrate must be grounded on concrete facts. Those facts, it ruled, must show a genuine danger to public order, and the restrictions could not be based on the police assumption that the combination of alcohol consumption and political opposition to the government would inevitably result in a disturbance of the public order.[12] Finally, a particularly strict test was established in a series of rulings relating to the controversial play *The Weaver*, which was suspected of being sympathetic to, and even stirring up, popular revolt against alleged capitalist exploiters. The PSAC ruled that the police could not ban performances of the play based on the remote possibility that they would lead to a disturbance of the public order. Rather, the police needed to prove "an actual, near and impending danger" to justify such censorship.[13]

Proportionality, natural law, and formalism

In the absence of explicit protection of constitutional rights in Germany, many liberal reformists resorted to natural rights rhetoric to justify the introduction of rights into German public law. This rhetoric dominated the writings of liberal Prussian legal scholars of the time, such as Carl Gottlieb von Svarez, a famous reformist jurist. Von Svarez, who was extensively involved in the drafting of the 1794 ALR, stated that the monarch "must limit the natural freedom of his subjects only to such an extent that it is necessary to protect and maintain the security and freedom of all."[14] Two other leading scholars, von Berg and Mayer, who later went on to develop the principle of proportionality in their writings, directly linked proportionality to natural rights. In 1802, von Berg wrote, "The police power may abridge the natural freedom of the

[11] Decisions of the Prussian Administrative Law Court, 9 (1882) 353. It should be noted that in Germany the requirement that the government pursue a legitimate objective is part of the proportionality requirement.
[12] Vernon L. Lidtke, *The Outlawed Party: Social Democrats in Germany 1878–1890* (Princeton, NJ: Princeton University Press, 1966) 241–62.
[13] Ledford, "Formalizing the rule of law in Prussia: the Supreme Administrative Law Court (1876–1914)" 220.
[14] Carl Gottlieb Svarez, *Vorträge über Recht und Staat* (Cologne and Opladen: Westdeutscher Verlag, 1960) 9 f; Karl-Peter Sommermann, *in v. Mangoldt/Klein/Starck Kommentar zum Grundgesetz Band 2* (Munich: Verlag Franz Vahlen, 2010) Art. 20 Rn. 309.

subject, but only to such a degree as its legitimate purpose requires,"[15] adding that "in any case, it is obvious that the one who is forced to offer ... a sacrifice to the community, has to be compensated proportionately."[16] Mayer made similar statements, writing, for example, that "natural rights demand that the use of police powers by the government be proportionate."[17] It is important to keep in mind the fact that in the nineteenth century natural rights were perceived in Germany as libertarian in nature, imposing constraints on the use of governmental powers, and expanding the protection of political and economic freedoms. The liberal bourgeoisie therefore had a deep economic and political interest in promoting legal developments such as the principle of proportionality and the *Rechtsstaat*.[18]

It should be noted, also, that despite the linking of proportionality and natural law concepts, the PSAC judges continued to apply a methodology that was essentially formalistic. The judges regarded themselves to be acting within the framework of the formalist tradition of German law.[19]

In general, the administrative judges refrained from presenting themselves as conducting a balancing-like, commonsense cost-benefit analysis.[20] Although the PSAC did not split the proportionality

---

[15] Cited in Stone Sweet and Mathews, "Proportionality, balancing and global constitutionalism" 17.

[16] Günter Heinrich von Berg, *Handbuch des Teutschen Policeyrechts. 1. Teil* (Hannover: Verlag der Gebrüder Hahn, 1802) 88 ff.

[17] Otto Mayer, *Deutsches Verwaltungsrecht* 1. Bd. (Munich: Duncker & Humblot, 1895) 267.

[18] David Blackbourn, "The discreet charm of the bourgeoisie: reappraising German history in the Nineteenth Century," in David Blackbourn and Geoff Eley (eds.), *The Peculiarities of German History* (Oxford: Oxford University Press, 1984) 157 (noting that the *Rechtsstaat* principle was necessary for the creation of a solid middle-class society and promoted capitalist modernization in nineteenth-century Germany).

[19] For an excellent overview of the radical formalist characteristics of German legal thought in the nineteenth century, see Mathias Reiman, "Nineteenth-Century German legal science" (1990) 31 B.C.L. Rev. 837.

[20] This is not to say that the PSAC totally refrained from balancing, but it did not conduct the sort of full-blown balancing that is applied today in the context of proportionality in its strict sense. Rather, there was balancing in the form of small–large tradeoffs, of the type that arises only in extreme cases where great harm is done to a right for a minor gain to the public interest. For one version of the "small–large tradeoffs" in PSAC jurisprudence, see Stefan Naas, *Die Entstehung des Preußischen Polizeiverwaltungsgesetzes von 1931* (Tübingen: Verlag Mohr Siebeck, 1st edn., 2003) 301 ("The police must not kill a valuable dog that damages a public park of no high value by scratching the lawn, even if it cannot avoid the damage in a different way."). However, the rhetoric of balancing was not

requirement into three or four sub-tests (as is current practice in German public law), it seems that a central underlying component of its jurisprudence was the consistent adherence to a more formal means–ends analysis rather than the more substantive (balancing) inquiry typically conducted in the framework of proportionality in its strict sense, as we think of it today. The Court focused on the strictness of the application of the necessity test *vis-à-vis* the government.[21] Any reference to balancing was incidental in the Court's judgments, appearing only when the police's choice of means was "extremely disproportional" to its stated aims.[22]

The tendency of the administrative judges to focus on a formal analysis of proportionality was consistent with German mainstream formal legal science of the day (*Rechtswissenschaft*). The nineteenth-century *Rechtswissenschaft* movement, led by Savigny, borrowed from the natural sciences to exemplify the logic of the law and the systematic way in which legal rules are created and function. For example, just as the length of one side of a triangle can be derived from the lengths of its two other sides so, they claimed, can missing rules be deduced from the existing rules of law.[23] Similarly, some legal scientists analogized the science of law to chemistry: if under the logic of chemistry, matter can be created from certain basic elements, so can new rules be created in law from the basic rules of law. Even the Darwinist theory influenced how German legal science presented the law, comparing its emergence to the development of an organism.[24]

---

pervasive in the Court's decisions, with the legal analysis focusing more on the empirical and logical connections between means and ends. See Jürgen Schwarze, *European Administrative Law* (London: Sweet & Maxwell, 2006) Ch. V, C5.

[21] Naas, *Die Entstehung des preußischen Polizeiverwaltungsgesetzes von 1931* 302. It should be noted, however, that in the 1920s, there was a shift in the Court's jurisprudence from a strict application of the test, where the government bore the burden of proof to show that no less restrictive means are available, to an approach more deferential to the government, with the plaintiff now bearing the burden of proof. Compare OVG, IV. Senat vom 6.4.1924, E 79, 393, 397 (when there are several measures available to the police to achieve its objective that are equally effective, the police must give the plaintiff the choice of which one will be used, since "the limitation on one certain measure is not likewise necessary to achieve the purpose. The police are not obligated to investigate which measure is available or which one seems to be less burdening for the obligated party from his point of view."), with OVG, III. Senat vom 13.11.1930, E 86, 273, 279 ("The plaintiff wrongfully denies that the necessary measure was applied. If he thought that a less burdening measure could be employed ..., so it was on him to offer it.").

[22] OVG, III. Senat vom 29.12.1932, E 90, 270, 273.

[23] Mattias Reimann, "Nineteenth century German legal science" (1990) 31 Boston College L. Rev. 837, 876–83.

[24] *Ibid.*

The formalism of the PSAC jurists was also in line with the ideas of libertarianism, formulated later by early twentieth-century liberals such as Weber and Kelsen. These writers regarded the formalistic analysis of the kind described above as both a crucial means for ensuring a more effective governmental system as well as an important tool for maximizing individual freedom, for it sets clear limits on state action and thus allows the individual a wider space of activity.[25]

The formal interpretation of proportionality in the PSAC judgments described should be contrasted with the notion of "balancing of interests" that developed concurrently (though unrelatedly) in German law. During the nineteenth century, a radical anti-formalistic movement gained ground in German legal jurisprudence, known as the *Freirechtsschule*, which criticized formalism and conceptualism, albeit mainly in the context of private law.[26] The proponents of *Freirecht* ("free law") viewed law to be a domain whose purpose is to settle conflicts between competing interests by way of balancing.[27] Von Jhering, writing at the same time, mounted a similar attack on German legal conceptualism, relying on the notion of balancing of interests.

It seems that there has never been any direct link between balancing and proportionality in German law and that, in a certain sense, they were even associated with opposing legal movements. First, balancing of interests has its origins in German private law, whereas proportionality originated in German public law. Second, in contrast to the influence of the twentieth-century American legal realists, the *Freirechtsschule*, and von Jhering's critique constituted a radical departure from the dominant formalistic tradition of German law of the time and, thus, had no

---

[25] Weber viewed formal rationality as almost the "twin brother of liberty," since it prevents the government from taking arbitrary action. Max Weber, "Diskussionerede zu dem Vortag von H. Kantorowicz Rechtswissenschaft und Soziologie," in *Gesammelte Aufsätze zur Sociologie und Sociopolitik* (Tübingen: Mohr, 1921) 477–81. The translation into English of parts of the article can be found in Arthur J. Jacobson and Bernhard Schlink (eds.), *Weimar: A Jurisprudence of Crisis* (Berkeley, CA: California University Press, 2000) 50, 53. For similar reasons, Hans Kelsen opposed the inclusion of a Bill of Rights in the German Constitution. Because rights are drafted in an open-ended manner, their inclusion in a constiutution would give judges too much power to interpret their meaning. See Stone Sweet, "Investor–state arbitration: proportionality's new frontier" (2010) 4(1) L. & Ethics Hum. Rts. 16.

[26] For a comparison of the *Freirechtsschule* and American realism, see James E. Harget and Steohen Wallace, "The German free law movement as the source for American legal realism" (1987) 73 Va. L. Rev. 399.

[27] Mathias Reimann, "Free law school," in David S. Clarck (ed.), *Encyclopedia of Law and Society* (Los Angeles, CA: Sage, 2007) 605.

significant impact on German jurisprudence.[28] The administrative courts obviously did not embrace this radical movement. Instead, they positioned themselves deeply within the framework of mainstream German formal thought. Third, the ideas of the *Freirechtsschule* were considered by liberal formalists such as Weber to pose a concrete threat and in ideological opposition to the principles of liberalism and democracy, on which *Rechtsstaat* and proportionality were grounded.

Conclusion

Several conclusions can be drawn from the development of the principle of proportionality in German public law during the nineteenth century. First, in Germany, the proportionality doctrine originated in administrative law, not private law. Second, proportionality was a vehicle by which the idea of rights was introduced into German law. Consequently, in Germany, the principle of proportionality stands for rights protection. Third, proportionality served to further the protection of political and economic rights, at the time considered to be "natural" rights. The German liberal bourgeoisie was obviously strongly motivated to maximize protection of these rights. Finally, the legal doctrine of proportionality was not related to theories of law, such as those advanced by the *Freirechtsschule* and American legal realism. Rather, German proportionality was rooted in the formalistic approaches deeply imbedded in the German legal tradition.

The origins of balancing in American constitutional jurisprudence

Balancing in American constitutional law had very different origins and path of development than proportionality in German administrative law. To begin with, in Germany, the notion of proportionality enabled the incorporation of rights protection into a system that provided limited formal protection of rights. In contrast, balancing was developed in the USA to contend with the very opposite problem. In the USA, there was strong textual support for the protection of rights but little textual basis for *limiting* rights. Balancing was therefore an important interpretative

---

[28] *Ibid.* (showing that the *Freirecht* movement was not part of mainstream German jurisprudence).

tool for preventing absolutism in rights protection, by requiring that rights be balanced against other important interests. In addition, unlike proportionality in Germany, balancing sprang from the anti-formalist movement and originated in private, not public law. Finally, balancing emerged completely unrelated to the natural rights theory that was associated with proportionality in Germany. In fact, natural rights theories were criticized by the Progressives who introduced balancing into American constitutional law. We discuss these differences and their ramifications below.

Balancing as a critique of formalism and Langdellianism

The notion of balancing entered American legal thought through the writings of Oliver Wendell Holmes, in his critique of formalism and Langdellianism in American private law.

Langdellianism

Christopher Columbus Langdell, who was Dean of Harvard Law School in the latter part of the nineteenth century, was one of the foremost proponents of formalism in American jurisprudence. Influenced by the German legal science movement and aspiring to promote law's status as an academic discipline, he set out to establish it as a serious and rigorous scientific enterprise, similar to physics or geometry.[29] The Langdellian conception of law thus depicted the legal sphere as featuring the following three scientific characteristics: (1) law is determinate, and therefore legal conclusions can be arrived at with certainty and are only minimally subject to individual discretion; (2) law is systematized, based on a coherent and limited set of abstract principles; and (3) law is an autonomous sphere of life, distinct from other spheres such as society, politics, and morality.[30] Langdellianism also emphasized categorical distinctions between different areas of law and different legal concepts,

---

[29] See Duncan Kennedy, "Towards a historical understanding of legal consciousness: the case of classical legal thought in America, 1850–1940" (1980) 3 Res. L. & Soc'y 3; Thomas Grey, "Langdell's orthodoxy" (1983) 45 U. Pitt. L. Rev. 1, 50 n. 180; Neil Duxbury, *Patterns of American Jurisprudence* (Oxford: Clarendon Press, 1995) 10.

[30] See Thomas Grey, "The new formalism," Stanford Law School, Public Law and Theory Working Paper 4 (1999). See also Morton J. Horowitz, *The Transformation of American Law 1870–1960: The Crisis of Legal Orthodoxy* (New York: Oxford University Press, 1992) 17–19, 198–9.

rather than distinctions of degree, absolute rather than relative rights, and the conceptual meaning of rights rather than their social function.[31]

Langdell's claims for law as a legal science were applied mainly in the sphere of private law, guided by an idealized conception of private law. He regarded constitutional law, in contrast, to be "soft" law and not a field of serious, scientific legal thought.[32] The mailbox rule is one of the more well-known examples of Langdellian jurisprudence: through a process of logical deductions based on the legal concepts of promise and contract, Langdell resolved the question of whether an insurance contract is valid from the time the insured drops it into a mailbox or from the time it is received by the insurance company. In order to become a binding contract, a promise must be met with consideration in the form of a return promise by the offeree. However, by definition, a promise must be communicated. Therefore, unless an acceptance letter is received and read by the promissor, there is no return consideration and, therefore, no valid contract. Factors such as customary practice and practical difficulties, what Langdell termed "the balance of convenience," he considered to be legally irrelevant.[33]

Balancing as anti-Langdellianism

Beginning with the writings of Holmes, the Langdellian set of beliefs regarding the nature of law was challenged by the Progressive movement. The idea of balancing was a central conceptual element in this critique. Rather than a process of logically deducing outcomes from abstract rights and principles, Holmes believed that the law should be viewed as a means to a social end and that the best legal rule would be arrived at through a balancing of the various social interests that would be affected by that rule. Thus, for example, the mailbox rule should have been determined through a balancing of the interests of the insured and insurer, taking into consideration actual business practices and market relations.[34]

---

[31] See Grey, "The new formalism" 5–6. See also Horowitz, *The Transformation of American Law 1870–1960: The Crisis of Legal Orthodoxy*.

[32] See Grey, "The new formalism" 6–7. See also Horowitz, *The Transformation of American Law 1870–1960: The Crisis of Legal Orthodoxy*.

[33] See Grey, "The new formalism" 3–4.

[34] Holmes wrote with regard to the consideration doctrine that framed Langdell's discussion of the mailbox rule: "The doctrine of consideration is merely historical ... Consideration is a mere form. Is it a useful form? If so, why should it not be required in all contracts? ... Why should any merely historical distinction be allowed to affect the rights and obligations of business men?" Oliver W. Holmes, "The path of the law" (1897) 10 Harv. L. Rev. 457, 465.

Holmes wrote as early as 1870, in his *Common Law*, that when "two rights run against one another ... a line has to be drawn," and the decision must be based on "distinction of degree" rather than "logical deduction" from conceptions of absolute rights,[35] adding in "The path of the law" that "[j]udges ... have failed adequately to recognize their duty of *weighing* considerations of social advantage."[36] Holmes did not conceive of rights and legal principles as discrete entities. Rather he understood them to be in conflict with one another, but with areas of convergence and overlap.

This view was prominently expressed in *Hudson County Water Co.*,[37] where Holmes, writing for the Court, used the language of balancing to uphold a New Jersey statute against claims that it "impairs the obligation of contracts, [and] takes property without due process of law":[38]

> All rights tend to declare themselves absolute to their logical extreme. Yet all in fact are limited by the neighborhood of principles of policy which are other than those on which the particular right is founded, and which become strong enough to hold their own when a certain point is reached. The limits set to property by other public interests present themselves as a branch of what is called the police power of the state. The boundary at which the conflicting interests balance cannot be determined by any general formula in advance, but points in the line, or helping to establish it, are fixed by decisions that this or that concrete case falls on the nearer or farther side.[39]

The intention of the language is unmistakable. The right to property, Holmes tells us, though formulated in absolute terms, is limited by considerations of policy and should be regarded itself as a policy interest (when Holmes speaks of "[t]he boundary at which the conflicting *interests* balance," he is referring to the boundary between the right to property and the public interest). The conflict is furthermore decided not by some formula but by "points in the line," which represents a balancing process.[40]

Legal Progressives Benjamin Cardozo and Roscoe Pound were also proponents of balancing. Cardozo asserted that legal decisions depend

[35] Oliver W. Holmes, "Privilege, malice, and intent," in *Collected Legal Papers* (Orlando, FL: Harcourt Brace, 1920) 122.

[36] Holmes, "The path of the law" 184.

[37] *Hudson County Water Co.* v. *McCarter*, 209 US 349, 355 (1908).

[38] *Ibid.* 353. The statute was attacked on commerce clause grounds as well.

[39] *Ibid.* 355 (emphasis added).

[40] *Hudson County Water Co.* v. *McCarter*, 209 US 349, 355 (1908).

"largely upon the *comparative importance* or value of the social interest that will be thereby promoted or impaired."[41] Pound, for his part, wrote emphatically in favor of "weighing social interests" and argued that the law "is an attempt to satisfy, to reconcile, to harmonize, to adjust ... overlapping and often conflicting claims and demands."[42]

The Progressive movement was influenced by philosophical movements originating from both inside and outside the USA. One of the major domestic influences was pragmatism and the thinking of William James and James Dewey, which provided the intellectual grounding for both Progressivism and balancing. Pragmatism held truth to be a social construct, with the only basis for the truth of a concept being its pragmatic application in human affairs. Rather than turning to metaphysics for answers, pragmatism required the identification and balancing of actual interests in order to determine the truth.[43] From abroad, Progressives were influenced by the German *Freirechtsschule*, described above, which challenged formalism and conceptualism in German private law. In particular, Roscoe Pound, in forming his jurisprudence of interests, was directly influenced by the notion of balancing interests propounded by von Jhering and the *Freirechtsschule*[44] in response to Savigny's legal metaphysics.[45]

It is important to note that the intellectual soil from which balancing in American law grew, even before it was introduced into constitutional law, was quite different from the background of German proportionality. American balancing was associated with anti-formalism and pragmatism, whereas German proportionality had a far more modest intellectual

---

[41] Benjamin Cardozo, *The Nature of the Judicial Process* (New Haven, CT: Yale University Press, 1921) 112.

[42] Roscoe Pound, "A survey of social interests" (1943) 57 Harv. L. Rev. 1, 4.

[43] See generally Robert S. Summers, *Instrumentalism and American Legal Theory* (Ithaca, NY: Cornell University Press, 1982).

[44] See John M. Kelly, *A Short History of Western Legal Theory* (Oxford: Oxford University Press, 1992) 330 (describing the origins of the conception of law as an arena for balancing conflicting social interests, beginning with August Comte and Rudolf von Jhering); James E. Harget and Steohen Wallace, "The German free law movement as the source of American legal realism" (1989) 73 Va. L. Rev. 799. Cf. Carl J. Friedrich, *The Philosophy of Law in Historical Perspective* (Chicago, IL: Chicago University Press, 1963) 156–7 (arguing that the Progressives' adoption of the German conception of balancing involved a shift from the original understanding of balancing).

[45] Von Jhering sarcastically described Savigny's metaphysics as a "heaven of legal concepts." See Rudolf von Jhering, "In the heaven of legal concepts," trans. in Morris R. Cohen and Felix S. Cohen (eds.), *Readings in Jurisprudence and Legal Philosophy* (Washington, DC: Beard Books, 1951) 678.

purpose, intended only as a mechanism to be applied within the general formalistic conception of law. As noted, the German legal thinkers who influenced American balancing (von Jhering and the *Freirecht* scholars) were in no way identified with the principle of proportionality in Germany.

Progressive balancing in constitutional law: balancing and anti-formalism in constitutional law

The Progressive anti-formalist movement that began as anti-Langdellianism in private law soon expanded to constitutional law, in the form of an attack on the US Supreme Court's formalistic interpretation of constitutional rights. There have been two prominent waves to the Progressive push to introduce balancing into constitutional law. The first was in the form of anti-Lochnerism, advocating the application of balancing in Fourteenth Amendment jurisprudence; the second context was the McCarthy era, when Progressives called for incorporating balancing into First Amendment jurisprudence. In both cases, the proponents of balancing called for judicial restraint and treating rights as social interests to be balanced against other social interests.

Lochnerism

The Lochner Court is commonly used to refer to the US Supreme Court roughly between the years 1900 and 1937. The *Lochner*[46] decision, which lent its name to the entire period, exemplifies both the Court's formalist methodology and its libertarian ideological inclinations.

In *Lochner*, the Supreme Court struck down a New York state law that limited the working hours of bakery employees to ten hours per day and sixty hours per week. The Court ruled that the Fourteenth Amendment right to liberty includes the right to freedom of contract and that this right is absolutely protected from legislative incursions, except in the limited context of "police powers of the state."[47] This decision was formalistic in two senses. First, the Court sought (and found) its solution to the legal issue at hand through logical deduction from what it deemed to be the proper meaning of one concept: liberty. Second, it arrived at its legal conclusion without any reference to the social realities of labor

---

[46] *Lochner v. New York*, 198 US 45 (1905).   [47] *Ibid.* 53.

relations at the time, wherein workers had no meaningful "liberty" to accept or reject the working conditions that were in fact imposed on them by their employers.

The decision similarly revealed the ideological orientation of the Lochner Court and its philosophical penchant for natural rights. Its interpretation of the right to liberty was framed in a conception of state intervention in individual liberties as being justified only for the purpose of protecting a limited set of crucial interests, what the Court termed "police powers of the state."[48] In the Court's view, individual liberty was protected from such state intervention as part of a person's inalienable natural rights. This natural rights theory had obvious libertarian implications for state intervention in the market.[49] Indeed, the Court opposed state intervention for purposes of economic redistribution or social equality and struck down any legislative attempts to regulate the economy such as Roosevelt's New Deal initiatives.

Balancing as anti-Lochnerism

Balancing was an integral element of the Progressive criticism of Lochnerism and formalism in constitutional law. First, as in the anti-Langdellianism context, here too balancing was construed as the alternative to formalism. As opposed to a process whereby the legal outcome is deduced logically from the meaning of the right to liberty, balancing entails a weighing of the conflicting interests to arrive at a decision. Thus, in his landmark dissent in *Lochner*, Holmes wrote that "general propositions do not decide concrete cases" and that "the word 'liberty,' in the 14th Amendment, is perverted" by the Supreme Court's interpretation of it, insofar as the Court understands liberty as leading directly to the legal conclusion that it reached.[50] In fact, Holmes suggested, the Court had applied its own balancing of interests (in this case, preferring a laissez-faire economic policy to social equality), while hiding behind the fig leaf of formalism.[51]

Second, championing balancing was the Progressive movement's way of signaling that in its view certain rights are in fact social interests and the Supreme Court's reliance on rights rhetoric resulted in an unjust emphasis on particular interests (mainly those of the affluent) at the expense of other interests. Pound made this point very succinctly in

[48] *Ibid.*
[49] Morton J. Horowitz, "The rule of law: an unqualified human good" (1977) 88 Yale L.J. 10.
[50] *Lochner*, 198 US at 75-6.   [51] *Ibid.*

"A survey of social interests."[52] In his most comprehensive piece on balancing, he was responding to Justice McKenna's attempt to protect the right of contractual freedom from legislative encroachment. McKenna had asserted a "menace in the ... judgment of all rights, [in] subjecting them unreservedly to conceptions of public policy."[53] Pound thought otherwise, criticizing the Lochner Court's exaggerated concern for private rights at the expense of public rights:

> It was only the ambiguity of the term "right" ... that made it possible to think of the decision in question in such a way ... The "rights" of which Mr. Justice McKenna spoke were ... individual wants, individual claims, *individual interests*, which it was felt ought to be secured through legal rights or through some other legal machinery ... Thus, *the public policy* of which Mr. Justice McKenna spoke is seen to be something at least *on no lower plane than the so-called rights ... There is a policy in the one case as much as in the other.*[54]

The conception of rights as a type of interests clashed with the Lochner Court's idea of natural rights. There was nothing natural in preferring private property over public interests. These were two interests in conflict with each other that needed to be balanced against one another. The invocation of natural rights was thereby exposed as a manipulative favoring of one interest over another.

The balancing methodology was also an integral part of a general conception that constitutional rights should be interpreted as standards rather than categorical and absolute restrictions on government action. This approach thus supported giving the legislature a certain degree of latitude in the infringement of rights and a comparable measure of judicial self-restraint in reviewing legislative action. Again, Holmes led the charge in advancing this approach, arguing that "[a]ll rights tend to declare themselves absolute to their logical extreme. Yet all in fact are limited by the neighborhood of principles of policy which are other than those on which the particular right is founded, and which become strong enough to hold their own when a certain point is reached."[55] Similarly, Pound wrote that the Fourteenth Amendment constitutes only a standard for the legislator:

> It sa[ys] to him that if he trenched upon these individual *interests* he must not do so arbitrarily. His action must have some basis in reason. It is

---

[52] Pound, "A survey of social interests."
[53] *Arizona Cooper Co. v. Hammer*, 250 US 400 (1919) (Justice McKenna, dissenting).
[54] Pound, "A survey of social interests" 4 (emphasis added).
[55] *Hudson County*, 209 US 355 (1908).

submitted that that basis must be the one upon which common law has always sought to proceed, the one implied in the very term "due process of law," namely, *a weighing or balancing* of the various interests which overlap or come in conflict and a rational reconciling or adjustment.[56]

Latter-day Progressives writing in the 1930s, such as Justice Harlan Fiske Stone and Judge Learned Hand espoused balancing as part of their view that all constitutional provisions were in fact standards rather than exact rules that impose concrete limits on government action. Stone wrote:

> The great constitutional guarantees of personal liberty and of property ... are but statements of standards ... The chief and ultimate standard which they exact is reasonableness of official action and its innocence of arbitrary and oppressive exactions ... *They do not prescribe formulas to which governmental action must conform* ... [They do not subject] government to inexorable commands imposed upon it in another age. [They should] enable government, in "all the various crises of human affairs," to continue to function and to perform its appointed task within the bounds of reasonableness ...[57]

Progressive balancing was, therefore, hostile to constitutional rights in two important and related ways. First, it equated rights with interests: rights are nothing more than specific social interests and should thus be balanced against other interests. Elevating rights above interests as a separate category was considered by Progressives to be a rhetorical or manipulative move whose sole purpose was to further the ideological goals of the Supreme Court. Second, Progressives believed that balancing should be left to the legislature. Professor Morton Horowitz makes this view clear: "[I]f law is merely a battleground over which social interests clash, then the legislature is the appropriate institution for weighing and measuring competing interests." He adds further that "by the time 'The path of the law' was written, the focus of Holmes's Darwinism had shifted from courts to legislatures."[58]

Holmes' dissent in *Lochner* is the clearest example of this conclusion being applied to constitutional law: "I do not conceive that to be my duty to determine which economic theory should prevail, because I strongly believe that my agreement or disagreement has nothing to do with the right of a majority to embody their opinions in law ... [A] Constitution is

---

[56] Pound, "A survey of social interests" (emphasis added).

[57] Harlan F. Stone, "The common law in the United States" (1936) 50 Harv. L. Rev. 4, 23–4 (emphasis added).

[58] Horowitz, "The rule of law: an unqualified human good" 142.

not intended to embody a particular economic theory, whether of pater-nalism and the organic relation of the citizen to the state or of *laissez faire*. It is made for people of fundamentally differing views."[59] Since Holmes identified the issue in *Lochner* as a matter of balancing rather than something determined by the Constitution, he concluded that it was not the Court's role to decide it, but the legislature's.

Progressive balancing during the McCarthy era

In the 1950s and early 1960s, during the McCarthy era and the early days of the Warren Court, balancing continued to be associated with an attack on the formalistic and absolutist conception of rights and with judicial restraint. The Supreme Court justices who applied balan-cing principles during this period were also Progressivists, but unlike their earlier counterparts from the Lochner era, they were associated with conservatism rather than liberalism. This was so since the liberal–conservative divide during the McCarthy era ran down different lines from the Lochner Court period. It was now the legislature and execu-tive which were conservative and reactionary, rather than the Supreme Court, so that judicial deference meant conservatism rather than liberalism.[60]

Justice Frankfurter's opinion in *Dennis*[61] is the leading example of the use of balancing during the McCarthy era. This case, decided at the height of the anti-communist campaign, revolved around the appeal, on constitutional free speech grounds, of the conviction of members of the American Communist Party under the Sedition Act. Frankfurter, writing in concurrence, applied balancing to First Amendment freedom of speech very similarly to how the earlier Progressives had applied it to freedom of contract under the Fourteenth Amendment. He argued that the right to free speech should not be read formalistically and in absolute terms: "[T]here are those who find in the Constitution a wholly unfet-tered right of expression. Such literalness treats the words of the Consti-tution as though they were found on a piece of outworn parchment."[62]

---

[59] Lochner, 198 US at 76.

[60] For a general review of the use of balancing during the McCarthy era and for objections on the Court, see Melvin I. Urofsky, *Division and Discord: The Supreme Court under Stone and Vinson, 1941–1953* (Columbia, SC: University of South Carolina Press, 1997). See also Laurent B. Frantz, "The First Amendment in the balance" (1962) 71 Yale L.J. 1424; Wallace Mendelson, Justices Black and Frankfurter, *Conflict in the Court* (Chicago, IL: University of Chicago Press, 1961).

[61] *Dennis v. United States*, 341 US 494 (1951).   [62] *Ibid.* 524.

Instead, he argued, the right should be understood as a standard and as espousing one of many social interests that can come into conflict and should be balanced against one another:

> The demands of free speech in a democratic society as well as the interest in national security are better served by candid and informed weighing of the competing interests, within the confines of the judicial process, than by announcing dogmas too inflexible for the non-Euclidian problems to be solved.[63]

Similar to the earlier Progressives, Frankfurter also argued that the balancing of interests should be left to the legislature and that the Court should exercise judicial restraint: "Primary responsibility for adjusting the interests which compete in the situation before us, of necessity, belongs to the Congress."[64]

Dennis was followed by a series of judgments that applied balancing in the same way.[65] These subsequent cases very clearly manifested all three features of Progressive balancing noted earlier: anti-formalism and anti-absolutism; the association with judicial restraint; and, most importantly, hostility towards the preference of rights over interests and the idea that rights are exempt from public interest considerations. Not coincidentally, *Dennis* symbolizes to this day the most troubling risk of balancing: the danger of judicial capitulation to the legislature's determination of the balance of interests in times of national security crisis. Nor should it come as any surprise that in the later days of the Warren Court, as the Court became more and more liberal, it dissociated itself completely from the idea of balancing, in part as a consequence of the stigma of *Dennis*.[66] Thus, most of the major

---

[63] *Ibid.* 524–5.   [64] *Ibid.* 525–6.

[65] The major cases involved in this debate were *American Communications Ass'n* v. *Douds*, 339 US 382 (1950); *Barenblatt* v. *United States*, 360 US 109 (1959); *Konigsberg* v. *State Bar*, 366 US 36 (1961); *Communist Party of the United States* v. *Subversive Activities Control Bd.*, 367 US 1 (1961).

[66] See Horowitz, *The Transformation of American Law 1870–1960: The Crisis of Legal Orthodoxy* 68 ("As a result of this blatant misuse, the balancing test in civil liberties litigation deservedly acquired a bad reputation among liberal justices, and Warren Court opinions are filled with angry denunciation of its use."); Ely, "Flag desecration: a case study in the roles of categorization and balancing in First Amendment analysis" (1975) 88 Harv. L. Rev. 482, 1490–1 ("[Balancing] was hardly the attitude of the Warren Court, at least in its later years. During [that period] the Court was making clear its dissatisfaction with a general balancing approach …").

constitutional decisions of the Warren Court avoided balancing rhetoric,[67] and some even rejected balancing outright.[68]

Conclusion

The historical origins of balancing in American constitutional law are very different from – even antithetical to – how proportionality developed in German law. First, unlike proportionality, balancing entered a system in which constitutional guarantees were already present and in which judicial activism to protect rights was an established norm. Therefore, unlike proportionality, which was a way of ensuring that rights are not *harmed* unnecessarily, balancing was aimed at ensuring that rights are not *protected* unnecessarily by weighing them against public interests. Second, balancing emerged as part of the anti-formalist movement, which emphatically rejected categorical distinctions between rights and interests and according preference to rights over interests. In contrast, the focus of proportionality in the context of the *Rechtsstaat* was to find specific ways to restrict governmental action, grounded on a conception of the unique status of rights and the need for the government to provide special justification for infringing them.

Finally, the two concepts also differed significantly in their jurisprudential and ideological backgrounds. Proportionality was developed within the framework of the PSAC's well-organized and formalist jurisprudence without any aspirations of creating a sweeping theory. Balancing, on the other hand, was part of a revolutionary anti-formalist conception of law that sought to call into question the prevailing legal philosophy and eventually transformed the face of American law. Ideologically, proportionality was based on natural rights liberalism and libertarianism, whereas balancing sought to undermine the primacy of natural rights and opposed the libertarian conception of property and liberty rights.

---

[67] *See* Aleinikoff, "Constitutional law in the age of balancing" (1987) 96 Yale L.J. 998 (arguing that the major constitutional cases of the Warren Court were not balancing cases, and referring to *Brown* v. *Board of Education*, 347 US 483 (1954), claiming, "Of course ... there were competing interests at stake. But the Court based its decision – as has society – not on the balance of those interests, but on the intolerability of racial discrimination.").

[68] See, for example, Chief Justice Warren's opinion in *United States* v. *Robel*, 389 US 258, (1968): "[I]t has been suggested that this case should be decided by 'balancing' the governmental interests ... against the First Amendment rights ... This we decline to do." *Ibid.* 268 n. 20.

3

Culture

Chapter 2 addressed differences in the historical origins of American balancing and German proportionality. This chapter will add another layer to the contextual understanding of these two concepts, by examining the general political culture of the German and US legal systems over time, and the way they are reflected in the structure of their respective constitutional systems. The two layers of context – history and political culture – are of course interrelated. This interrelation can be understood by looking at the relevant political culture as the general background against which balancing and proportionality historically emerged. In addition, whereas the historical review is confined to a relatively defined period of time – the late nineteenth and early twentieth centuries, when these doctrines first appeared and began to develop – the examination of political culture considers earlier as well as later periods that are relevant to understanding this layer of context.

The German communitarian and organic conception of the state

The terrible outcome of the Second World War ignited a debate over what political morality should guide the constitution of the new Germany. In his seminal work *The German Idea of Freedom*, Leonard Krieger argued that in light of the moral bankruptcy of nationalism, Germany should break away from its communitarian heritage and adopt a more neutral, suspicion-based constitution, one that would guarantee negative liberties for all its citizens and set strict limits on the government.[1]

---

[1] Krieger, *The German Idea of Freedom* (Boston, MA: Beacon Press, 1957) 470 (arguing for an approach that "views the state as a morally neutral, purely utilitarian organization of public power"); see also Donald P. Kommers, *The Constitutional Jurisprudence of the Federal Republic of Germany* (Durham, NC: Duke University Press, 2nd edn., 1997) 33; Girish N. Bhat, "Recovering the historical Rechtsstaat" (2007) 32 Rev. Cent. & E. Eur. L. 65, 88–9.

Although sound at first glance, it appears that this "American-style" solution of state neutrality and negative rights would have been inappropriate for postwar Germany. First, adhering to state neutrality would have entailed neutrality also towards the racist attitudes that were prevalent in a society in which the large majority of the population had been raised on the notion of Aryan superiority. Indeed, an ambitious project lay behind the formulation of the postwar German Constitution: to bring about a profound transformation of German consciousness and attitudes so that the values upon which human rights are founded would become acknowledged and internalized in German society.[2] This goal could only be realized by according the state a non-neutral stance in society.

Secondly, the "neutral" approach does not conform to traditional German political theory, which is Hegelian and Aristotelian in orientation. Under this tradition, the state is conceived not as merely an aggregate of the individuals who live in a given territory and coordinate their activities, but as a union of people who share a common value system and seek to promote those values.[3] As opposed to the atomized conception of the self and the idea of the "separateness of the person,"

---

[2] See Clemens Jabloner, "Hans Kelsen: Introduction," in Arthur J. Jacobson and Bernhard Schlink (eds.), *Weimar: A Jurisprudence of Crisis* (Berkeley, CA: California University Press, 2000) 67, 73 (relating to the arguments that the concepts of formal democracy and neutrality that guided the Weimar Republic were conceived of as one of the reasons for its constitutional collapse); Donald P. Kommers, "German constitutionalism: a prolegomenon" (1991) 40 Em. L.J. 837, 852–3, 861 (explaining that the trauma of the Second World War led many German theorists to suggest a departure from neutral principles of formalism and the adoption of a natural law approach).

[3] As mentioned in Chapter 2, the German fundamental concept of the *Rechtsstaat* – "a state governed by law" – differs from the common law concept of the rule of law, in that the former is tied to an organic conception of the state that seeks to integrate state and society. See Kommers, *The Constitutional Jurisprudence of the Federal Republic of Germany* 36; Hans Rosenberg, "Politische Denkströmungen im deutschen Vormärz," in *Kritische Studien zur Geschichtswissenschaft 3* (Göttingen: Verlag Vandenhoeck & Ruprecht, 1972) 37 (arguing that the state is viewed not only as an institutional safeguard to protect individual rights but also as the "Vaterland"); Rudolf Smend, *Verfassung und Verfassungsrecht* (Munich: Duncker & Humblot, 1928) (stating the role of the constitution and of constitutional interpretation is to integrate society around shared values); Otto von Gierke, *The Development of Political Theory* (Bernard Freyd trans., New York: Howard Fertig, Inc., 1966) (first published 1939) (original German version 1880); Reimann, "Nineteenth century German legal science" (1990) 31 B.C.L. Rev. 837 (discussing the influence of Hegelian and communitarian ideas on nineteenth-century German legal science). On Smend's influential integration theory, see Stefan Korioth and Rudolph Smend, "Introduction," in Arthur J. Jacobson and Bernhard Schlink (eds.), *Weimar: A Jurisprudence of Crisis* (Berkeley, CA: California University Press, 2000) 207.

which are predominant in liberal political theory,[4] German political theory emphasizes that a person is embedded in a community with shared values that expresses solidarity towards all of its members and holds an "organic" conception of the state and its relationship with the individual. The organic conception is the institutional manifestation of the communitarian idea in which all the state organs including the citizens act in harmony and coordination to fulfil and realize their shared values. Accordingly, in 1954, the Federal German Constitutional Court (FGCC) ruled:

> The Basic Law's idea of man is not the idea of an isolated sovereign individual; rather, the Basic Law has decided the tension between individuals and society in favor of the individual being community related and community bound – while not touching its intrinsic value.[5]

Based on this ruling, some commentators have argued that communitarianism is the underlying constitutional theory of the German Basic Law.[6] This does not mean that German constitutional law can be reduced to mere conservatism and traditionalism. Rather, German constitutional jurisprudence can also be conceived of as manifesting liberal, egalitarian, and republican strands of communitarianism.[7] What is common to all these strands, however, is the essential role played by the state in realizing shared values. In this sense, German political theory can be characterized as *perfectionist*, in contrast to the *anti-perfectionist* political theory predominant in the USA, which emphasizes state-neutrality.[8]

---

[4] The concept of the separateness of the person is central in liberalism and libertarianism. See Robert Nozick, *Anarchy, State, and Utopia* (New York: Questia, 1974) 32–3; John Rawls, *A Theory of Justice* (Cambridge, MA: Harvard University Press, 1971) 27.

[5] *Lüftsicherheitsgesetz* Case, BVerfGE 4, 7, www.servat.unibe.ch/dfr/bv004007.html.

[6] See, e.g., Walter Reese-Schäfer, *Politisches Denken heute: Zivilgesellschaft, Globalisierung und Menschenrechte* (Munich: Oldenbourg, Wissenschaftsverlag GmbH, 2007) 23; Rainer Nickel, "Gleichheit in der Differenz? Kommunitarismus und die Legitimation des Grundgesetzes," in *Legitimation des Grundgesetzes aus Sicht von Rechtsphilosophie und Gesellschaftstheorie* (Baden-Baden: Nomos Verlag, 1996) 401 ff.

[7] For such a distinction, see Winfried Brugger, "Zum Verhältnis von Neutralitätsliberalismus und liberalem Kommunitarismus. Dargestellt am Streit über das Kreuz in der Schule," in Winfried Brugger and Stefan Huster (eds.), *Der Streit um das Kreuz in der Schule: Zur religiös-weltanschaulichen Neutralität des Staates* (Baden-Baden: Nomos Verlag, 1. Auflage, 1998) 123; Nickel, "Gleichheit in der Differenz? Kommunitarismus und die Legitimation des Grundgesetzes" 401 ff.

[8] For a distinction between liberal perfectionism and liberal anti-perfectionism, see Joseph Raz, *The Morality of Freedom* (Oxford: Clarendon Press, 1986).

This communitarian aspect of German constitutionalism is manifested in various frameworks. First, Article 20(1) of the Basic Law entrenched the fundamental institutional and unamendable principle that Germany is a social state. This defining feature of German constitutionalism has shaped the *Soziale Marktwirtschaft* ("social market economy") principle, one of the most important organizing principles of the German economy, which obliges the state to maintain a collective safety net. Second, in contrast to American constitutionalism, which requires a relatively strict separation between state and religion, the German model espouses cooperation (*Kooperation*) between the two. In Germany, religious beliefs are sometimes seen as instilling solidarity with the poor and as enhancing constitutional values relating to civil rights, which are also linked to the ideals of solidarity and membership in society.[9] Third, Article 6 of the Basic Law assigns a major role to traditional notions of the family, motherhood, and marriage. Under Article 6(1), "marriage and the family" are extended "the special protection of the state," with Article 6(4) providing further that "every mother shall be entitled to the protection and care of the community." It is small wonder that some feminist scholars see these features of German constitutionalism as undermining women's rights.[10]

The state and its various organs and documents, then, play an important role in realizing common values and are perceived as having an organic relationship with the citizens. This organic conception of the state is trust-oriented: it is constructed on a premise of reciprocal cooperation and trust among all state organs and assumes that all state organs have legitimate interests that should be optimized. The functioning of the FGCC should be understood in light of this organic conception. Unlike the US perception of courts, constitutional judges in Germany are not expected to fulfill a classic anti-majoritarian task. As Alec Stone Sweet explains, in Germany, as in Europe in general, the Constitutional Court does not conduct judicial review in the typical anti-majoritarian sense that many Europeans oppose. Instead, the Court is viewed as a political organ that is an integral part of the state and shares in the task of

[9] Winfried Brugger, "Liberaler Kommunitarismus im Grundgesetz: Eine Theorieskizze und das Kreuz in der Schule als praktisches Beispiel," in *Die Idee des Rechts und soziale Verantwortung als Handlungsgrundlage der modernen Staatenwelt* (Speyer: Deutsche Hochschule für Verwaltungswissenschaften, 2010) 83 (arguing that these virtues merit state support for religion).

[10] See, e.g., Gila Stopler, "The liberal bind: the conflict between women's rights and patriarchal religion in the liberal state" (2005) 31 Soc. Theory & Prac. 191.

elaborating and shaping social values and norms.[11] This approach to the court's role, which reflects and derives from the organic conception of the state, may account for the fact that, in Germany, there is far less criticism of judicial review for being countermajoritarian.[12] As Dieter Grimm has elucidated, "There is no preestablished difference between court and legislatures which a particular contribution has to adopt and which an interpreter has to enforce regardless of what the constitution says. In addition, constitutional courts inevitably cross the line between law and politics."[13]

It is important to note that the organic conception was adapted to the shift of values in German society after the Second World War. Shortly after its establishment, the FGCC ruled that the Constitution is governed by a set of objective and hierarchal values, what has been termed the *Objektive Wertordnung*.[14] This ruling did not mark a departure in any way from traditional German thought, which assigns

[11] Alec Stone Sweet, *Governing with Judges: Constitutional Politics in Europe* (Oxford: Oxford University Press, 2000) 32, 40.

[12] It is true that in the 1960s, there was some criticism of the Constitutional Court's broad role and its extensive reference to abstract values. Carl Schmitt and other German legal scholars attacked the Court's functioning on the grounds that it leads to the "tyranny of values," primarily because values are of an abstract nature and their realization quite often leads to rulings that correspond with the particular judge's own personal value system. Ernst Forsthoff, *Zur Problematik der Verfassungsauslegung* (Stuttgart: W. Kohlhammer Verlag, 1961) 19, 40; Carl Schmitt, "Die Tyrannei der Werte," in K. Doering and W.G. Grewe (eds.), *Säkularisation und Utopie: Ernst Forsthoff zum 65. Geburtstag* (Stuttgart: Ebracher Studien, 1967) 37, 39; Wolfgang Zeidler, "Grundrechte und Grundentscheidungen der Verfassung im Widerstreit," in *Verhandlungen des Dreiundfünfzigsten Deutschen Juristentages* (Munich: Beck Verlag, 1980) 6–29. This criticism, however, is the minority stance in current German legal scholarship. See Kommers, "German constitutionalism: a prolegomenon" 842 ("the source and authority of the Federal Constitutional Court are relatively undisputed"). But see Bernhard Schlink, "Der Grundsatz der Verhältnismäßigkeit," in Peter Badura and Horst Dreier (eds.), *Festschrift 50 Jahre Bundesverfassungsgericht* (Tübingen: Mohr Siebeck, 2001) 445, 460 (criticizing the extensive use of the third proportionality subtest – balancing – in FGCC jurisprudence).

[13] Kommers, *The Constitutional Jurisprudence of the Federal Republic of Germany* 44 (referencing Grimm's comments that appear in Dieter Grimm, "Comment," in Christian Landfried (ed.), *Constitutional Review and Legislation: An International Comparison* (Baden-Baden: Nomos, 1988) 169.

[14] Article 117 Case, Bundesverfassungsgericht [BVerfG] [Federal Constitutional Court] December 20, 1953, 3 Entscheidungen des Bundesverfassungsgerichts [BVerfGE] 3, 225 (232) (FRG), cited in Kommers, *The Constitutional Jurisprudence of the Federal Republic of Germany* 47–8 (noting that the Constitutional Court rejected "value-free legal positivism" and that, in its early years, "appeared to accept natural law as an independent standard of review").

the state a central role in realizing individual well-being and integrating individuals into a community with shared values. The Court did, however, change the contents of those common values in its ruling. Rather than nationalistic values – such as *Volksgeist*, or "the spirit of the people," which lay at the foundation of nineteenth-century German jurisprudence[15] – the Court deemed the dominant value of German society to be human dignity.[16] This value, which is the opening shot of the German Constitution, is absolute and can be considered its Archimedes Point.[17]

Proportionality as an intrinsic element of the communitarian and organic conception of the state

The doctrine of proportionality is understood to be inherent to the German constitution, despite the lack of any explicit reference to it therein.[18] The doctrine of proportionality is widely conceived as the main means by which the organic conception is realized in FGCC jurisprudence. Proportionality in Germany is a tool not only for resolving disputes, but also for harmonizing and integrating the various state organs around shared values.[19] German constitutional scholars do not speak of proportionality in terms of a pragmatic enterprise involving some sort of cost-benefit analysis. Rather, they take a more idealistic view

---

[15] Reimann, "Nineteenth century German legal science" 853. To Savigny, one of the leading legal scholars in nineteenth-century Germany, *Volksgeist* does not stand for "culture" in the anthropological sense but rather in the intellectual sense: *Volksgeist* was the organic development of the law's underlying intellectual principles.

[16] Article 1(1) of the German Basic Law, 1949, provides: "Human dignity shall be inviolable. To respect and protect it shall be the duty of all state authority." Grundegesetz [GG] [Constitution] art. 1(1) (FRG), www.bundestag.de/interakt/infomat/fremdsprachiges_-material/downloads/ggEn_download.pdf (English translation). In the *Microzensus* Case, BverfGE 27, 1, the FGCC ruled, "Human Dignity is at the very top of the value order of the Basic Law." *Ibid.* (author's translation).

[17] Kommers, "German constitutionalism: a prolegomenon" 855.

[18] Most post-Second World War constitutional and international documents include an explicit textual basis for proportionality analysis. See Grimm, "Proportionality in Canadian and German constitutional law jurisprudence" (2007) 57 U. Toronto L.J. 383–4 (in the Canadian Charter of Rights and Freedoms, "proportionality appears to be a genuine interpretation of the words 'reasonable limits … as can be demonstrably justified in a free and democratic society'"). In Germany, however, the constitutional text lacks any such explicit reference. The Constitutional Court derived the principle of proportionality from the *Rechtsstaat* principle, but without explaining why. See *ibid.* at 385.

[19] Michael Sachs (ed.), *Grundgesetz: Kommentar* (Munich: Beck, 1996) 94, 95.

of the doctrine, as necessary for the optimization of social values.[20]
Consequently, proportionality constitutes the primary methodology for
maintaining the integrity and "unity of values" of the Basic Law.[21] As
originally stated by the late Constitutional Court Justice Konrad Hesse:

> The principle of the constitution's unity requires the optimization of [the
> values in conflict]: Both legal values need to be limited so that each can
> attain its optimal effect. In each concrete case, therefore, the limitation
> must satisfy the principle of proportionality; that is, they may not go any
> further than necessary to produce a concordance of both legal values.[22]

Proportionality thus functions as a central mechanism for enhancing
harmony and cooperation between conflicting values in German society
and is closely related to the principle requiring harmonic interpretation
and practical concordance of the German constitution, known as "*prak-
tische Konkordanz.*"[23] Accordingly, When Winfried Brugger, a liberal
communitarian, refers to cases revolving around the constitutionality of
hanging up crucifixes in schools, he argues that the Constitution does not
give preference to any of the conflicting interests, but instead aims at
accommodating and harmonizing among the opposing views.[24] It is all
about balancing and proportionality, he asserts, as well as about weighing
the facts of the concrete case and seeking to moderate between the
different religious and secular worldviews.[25]

The fact that proportionality serves to ensure the realization of abstract
constitutional values and gives them meaning in concrete cases goes back
to the German conception of value order. Conflicts in Germany are
perceived as occurring entirely within the constitutional sphere – that
is, both interests and rights derive from the Constitution. The main

---

[20] See Kommers, *The Constitutional Jurisprudence of the Federal Republic of Germany* 46–7;
Konrad Konrad Hesse, *Grundzüge des Verfassungsrechts der Bundesrepublik Deutschland*
(Heidelberg: C.F. Müller Verlag, 1988) 27, translated in Kommers, "German constitu-
tionalism: a prolegomenon" 851 n. 43.

[21] The Constitutional Court first set the "unity of values" principle in the *Southwest State
Case*, Bundesverfassungsgericht [BVerfGE] [Federal Constitutional Court] October 23,
1951, 1 Entscheidungen des Bundesverfassungsgerichts [BVerfGE] 1, 14 (FRG), holding
that "every constitutional provision must always be interpreted in such a way as to render
it compatible with the fundamental principles of the constitution." *Ibid.* (author's
translation).

[22] Hesse, *Grundzüge des Verfassungsrechts der Bundesrepublik Deutschland, 27,* quoted and
translated in Kommers, *The Constitutional Jurisprudence of the Federal Republic of
Germany* 46.

[23] *Ibid.* 30–1.   [24] Winfried Brugger, "Liberaler Kommunitarismus in Grundgesetz" 84.

[25] *Ibid.*

concern of proportionality, then, is to determine which of the interests or rights in conflict best furthers the ultimate shared goals of the constitutional order. In addition, as already noted, the organic conception of the polity makes the policymaking aspects of proportionality less problematic in the German constitutional regime; it is the Constitutional Court's explicit task to instantiate the abstract values of the Constitution in specific cases. Thus, rather than being perceived as illegitimate judicial intervention in policymaking, balancing is viewed in Germany as the objective, systematic, and logical implementation of constitutional rights, while realizing values in everyday life is considered to be the Constitutional Court's ultimate task.[26]

The centrality of the proportionality doctrine in the Constitutional Court's jurisprudence is clearly evident in its declaration that proportionality emerges "basically from the nature of constitutional rights themselves."[27] Moreover, Robert Alexy has gone so far as to assert that proportionality "logically follows from the nature of [rights as] principles; it can be deduced from them."[28] The centrality of proportionality in German constitutionalism is also manifested in its close connection to *Rechtsstaat* (a state governed by law), which underlies the entire organization of the German state. It is also reflected in the frequent references in German legal literature to this principle, which – so it is claimed – fundamentally forms and maintains the state.[29]

Two FGCC judgments are illustrative of how proportionality analysis is guided by the organic conception of the state. In *Mephisto*, the court dealt with the constitutionality of a judicial order banning the distribution of Klaus Mann's novel *Mephisto*, on the grounds that it slandered the reputation of a deceased Nazi collaborator.[30] In balancing the right to reputation

---

[26] Jacco Bomhoff, "*Lüth*'s 50th anniversary: some comparative observations on the German foundations of judicial balancing" (2008) 9 Ger. L.J. 121, 124, www.germanlawjournal.com/pdf/Vol09No02/PDF_Vol_09_No_02_121-124_Articles_Bomhoff.pdf.

[27] Bundesverfassungsgericht [BVerfG] [Federal Constitutional Court] December 15, 1965, 19 Entscheidungen des Bundesverfassungsgerichts [BVerfGE] 19, 342 (348) (FRG) (author's translation).

[28] Robert Alexy, *A Theory of Constitutional Rights* (Oxford: Oxford University Press, Julian Rivers trans., 2002) 66.

[29] Bernd Grzeszick, in *Maunz/Dürig Grundgesetz Kommentar* (Munich: Verlag C.H. Beck 2009) Art. 20 Rn. 108.

[30] *Mephisto* Case, Bundesverfassungsgericht [BVerfG] [Federal Constitutional Court] February 24, 1971, 30 Entscheidungen des Bundesverfassungsgerichts [BVerfGE] 30, 173 (FRG), www.servat.unibe.ch/dfr/bv030173.html, summarized and partially translated in Kommers, *The Constitutional Jurisprudence of the Federal Republic of Germany* 301–4.

and free artistic speech, the Constitutional Court deliberated which of the conflicting values had the stronger link to the paramount value of human dignity.[31] The Court's decision in favor of the right to reputation, banning the distribution of the book, meant that the balancing process more strongly promoted the German value system prescribing "man as an autonomous person who develops freely *within the social community*."[32]

The Court's *Lebach* judgment is an example of a more nuanced application of the proportionality analysis.[33] In this case, the Court deliberated the matter of whether a television station could broadcast a documentary exposing the private information about a prisoner on the eve of his release.[34] In its decision, the Court weighed the extent to which the broadcast would harm the prisoner's right to privacy against the extent of harm to free speech that would ensue from banning the program in light of the paramount value of human dignity. The Court stressed that it would not abstractly rank the competing rights.[35] Instead, the mediation and harmonization between rights should be an ad hoc process, with the extent of harm to each measured in light of the circumstances of the case at hand.[36] Thus, the Court ruled that banning reference to the prisoner's private information in the broadcast would *best* serve human dignity.[37]

To sum up, proportionality analysis in Germany seems to have two distinct features. First, when conducting a proportionality analysis, the Constitutional Court considers which of the competing rights or values better optimizes the constitutional value order and, more specifically, which more strongly upholds human dignity. Second, the fact that German proportionality is always conducted in an ad hoc manner does not raise any issues of judicial legitimacy, because under the organic conception of the state in Germany, it is actually the Constitutional Court's duty to realize the constitutional values in concrete cases.

The American individualistic and suspicion-based conception of the state

Unlike Germany, American political culture did not have to adjust or change its course following the Second World War. The fundamental

---

[31] *Ibid.*   [32] *Ibid.* (emphasis added).

[33] *Lebach* Case, Bundesverfassungsgericht [BVerfG] [Federal Constitutional Court] May 2, 1973, 35 Entscheidungen des Bundesverfassungsgerichts [BVerfGE] 202 (FRG), www.servat.unibe.ch/dfr/bv035202.html, summarized and partially translated in Kommers, *The Constitutional Jurisprudence of the Federal Republic of Germany* 416–19.

[34] *Ibid.*   [35] *Ibid.*   [36] *Ibid.*   [37] *Ibid.*

premises and tenets on which it was founded remained very much intact. American society perceived itself even from the colonial period to be a refuge for religious minorities that were being persecuted in Europe and as a place where class distinctions would be minimized and alleviated. The abundance of land allowed for greater social mobility and for easier acquisition of land, while the opportunities of a New World created the common perception that even people from the middle or lower classes could build a life for themselves based on the ideals of personal merit and hard work.[38]

These premises and conceptions bred a political culture in which paramount value was accorded to liberty, personal responsibility, and individualism. In terms of liberty, there was emphasis on religious liberty from governmental oppression and personal liberty in the form of freedom to pursue one's goals and aspirations. The flipside of the coin is responsibility and individualism: liberty entails responsibility for the outcome of one's actions and decisions, without any right or claim to assistance from others or the state in the event of failure. Similarly, one is responsible only for the product of one's actions and not for injustices that are not the direct result of those actions, such as social inequality. This directly relates to the third value that characterizes American society: individualism. Every individual is free to shape his or her own life, free of the collective interests, but at the same time, bearing responsibility for his or her choices and with no resort to the collective for help. Taken together, these values shaped the system of government in the USA as based on strong faith in the potential of the individual and a deep-rooted wariness of government.[39]

As argued forcefully by Jed Rubenfeld, this aversion to government intervention and emphasis on popular democracy were not diminished by the outcome of the Second World War but rather reinforced by it. In Germany, popular democracy came to be viewed with great suspicion following the war, since it was felt that the masses could not be trusted to distinguish right from wrong, having chosen racist, fascist regimes. This led to the call to curb popular democracy in Germany and, to some extent, in European political culture generally. In the USA, in contrast, popular democracy had "stood the test." The masses had chosen democracy and, furthermore, to defend it even

---

[38] Michael Kazin et al., *The Princeton Encyclopedia of American Political History* (Princeton, NJ: Princeton University Press, 2010) vol. II 153–5.

[39] B. Wright (ed.), *The Federalist* (New York: Peter Lang, 1961).

overseas against fascism and totalitarianism. The message, therefore, did not change in the wake of the Second World War: leave power in the hands of the people and bolster democracy.[40] The starkest context in which the difference between the lessons of the Second World War for Europe and for America emerges is with regard to free speech. In Europe, the lesson learned was that harmful speech, in particular, hate speech and racist speech, had to be limited to prevent the recurrence of another world war. In America, it was Heinrich Heine's famous words that expressed the lessons learned: "where they burn books they will ultimately burn people also."[41] Thus, the prevailing approach in the USA remained that free speech should be as robust as possible, since democracy is the best response to totalitarianism.[42]

Four key tenets of American constitutional law express clearly the individualistic and suspicion-based conception of the state: (1) the separation of powers; (2) the conception of rights as trumps; (3) the notion of state neutrality; and (4) an emphasis on popular democracy.

First, as already described, the American conception of the state, unlike the German organic conception, is characterized by a distrust of government, deriving from the principles of individual autonomy and self-rule.[43] This wariness extends to all branches of government, including the judiciary, and lies at the base of the particularly American emphasis on separation of powers:[44] because no governmental organ can be trusted not to overstep its legitimate bounds, power must be decentralized by clearly defining the limits of each of the branches of

[40] See Jed Rubenfeld, "Commentary, *Unilateralism and Constitutionalism*" (2004) 79 N.Y.U. L. Rev. 1971.

[41] This line appears in Heine's 1823 play *Almansor: A Tragedy*, as trans. in Graham Ward, *True Religion* (Hoboken, NJ: Blackwell Publishing, 2003) 142.

[42] See, e.g., Frederick Schauer, "Freedom of expression adjudication in Europe and the United States: a case study in comparative constitutional architecture," in Georg Nolte (ed.), *European and US Constitutionalism* (Cambridge: Cambridge University Press, 2005) 49–51; Frederick Schauer, "The exceptional first amendment," in Michael Ignatieff (ed.), *American Exceptionalism and Human Rights* (Princeton, NJ: Princeton University Press, 2005) 29, 32.

[43] The most distinct exposition on the centrality of distrust in American political culture can be found in John Hart Ely, *Democracy and Distrust: A Theory of Judicial Review* (Cambridge, MA: Harvard University Press, 1980) 102–3.

[44] See, for example, Rachel Barkow's description of the American governmental system as one "whose hallmark is supposed to be the separation of powers." Rachel E. Barkow, "Institutional design and the policing of prosecutors: lessons from administrative law" (2009) 61 Stan. L. Rev. 869.

government and clearly separating them.[45] Consequently, American constitutionalism seeks to set limits on judicial power and to differentiate the judicial role from the roles of the other branches of government.[46] This, of course, stands in stark contrast to the conception of the German Constitutional Court as operating between the lines of politics and law.

Second, American constitutionalism is grounded on the conception of rights as trumps or as exclusionary reasons *vis-à-vis* the government that limits the scope of legitimate governmental ends.[47] The American culture of distrust of government power bred a similarly suspicion-based approach in the drafting of the Constitution: clear rules for government and clear rights for citizens were crafted as a means of limiting government power. Thus, formulating constitutional rights in absolute terms was preferred to the complexity of allowing limitations on rights in certain instances, and a clear-cut distinction between individual rights and governmental interests was favored over blurred boundaries, in order to safeguard individual autonomy and constrain governmental power.[48]

[45] See, e.g., Cass R. Sunstein, *The Partial Constitution* (Cambridge, MA: Harvard University Press, 1993) 21 (explaining the intention of the Framers that "[i]n a large republic, the various factions would offset each other").

[46] See, e.g., Alexander M. Bickel, *The Least Dangerous Branch* (Hartford, CT: Yale University Press, 1962) 46-7.

[47] The term "exclusionary reasons" is taken from Joseph Raz's practical reasoning philosophy. Joseph Raz, *Practical Reasons and Norms* (Princeton, NJ: Princeton University Press, 2nd edn., 1999) 35. It has been applied to describe American constitutional law. See, e.g., Richard H. Pildes, "Avoiding balancing: the role of exclusionary reasons in constitutional law" (1994) 45 Hastings L. J. 707; Iddo Porat, "The dual model of balancing" (2006) 27 Cardozo L. Rev. 1393; Iddo Porat, "On the Jehovah Witnesses cases: balancing tests, indirect infringement of rights and multiculturalism. A proposed model for three kinds of multicultural claims" (2007) 1 L. & Ethics of Hum. Rts. 429. Some authors, while not making direct use of the term, have a similar conception of rights in American law. See, e.g., Ronald Dworkin, *Taking Rights Seriously* (Cambridge, MA: Harvard University Press, 1977) (rights are constructs designed to exclude those instances where history has shown that the utilitarian tends to be corrupted by external preferences); Rubenfeld, "Commentary. *Unilateralism and Constitutionalism*" (advocating a non-balancing approach to free speech law in the USA); Donald H. Regan, "The Supreme Court and state protectionism: making sense of the dormant commerce clause" (1986) 84 Mich. L. Rev. 1091, 1103-4 (interpreting the Commerce Clause as "excluding" protectionist motives).

[48] C. Edwin Baker, "Limitations on basic human rights: a view from the United States," in Armand de Mestral *et al.* (eds.), *The Limitation of Human Rights in Comparative Constitutional Law* (Montreal: Les Editions Yvon Blais, 1986) 75, 76, 89 (describing the American categorical approach to rights as opposed to approaches that expressly allow for the limitation of rights).

Third, in contrast to the German conception of underlying values, the American concept of the polity is based on the Lockean notion of state neutrality and individual liberties.[49] While the Constitution provides the infrastructure for democracy, it cannot govern or impose ideas or ideologies; they must be hashed out through the democratic process. According to Justice Holmes, the Constitution should unite people with extremely divergent views under its umbrella.[50]

Finally, American constitutionalism is founded on a strong belief in representative democracy and the sovereignty of the people. Since *Marbury* v. *Madison*,[51] the democratic principle of self-rule has been the justification for judicial review and the judiciary's duty to uphold the Constitution. According to one popular perception, the Constitution represents a particularly long-lasting and fundamental means of democratic self-legislation; it represents the particular commitments that the American People undertook and set as higher law. This conception of democratic self-rule – more so than the organic conception of the state – views the constitutional text that expresses these commitments as of supreme importance. Rubenfeld has argued that in this context as well, the divergence between the USA and Europe is due in part to the lessons learned by each from the Second World War.[52] In Europe, one of the central understandings to emerge was that nationalism must be rejected and replaced by universalism and notions of international community. This significantly guided the preference in Europe of a universal conception of rights over a local conception. In the USA, however, nationalism did not present any problem in the context of the Second World War since it had generated the patriotic recruitment against totalitarianism. Rights, therefore, could remain local in nature and

---

[49] There is wide consensus on the significant influence of Lockean philosophy on the American Bill of Rights, though there is dispute as to the centrality of the right to property – as manifested in Locke's writings – in the Constitution. See, e.g., Richard Epstein, *Takings: Private Property and the Power of Eminent Domain* (Cambridge, MA: Harvard University Press, 1985) 17, 29; cf. Herman Schwartz, "Property rights and the constitution: will the ugly duckling become a swan?" (1987) 37 Am. U.L. Rev. 9, 14–19 (questioning the extent of Locke's influence on the Founding Fathers).

[50] See Holmes' famous statement in his *Lochner* dissent (*Lochner* v. *New York*, 198 US 45 (1905)): "[A] constitution is not intended to embody a particular economic theory, whether of paternalism and the organic relation of the citizen to the State or of *laissez faire*. It is made for people of fundamentally differing views." *Ibid.* 75–6 (Holmes, J., dissenting).

[51] 5 US (1 Cranch) 137 (1803).

[52] Rubenfeld, "Commentary, *Unilateralism and Constitutionalism*."

definition and derive their origin and legitimacy from "the people" rather than from universal and shared ideals.

The suspicion-based conception of the state and balancing

Whereas under an organic conception of the state, balancing is pivotal in the judicial enhancement of values, its corollary concept in America, balancing, is a problematic mechanism under a suspicion-based approach. First, balancing is in tension with the separation of powers doctrine and public wariness of the courts, because it entails a considerable amount of judicial discretion – greater, at any rate, than what is allowed under a rule-bound or categorical approach.[53] Moreover, separation of powers is further compromised by the fact that balancing appears to be strongly associated with policymaking, which is a function assigned to the elected branches of government.[54] Second, balancing is problematic also from the perspective of rights as a constraint on state power: blurring the distinction between rights and interests and giving more leeway for the infringement of rights to advance state interests result in weaker limits on government action.[55] Third, judicial balancing undermines state neutrality, for it requires that the constitutional court make substantive assessments of values, as well as decisions on the appropriate resolution of clashes between values. Lastly, balancing tends

---

[53] Burt Neuborne argues that "judicial balancing has been subjected to deserved academic criticism … because it licenses a judge to engage in overtly subjective decision-making that replicates and occasionally displaces, identical thought-processes already carried out by a politically responsible official." Burt Neuborne, "Notes for a theory of constrained balancing in First Amendment cases: an essay in Honor of Tom Emerson" (1988) 38 Case W. Res. L. Rev. 576, 578.

[54] Thus, Ducat argues, "The approach to judicial decision-making, taken by interest balancers, is much like that taken by political actors staffing coordinate institutions of government who must themselves choose between rival group interests on issues of the day." Craig R. Ducat, *Modes of Constitutional Interpretation* (St. Paul, MN: West Publishing, 1978) 119. Ducat continues, "[W]e need to know how the [balancing] technique of judicial review differs from legislative interest balancing" and whether the principled quality of the judicial process can be sustained at all with interest balancing. *Ibid.* 133.

[55] See Dworkin, *Taking Rights Seriously* 198 ("The metaphor of balancing the public interest against personal claims is established in our political and judicial rhetoric, and this metaphor gives the model both familiarity and appeal. Nevertheless, the model is a false one …"); see also Ronald Dworkin, Comment, "It is absurd to calculate human rights according to a cost-benefit analysis" *The Guardian*, 24 May 2006 (Debate & Comment) 28.

to inhibit non-textual analysis, in that it is forward looking and involves consequentialist, rather than interpretative, questions.[56]

As a result of the wariness regarding balancing and its incompatibility with some of the basic tenets of American constitutionalism, its status and character in American constitutional law differs considerably from that of proportionality in German law. In Germany, proportionality stands front and center as the most prominent constitutional doctrine, and is accorded an idealistic and scientific character, whereas in the USA balancing is generally relegated to a more residual and instrumental role and bounded by the categorical approach, and is accorded a pragmatic character. Chapter 4 will elaborate on the way in which balancing is residual and bounded by a categorical approach through a discussion of the intent-based nature of the American Constitution. The following sub-section will shed some light on the pragmatic nature of American balancing and will contrast it with the conceptual or "scientific" nature of German proportionality.

Pragmatic versus conceptual balancing

American balancing is generally based on a more pragmatic and minimalist approach than German proportionality, whose ambitious purpose is to enable the realization of the constitution's underlying values. As described in Chapter 2, balancing in US constitutional law has historical ties to the pragmatic American Progressive movement of the early twentieth century and to such figures as Holmes, Pound, and Cardozo, who conceived of law as a means of achieving social goals and balancing as the mechanism for implementing this aim. Thus, Holmes wrote in "The path of the law" about judges' "duty of *weighing* considerations of social advantage."[57] Cardozo invoked a similar balancing approach when

---

[56] Laurent Frantz, who strongly objected to balancing in free speech during the 1960s, maintained that rather than treating the Constitution as a higher law and applying it to the political organs, balancing treats the Constitution as if it were no law at all and simply allows the Court to second-guess the wisdom, as opposed to the legality, of certain governmental decisions. Laurent Frantz, "The First Amendment in the balance" (1962) 71 Yale L.J. 1433, 1441, 1443. Cf. Vicki C. Jackson, "Being proportional about proportionality" (2004) 21 Const. Commentary 843 (arguing with regard to proportionality that it "may have little or no role on constitutional issues generally regarded within the legal community as resolved by constitutional text itself").

[57] Oliver Wendell Holmes, "The path of the law," in *Collected Legal Papers* (Orlando, FL: Harcourt Brace, 1920) 167, 184 (emphasis added).

he asserted that legal decisions depend "largely upon the *comparative importance* or value of the social interests that will be thereby promoted or impaired."[58] Likewise, Roscoe Pound called for "a weighing of the social interest," arguing that "law is an attempt to satisfy, to reconcile, to harmonize, to adjust ... overlapping and often conflicting claims and demands."[59] Indeed, to this day, self-proclaimed pragmatists such as Posner associate themselves with balancing.[60]

German proportionality, in contrast, emerged from German formalist jurisprudence. German legal formalism, which was rooted in the tenets of nineteenth-century German legal science, conceives of law as an autonomous and logical discipline.[61] Thus, despite its lofty and abstract goals, proportionality is the product of a legal approach that is far more formalistic than the American one. Bomhoff has strikingly expressed the differences between American balancing and German proportionality in this respect, in the context of the German Constitutional Court's *Lüth* decision:

> *Lüth*, in this view, becomes the embodiment of the European legal culture's will to believe that a formal, legal conception of the judicial weighing of interests or values is possible. Balancing, in this German or Continental view, does not have to be about policy choices, compromises or *ad hocery*, but can be about interpreting constitutional rights within a pyramidal, "objective" system of values. Balancing is not a discretion or an option; it can be a necessity, a constitutional obligation. Balancing may very well not "rigidify" in the way American adjudication has according to Schauer, because it already is *highly formal in other ways*. And balancing does not need to be associated with ideology in the same way as Duncan Kennedy describes it for the US, because, put (perhaps too) bluntly: judicial balancing in constitutional cases does not have to be politics, *it can be law*.[62]

---

[58] Benjamin Cardozo, *The Nature of the Judicial Process* (Hartford, CT: Yale University Press, 1921) 112 (emphasis in original).

[59] Roscoe Pound, "A survey of social interests" (1943) 57 Harv. L. Rev. 1, 6, 39.

[60] See, for example, Posner's criticism of the rejection of balancing in First Amendment jurisprudence, in Richard A. Posner, "The free speech market," in Richard A. Posner, *Frontiers of Legal Theory* 62 (Cambridge, MA: Harvard University Press, 2001).

[61] A certain tension has always existed between radical formalism and idealism and values in German jurisprudence and, in fact, typifies it, particularly in the nineteenth century. German legal science during that period ("*Rechtswissenschaft*") made extensive use of exact science terminology to describe the scientific method by which the legal system operates; however, the legal scientist also sought to detect the moral, national, and historic core from which legal rules derived. On this tension, see Reimann, "Nineteenth century German legal science" 882–3.

[62] Jacco Bomhoff, "*Lüth*'s 50th anniversary: some comparative observations on the German foundations of judicial balancing" (Leiden University, 2008) (footnotes omitted).

In general, then, American balancing can be described as pragmatic and policy-oriented, as opposed to the more formal and conceptual German proportionality.

Political culture and the expansiveness of rights

In this section, we will show that in order to facilitate the transformation of German society following the Second World War, the rights in the German Constitution were broadly construed, assigning a major role to the state to give effect to the "new" humanistic values enshrined therein. In America, in contrast, the preference for state neutrality and a minimal role for the state shaped a narrowly construed Constitution, one that is generally hostile to the realization of "values" by the government. This difference in constitutional design has implications regarding the centrality or marginality of proportionality and balancing in their constitutional systems. In Germany, the expansive nature of constitutional rights creates a *structural* need for proportionality in its intrinsic sense; in the USA, the narrower scope of constitutional rights allows for a bounded type of balancing.

Rights are considerably broader in definition and scope in German constitutional law than in American law, a feature that was termed by Kumm the "total application" of the Constitution. This "total application" features three central characteristics. First, the wider scope of constitutional rights in Germany has resulted from the fact that the Constitution pronounces explicitly certain underlying values and does not limit itself to an enumeration of rights.[63] This has paved the way to an expansive conception of constitutional rights. Values are abstract entities in essence that, unlike rights, can have a very broad meaning. The enunciation of broad values in the German Constitution has meant that constitutional rights are similarly broadly construed in German constitutionalism. As a result, in Germany almost any legitimate individual or collective interest is grounded on a constitutional value and accorded constitutional status.[64] The concept of rights in Germany is so

---

[63] The German Basic Law's Constitution opens with the declaration "Human dignity shall be inviolable," with Clause 20(1) pronouncing, "The Federal Republic of Germany is a democratic and social federal state." See also Article 19(1), which provides, "In no case may the essence of a basic right be affected."

[64] Limits can be placed on any constitutional right in order to advance another value embedded in the Constitution, whether explicitly or implicitly, that holds a higher ranking *vis-à-vis* constitutional values.

broad that it has enabled the FGCC to consider even such trivial interests as riding horses in the woods, feeding pigeons, smoking marijuana, and importing a certain breed of dog as constitutionally guaranteed rights.[65]

By contrast, the American Constitution does not speak in terms of values but rather in terms of a set of rights. Moreover, those rights are oftentimes judicially interpreted more narrowly than is the case in Germany, by delimiting their scope or excluding certain activities from that scope. One prominent example is the right to free speech, where certain categories of speech have been excluded from the scope of its protection.[66]

A second feature of the "total application" constitutional approach in Germany is that the FGCC has ruled that rights have not only a negative function, but also a "protective function" – i.e. they are positive rights, too. This is in contrast to the American constitutional conception of rights as solely negative in function.[67] The German Court has held that constitutional rights oblige the state to take any necessary measures in order to ensure their realization.[68] In 1972, for example, it interpreted a constitutional provision that "all Germans shall have the right freely to choose ... their place of training"[69] as imposing a duty on the state to fund those studies.[70] In another case, the Court interpreted the

---

[65] Kumm, "Political liberalism and the structures of rights."

[66] Frederick Schauer, "The boundaries of the First Amendment: a preliminary exploration of constitutional salience" (2004) 117 Harv. L. Rev. 1765, 1783–4, 1771 (referring to expressions in the realm of criminal law, securities regulation, antitrust law, and labor law; the law of copyright and trademark, sexual harassment, fraud, evidence, regulation of professionals; and a considerable portion of tort law, that are not covered by the constitutional protection to free speech).

[67] *Bowers* v. *DeVito*, 686 F2d 616, 618 (7th Cir. 1982); *DeShaney* v. *Winnebago County*, 489 US 189, 195–6 (1989); *Jackson* v. *City of Juliet*, 715 F 2d 1200 (7th Cir.), cert. denied, 465 US 1049 (1983) 1203–4 (referring to the American Constitution as a "charter of negative rather than positive liberties"); Laurence Tribe, *American Constitutional Law* (La Habra, CA: Foundations Publishing, 2nd edn., 1988) 998.

[68] Dieter Grimm, "The protective function of the state," in George Nolte (ed.), *European and US Constitutionalism* (Cambridge: Cambridge University Press, 2005) 49, 137.

[69] Article 12(1) of the German Basic Law.

[70] 33 BverfG 33, 303, 330 (1972):

The constitutional protection of basic rights in the field of education is not limited to the protective function against governmental intervention traditionally ascribed to the basic rights. Because the right would be worthless without the actual ability to make use of it, the entitlement of every German to carry out his chosen study program if he demonstrates the requisite qualifications ... is not in the discretion of the lawmakers.

See David Currie, "Positive and negative constitutional rights" (1986) 53 U. Chicago L. Rev. 864.

constitutional provision guaranteeing the right to life as imposing an active duty on the state to enact criminal legislation banning abortion.[71] In a subsequent case, it further ruled that the state should also act to ensure that the mother's economic and occupational security are not impaired if she decides not to abort.[72]

In the USA, however, the Supreme Court has taken the opposite course, ruling in an abortion case that while "government may not place obstacles in the path of a woman's exercise of her freedom of choice, it need not remove those *not of its own creation*."[73] That is to say, the fact that women have the right to free choice and the state is therefore prohibited from banning abortions does not impose on the state a positive obligation to fund abortions.

Third, unlike the American reading of the US Constitution, the German Constitutional Court has ruled that constitutional rights apply indirectly also in the context of relations between individuals; namely, the interpretation of the rules of private law should be consistent with the values of the Constitution (the *Drittwirkung* doctrine).[74] The American Constitution, on the other hand, is not interpreted as granting rights protection to individuals in their relations with others, but only to individuals *vis-à-vis* the state.[75]

Clearly, the broader the scope of constitutional rights, the more often they will clash. Therefore, the more expansive the conception of rights, the greater the need for a mechanism such as proportionality or balancing for resolving conflicts among rights. Since everything counts in German constitutional adjudication, rights are often conceived there as a "requirement for optimization."[76] In the USA, the narrower conception of rights makes conflict less pervasive.

---

[71] 39 BVerfGE 1 (1975) (the first abortion case).

[72] The second abortion case can be found in 88 BverfGE 88, 203 (1993) (a translation into English of parts of this decision can be found in Kommers, *The Constitutional Jurisprudence of the Federal Republic of Germany* 349).

[73] *Harris* v. *MacRea*, 448 US 297, 316 (1980). (Emphasis added.)

[74] *Lüth* Case, 7 BVerfGE 7, 198 (1958). See also Stephen Gardbaum, "The 'horizontal effect' of constitutional rights" (2003) 102 Mich. L. Rev. 387, 415.

[75] *Lugar* v. *Edmondson Oil Co.*, 457 US 922, 936 (1982). An exception to this rule can be found in *Shelley* v. *Kraemer*, 334 US. 1 (1948) (the Court will not enforce a racist restrictive covenant, as court decisions constitute "state actions"). For criticism of Shelley, see Herbert Wechsler, "Toward neutral principles of constitutional law" (1959) 73 Harv. L. Rev. 1, 29–31.

[76] Alexy, *A Theory of Constitutional Rights*; Hesse, *Grundzüge des Verfassungsrechts der Bundesrepublik Deutchland*.

In conclusion, this chapter has shown that proportionality in Germany is based on an organic conception of the state and works to moderate and navigate the realization of commonly shared social values and interests. In the USA, in contrast, a culture of public suspicion of the judiciary and government has relegated balancing to a more minor and subsidiary role, bounded by a categorical approach towards rights. In addition, balancing in America is tied to the pragmatic and realistic tradition that goes back to Holmes, Pound, and Cardozo.

4

Impact, intent and indifference

Chapters 2–3 discussed the way in which balancing and proportionality are set within different historical and cultural settings. This chapter will examine more closely how the two doctrines relate to a particular divide between two types of constitutional models. In this context, we will distinguish between the German/European impact-based constitutional model in which proportionality is set and the US intent-based constitutional model that serves as the setting for balancing, and show how this makes balancing "bounded" and proportionality "inherent."

Impact-based and intent-based constitutional models: the ideal types

The European impact-based model

European constitutional systems and the German system, in particular, can be characterized ideally as "impact-based" in that they concentrate on assessing and optimizing the constitutional effects of governmental action. This is a consequentialist conception of constitutional law since it is concerned mainly with the consequences of government actions rather than the intentions behind them. It also accords the doctrine of proportionality a central, almost inherent role in the constitutional system, since proportionality addresses directly the impact, and not the intention, of government action.

As we described in Chapter 3, from the perspective of German political culture, the state is understood to strive to realize a common *telos* based on the shared values of the specific community.[1] Under such a model,

---

[1] For modern versions of communitarianism, see Micheal Sandel, *Liberalism and the Limits of Justice* (Cambridge: Cambridge University Press, 1998); Alasdair MacIntyre, *After Virtue* (Notre Dame, IN: Notre Dame University Press, 2nd edn., 1985); Charles Taylor, *The Sources of the Liberal Self* (Belmont, CA: Wadsworth Publishing, 1990).

rights are framed and defined as goods or values that should be optimized, rather than as setting boundaries for legitimate state purposes. The constitutional discourse in Germany, especially since the Second World War, has been a value discourse, and values that are positive in nature require optimization and harmonization among them.[2] In addition, the various state organs are conceived of as working in relative harmony and towards a common purpose, with no inbuilt animosity or distrust between the state and individual or between the legislature and the courts.

There is a clear link between these characteristics of German political culture and the impact-based nature of German constitutional law. Since under this culture, promoting positively shared values, including rights, is the ultimate and utmost goal, the judiciary's task is to ensure that the government optimally realizes those values – namely, to review the impact, rather than intentions, of government action. Moreover, as the government is viewed more with trust than with suspicion, there is less need to look for illicit or hidden intentions lying behind its actions.[3]

From this perspective, the function of a constitution under an impact-based conception of rights is not that categorically different from regular legislation: both are concerned with promoting shared values and substantive ideas.[4] The two differ only at the level of generality, perspective,

---

[2] The value discourse was dominant in postwar Germany. See Horst Dreier, *Dimensionen der Grundrechte – Von der Wertordnungsjudicatur zu den objectiv-rechtlichen Grundrechtsgehalten* (Hannover: Hennies & Zinkeisen, 1993) 19; Helmut Georlich, *Wertordung und Grundgesetz* (Baden-Baden: Nomos Verlag, 1973) 140. For a criticism of this value rhetoric, see Carl Schmitt, "Die Tyrannei der Werte," in Karl Doering und Wilhelm Grewe, *Säkularisation und Utopie: Ernst Forsthoff zum 65. Geburtstag* (Stuttgart: Verlag W. Kohlhammer, 1967) 37, 39.

[3] On the relationship between trust and communitarianism, see Stanford Encyclopedia of Philosophy, "Communitarianism," http://plato.stanford.edu/entries/communitarianism/. On the connection between republicanism and trust, see Philip Petit, "Republican theory and political trust," in Valerie Braithwaite and Margaret Levi (eds.), *Trust and Governance* (New York: Russell Sage Foundation, 2003) 295.

[4] For the seemingly political role of constitutional judges in Europe, see generally Alec Stone Sweet, *Governing with Judges: Constitutional Politics in Europe* (Oxford: Oxford University Press, 2000). As Dieter Grimm has made clear, "There is no preestablished difference between court and legislatures which a particular contribution has to adopt and which an interpreter has to enforce regardless of what the constitution says. In addition, constitutional courts inevitably cross the line between law and politics." Kommers, *The Constitutional Jurisprudence of the Federal Republic of Germany* (Durham, NC: Duke University Press, 2nd edn., 1997) 44 (referencing Grimm's comments that appear in Dieter Grimm, "Comment," in Christian Landfried (ed.), *Constitutional Review and Legislation: An International Comparison* (Baden-Baden: Nomos, 1988) 169.

and time-frame. The task of the Constitution and the courts that enforce it is to ensure that the legislature works to promote the deep-rooted and longstanding values rather than short-term interests and particularly those values that further the general good rather than particular interest groups favored by individual legislators. Yet this difference notwithstanding, the Constitution and legislation alike are concerned with the promotion of goods and values and essentially, therefore, with outcomes rather than intentions.

Lastly, the impact-based rather than the intent-based nature of German constitutionalism is also reflected in the relative marginality of the purpose review stage in the constitutional analysis. In Germany it is quite rare for a law to be struck down at the purpose review stage, the tendency being to accept the legitimacy of the government's alleged objective and not to question it or try to show that it is not the true purpose and that the actual purpose is an illegitimate one.[5] The emphasis is, therefore, on impact, rather than intent (purpose review). Moreover, as Dieter Grimm has shown, German constitutional review concentrates on the final proportionality subtest, which is proportionality *stricto sensu*,[6] and not the necessity subtest, which is more formal and does not involve balancing. The latter test, as we show in the next section, is more directly related to the use of balancing to smoke-out illicit purposes, whereas the strict proportionality test, which is the central test in German jurisprudence, is more strictly an optimization test.[7]

The American intent-based model

In contrast to the German and European systems, the American constitutional system can be classified as intent-based and as embedded in a suspicion-oriented legal and political culture: it centers on classifying the intentions or motives behind government action as permissible or impermissible and construes the Constitution and judiciary as the mechanisms for striking down wrongly motivated actions.

---

[5] Dieter Grimm, "Proportionality in Canadian and German constitutional law jurisprudence" (2007) 57 Univ. Toronto L.J. 383, 388 ("Cases in which the legislature pursues a constitutionally prohibited purpose (e.g. racial discrimination) are extremely rare.")

[6] Grimm, "Proportionality in Canadian and German constitutional law jurisprudence" 383, 393 ("The most striking difference between [Canada and Germany] is the high relevance of the third step of the proportionality test in Germany and its more residual function in Canada.").

[7] But see also pp. 68–70 for uses of this test, albeit in a more limited sense, to smoke-out illicit purposes and detect total disregard of the constitutional norm.

The intent-based model is rooted in an individualistic rather than communitarian worldview that, as described in Chapter 3, places a premium on liberty and personal responsibility. Unlike the communitarian model, the individualistic model is not premised on promoting shared values. Values are viewed as contested and should, therefore, be decided on in the free market of ideas and through popular democracy, rather than being imposed from above. Any attempt by the state to impose on society a set of values is regarded as an unacceptable limitation on individual liberty and freedom. Consequently, under the individualistic approach, the constitution and legislature are charged with very different tasks. Rather than promoting substantive values, the Constitution is aimed at ensuring that the legislature does not step outside its democratic bounds, and abides by the rules of the game.[8] It is the legislature, rather, that engages in the promotion of substantive goods and values.

Whereas the ideal-type German constitutional system is rooted in a teleological moral philosophy, the ideal-type American intent-based model is based on a deontological ethics. For Kantian deontologists, moral action is evaluated through the intentions and motives of the action, and the impact or results are of no inherent moral importance.[9] Accordingly, the intent-based model focuses on the decisionmaking process and restricts the permissible reasons and intentions for action.[10]

Put differently, constitutional rights function as exclusionary reasons, in that they determine which reasons for government action are impermissible rather than which reasons should be promoted and realized in

---

[8] Robert Post, "Constitutional scholarship in the United States" (2009) 7 Inst. J. of Const. L. 16, 422 (arguing that constitutional law scholarship is primarily driven by the need to ensure that constitutional law remains responsive to changing political conditions, whereas consequentialist law and economics scholarship is driven by its own internally generated *telos* of efficiency, which is relatively unresponsive to the evolution of political commitments).

[9] Immanuel Kant, *Foundations of the Metaphysics of Morals*, trans., with an introduction by Lewis White Beck (Indianapolis, IN: Bobbs-Merrill, 1959). See also Andrew Levine, "Rawls' Kantianism" (1974) 3 Soc. Theory & Prac. 47–63; Allen Wood, *Kant's Ethical Thought* (New York: Cambridge University Press, 1999); Onora O'Neill, *Acting on Principle* (New York: Columbia University Press, 1975).

[10] Eyal Zamir and Barak Medina, "Law, morality, and economics: integrating moral constraints with economic analysis of law" (2008) 96 Cal. L. Rev. 323. For the application of deontological moral theories to balancing and proportionality, see Mattias Kumm, "What do you have in virtue of a constitutional right? On the place and limits of the proportionality requirement," in S. Paulsen and G. Pavlakos (eds.), *Law, Rights, Discourse: Themes of the Work of Robert Alexy* (Oxford: Hart Publishing, 2007) 131.

government action. The intent-based model, therefore, is categorical in nature and focuses on identifying and nullifying actions based on the wrong intentions.

In free speech cases, for example, a court will typically consider whether a restrictive law is directed at the content of speech in order to regulate the market of ideas, rather than concentrating on the legislation's impact on speech in general. The test famously set in *O'Brien*, for instance, established a much stricter level of review for state restrictions aimed at silencing speech than for restriction that are merely a by-product of motives unconnected to silencing speech.[11] In *O'Brien*, the court left the ban on burning draft cards intact, despite its restrictive effect on speech, since it was determined that the motive behind the ban was not related to speech and there was no silencing intention involved. In equal protection law cases, as well, disparate impact is not included in the constitutional analysis, which concentrates solely on evidence of intention to discriminate.[12]

The intent-based model also shapes American constitutional cases by channeling balancing to the function of an evidentiary tool to smoke-out hidden illicit government motives.[13] We term this use of balancing the "bounded" sense of balancing, since the use of balancing is bounded by the categorical approach to rights. In many cases, the judicial decision-making process can be understood as a categorical one, in that it identifies prohibited governmental purposes that are absolutely banned under the Constitution and deems them unconstitutional. There is no balancing in the reasoning underlying this process. However, because prohibited purposes and motives of this kind can be camouflaged by the government as legitimate, and because it is difficult to find concrete evidence of prohibited purposes underlying governmental action, balancing becomes necessary. Thus, in many instances, what is referred to as "balancing" becomes a necessary tool for smoking-out illegitimate governmental objectives.

Balancing can be used in two ways in this respect. First, smoking-out balancing can be conducted through its means–ends tests, which are aimed at discerning when the means do not match the ends. Assuming government rationality, a lack of means–ends correlation can be understood as indication that the stated purpose is not the genuine one. There

---

[11] *United States* v. *O'Brien*, 391 US 367 (1968).

[12] *Washington* v. *Davis* 426 US 229 (1976).

[13] We borrow here from Fallon, "Strict judicial scrutiny" (2007) 54 UCLA L. Rev. 1302–11.

are two principal requirements to the means–ends test: first, the existence of a close connection between the means and the end and, second, that the means chosen are the least restrictive alternative. Cass Sunstein's description of these two tests in the context of heightened scrutiny expresses well how they are used to smoke-out illegitimate purposes:

> Heightened scrutiny involves two principal elements. The first is a requirement that the government show a close connection between the asserted justification and the means that the legislature has chosen to promote it. If a sufficiently close connection cannot be shown, there is a reason for skepticism that the asserted value in fact accounts for the legislation. The second element is a search for less restrictive alternatives – ways in which the government could have promoted the public value without harming the group or interest in question. The availability of such alternatives also suggests that the public value justification is a facade.[14]

An illustrative example of this smoking-out process is the *Ho Ah Kow* Case, involving what was known as the Queue Ordinance from 1873 that required that the heads of all inmates in San Francisco prisons be shaved.[15] The alleged reason for this Ordinance was prison hygiene – to prevent lice and flea outbreaks – but in a lawsuit challenging the Ordinance, the state court exposed this alleged justification to be "mere pretense."[16] Using a means–ends analysis, the court reasoned that if hygiene were the actual purpose, the Ordinance was both underinclusive (it applied to only men and convicts and not women or detainees) and overinclusive (inmates could be checked for lice instead of the sweeping measure of shaving their heads).[17] The real objective, the court revealed, was to stop the influx of impoverished Chinese immigrants – who were desperate for food and shelter – into the prisons by requiring them to remove an important symbol in their culture.[18] Thus, in showing incompatibility between the means and the end, the court smoked-out the racist and unconstitutional motives behind the Ordinance's enactment.

Second, even if the means and ends are sufficiently correlated, courts can apply balancing in a stricter sense by weighing the importance of the end (the urgency of the government's need) against the extent of harm to the right. Courts will strike down a violation of a right when the harm is disproportionate to either the actual enhancement of the interest, if only

---

[14] Sunstein, *The Partial Constitution* (Cambridge, MA: Harvard University Press, 1993) 30.
[15] *Ho Ah Kow* v. *Nunan*, 12 F. Cas. 252, 253 (CCD Cal. 1879) (No. 6546).
[16] *Ibid.* 254.   [17] *Ibid.*   [18] *Ibid.* 255.

marginal, or the significance of the interest, if it is trivial. This balancing analysis can also be considered a smoking-out process. Because a rational actor would not ordinarily make an extremely poor tradeoff, it can be assumed that the government actor in such circumstances was motivated by goals other than what was alleged. An argument in a similar vein can be made regarding the hypothetical scenario of a teacher segregating black pupils from white pupils in the classroom for aesthetic reasons.[19] Although there is apparently a perfect fit between the means (segregation) and the end (aesthetics), the fact that the goal is so trivial raises suspicion that this is no more than an attempt at concealing the true, racist motive and purpose of the action.

This type of smoking-out process appears in the well-known *Schneider* Case, discussed earlier, from the 1930s. In *Schneider*,[20] the Court used balancing to find unconstitutional municipal bans on distributing handbills in public streets. In its decision, the Court weighed two considerations, protection of free speech and street cleanliness, and ruled that the latter is of such negligible weight that it is easily overridden by the former.[21] Thus, in this particular case, in the balance between free speech and cleanliness, free speech prevailed over cleanliness. The balancing applied in *Schneider* can be understood as bounded because it was used to smoke-out illegitimate purposes rather than actually balance between the two interests.[22] The Court undoubtedly suspected that the motivation for the regulations in question was not truly due to concern for cleanliness, but rather an objection to the messages printed on the handbills, especially given that the handbills were being distributed principally by Jehovah's Witnesses, whose views were disturbing to many people at the time.[23] However, as the Court could not easily find prejudice to be underlying the bans, it resorted to balancing to determine whether there was a message-related purpose, which ran counter to First Amendment protections.[24] The triviality of the cleanliness interest relative to the interest in free speech was proof that the true motive behind the regulations was the desire to exclude unpopular religious views.[25]

---

[19] Paul Brest, *Processes of Constitutional Decisionmaking: Cases and Materials* (Boston, MA: Little, Brown, 1975) 489; Ely, *Democracy and Distrust: A Theory of Judicial Review* (Cambridge, MA: Harvard University Press, 1980) 147–8.

[20] *Schneider* v. *State*, 308 US 147, 165 (1939).   [21] *Ibid.* 163.

[22] Cf. Jed Rubenfeld, "The First Amendment's purpose" (2001) 53 Stan. L. Rev. 767, 831–2 (arguing that the ordinance in *Schneider* v. *State*, 308 US was targeted at speech).

[23] *Schneider*, 308 US at 158.   [24] *Ibid.* 163–5.   [25] *Ibid.*

Impact-based and intent-based: exceptions

The previous section portrayed the ideal-type models of intent-based and impact-based constitutionalism. The premise in that section was that the American model involves only cases in which there are illicit intentions and that even when balancing is employed, it is used only as an indirect tool for smoking-out such intentions. Another premise of the discussion was that German constitutional law is predominantly concerned with outcomes rather than intentions. This section will show that while these assumptions are the general rules, exceptions can be found in both American and German constitutional law.

Richard Fallon has argued that there is a category of cases in American jurisprudence in which the strict scrutiny test operates much more like a rule that prohibits the weighing of certain types of considerations, such as racial considerations. In extreme or exceptional cases, the rule is to be set aside and balancing is to be allowed in order to avoid drastic outcomes.[26] A second example is the clear and present danger test developed in free speech jurisprudence in the early 1900s.[27] This test allowed free speech to be balanced against security or public safety concerns, but only when there was a "clear and present danger" of public disorder.[28] Free speech was in effect held to set a high bar for the regulation of opinions, and balancing was to be used only in exceptional cases.[29]

---

[26] See Fallon, "Strict judicial scrutiny" 1303–6 (arguing that strict scrutiny often functions as a "[n]early [c]ategorical [p]rohibition" on certain types of infringements of rights and that balancing enters the analysis only in extreme circumstances and as an exception to the categorical rule). See also Gerald Gunther, "The Supreme Court, 1971 term – foreword: in search of evolving doctrine on a changing court: a model for a newer equal protection" (1972) 86 Harv. L. Rev.1, 8.

[27] *Abrams* v. *United States*, 250 US 616, 627–8 (1919) (Holmes, J., dissenting); *Schenck* v. *United States*, 249 US 47, 52 (1919); *Gitlow* v. *New York*, 268 US 652, 671 (1925); *Whitney* v. *California*, 274 US 357, 376 (1927).

[28] Jonathan S. Masur, "Probability thresholds" (2007) 92 Iowa L. Rev. 1293, 1297 ("True balancing – a full accounting on each side of the ledger – simply will not take place unless the probability of the asserted harm crosses the threshold.").

[29] In addition, see Rubenfeld, "The First Amendment's purpose" 829:
Despite appearances, the [clear and present danger test] cannot be understood as a balancing test. It should be understood rather as a test to determine whether an individual has intentionally used speech so closely and directly engaged with a particularized course of prohibited conduct that the individual may be treated as having participated in that conduct.
Moreover, Rubenfeld continued,
[The individual] can be punished for [participating in that conduct] – and not because the harmfulness of his speech outweighs its benefits. The same line of thought explains

What we see, therefore, is that when the effect of legislation crosses a certain threshold and has extremely detrimental effects, American constitutional law looks at the impact and not only the intention of the action. This can be termed a "consequentialist constraint" in an otherwise deontologically oriented system.

Divergence from the basic constitutional design in extreme cases occurs also in impact-based models such as the German constitutional system. In such systems, intention could still insert itself as a sort of deontological constraint in extreme cases of morally reprehensible intention, despite the potentially desirable impact of the government action. One illustrative case in Germany dealt with a law that permitted the downing of a passenger aircraft hijacked by terrorists to commit a 9/11 type of attack. The law in question effectively allowed the intentional killing of civilians in order to protect other civilians from harm. This intention was deemed unacceptable and in violation of the value of human dignity, which is the most central value in German constitutional law.[30] This case, therefore, demonstrates how motive can serve as a deontological constraint in judicial review, when exceptional circumstances of an intolerable underlying intention shift the focus from impact to intent.

Another example in which deontological constraints were imposed on the consequentialist calculus in judicial review is the FGCC's landmark ruling on abortion from the mid 1970s. In its judgment, the Court held that the Constitution imposes a ban on abortion given the paramount importance of the right to life, especially in light of the Nazi atrocities in the Second World War. This fundamental right extends to fetuses as well, the Court ruled, and the state has a positive duty to protect them by criminalizing abortions.[31] Underlying the decision in this case was a

---

the unprotectedness of an entire set of speech acts "brigaded" with prohibited conduct: agreements to commit unlawful acts (conspiracy), solicitations of unlawful acts, threats, and so on.

    Ibid. 828.

[30] BVerfGE, 1 BvR 357/05 (2006) (striking down the Air-Transport Security Act that authorized the Minister of Defense to order that a passenger airplane be shot down, if it can be assumed that the aircraft will be used against the life of others and if the downing is the only means of preventing this present danger, with the Court ruling that the law violates the absolute constitutional guarantee of human dignity), English translation available at www.bundesverfassungsgericht.de/en/decisions/rs20060215_1bvr035705en. htm. For an overview of the case, see Oliver Lepsius, "Human dignity and the downing of aircraft: the German federal constitutional court strikes down a prominent anti-terrorism provision in the new Air-Transport Security Act" (2006) 7(9) German L.J. 761.

[31] BVerfGE 39, 1 (1975).

deontological constraint on the social value of promoting the general welfare. The principle advanced by the ruling is that regardless of the desirability of the consequences, some actions are strictly forbidden since they violate absolute deontological prescription.[32]

Intent-based: indifferent infringement of the Constitution

It could be argued that our description of American constitutional law thus far overlooks a much more far-reaching phenomenon of the use of balancing in American constitutional law than what has been presented. Indeed, balancing arises not only in the limited contexts of smoking-out bad intentions, or as an exception to categorical rules, in cases of extreme consequences. Rather, there is a third category of balancing cases that could be responsible for the broader manifestation of balancing in US constitutional law that we identify and term as cases of "indifference" to the infringement of constitutional values. While balancing in cases of indifference does not involve bad intention, it is concerned not only with the impact of government action but also with the state of mind of the decisionmaker. In such cases, balancing is not aimed, therefore, at the impact of legislation and governmental action or at optimizing results; rather, it is applied to strike down legislative and governmental actions that show no regard for constitutional values.

Two illustrations: Minnesota v. Barber and the indifferent bomber

A US Supreme Court case relating to interstate commerce exemplifies this category of balancing cases. Under the intent-based approach of American constitutional law, interstate commerce cannot be intentionally burdened by the government, since the Constitution excludes state protectionism as a reason for any governmental action.[33] In other words, if a state imposes a burden on commerce with other states with the

---

[32] This decision was later modified (88 BVerfGE 203, 1993) (the Constitution does not require the criminalization of abortion but, instead, imposes other limits on it). However, the ruling that the Constitution denounces abortion still stands. For a comparison of the German and American approaches to abortion, see Gerald L. Neuman, "Casey in the mirror: abortion, abuse and the right to protection in the United States and Germany" (1995) 43 Am. J. Com. L. 273.

[33] See, e.g., *Hunt v. Washington State Apple Advertising Comm.*, 432 US 333 (1977) (excluding simple economic protectionism); *City of Philadelphia v. New Jersey*, 437 US 617 (1978).

intention of protecting its own commerce from competition, this is construed as intentionally harming interstate commerce and, therefore, forbidden; in contrast, any restriction on interstate commerce for reasons unrelated to the free flow of commerce between states is not regarded as intentionally causing harm to interstate commerce and, therefore, permitted.[34] While this conclusion is not always explicit in American commerce clause doctrine, it has been forcefully argued that this depiction of US case law best exemplifies actual judicial results in the cases.

In *Minnesota v. Barber*,[35] at issue was a Minnesota statute that prohibited the sale of dressed meat unless it had been inspected a minimum of twenty-four hours before its sale, within the state. This legislation in effect barred the sale of meat from neighboring states' slaughterhouses, because it was implausible for the latter to transfer their cattle for inspection, ship them back for processing, and then transport the meat to Minnesota for sale, all within twenty-four hours. In this case, the Minnesota legislature had not intended to prohibit the selling of meat from out-of-state slaughterhouses, nor to protect its own commerce, but rather seemed to have been motivated by another interest altogether: the protection of public health.

In its decision, however, the Supreme Court deviated from the intent-based model and weighed the impact of the legislation on interstate commerce against its public health impact. On the basis of this balancing process, it found the statute to be in violation of the Constitution and void, reasoning that Minnesota had readily available alternatives that would promote health almost as effectively but would not burden interstate commerce.[36] This followed a similar line of reasoning taken in other commerce clause cases.[37]

Did this decision signal a shift towards an impact-based model that balances the potential effects of government or legislative acts, similar to the European one? We suggest that the answer is "no." For the Supreme Court's decision can still be interpreted as concerned with legislative state of mind rather than balancing the favorable and unfavorable consequences of the statute. By ruling that the legislature could have just as

---

[34] The Court has defined "protectionist" state legislation as "regulatory measures designed to benefit in-state economic interests by burdening out-of-state competitors." *New Energy Co. of Indiana v. Limbach*, 486 US 269, 273–4 (1988).

[35] *Minnesota v. Barber*, 136 US 313 (1890).   [36] *Ibid.* 322.

[37] For an overview, see Alec Stone Sweet, "All things in proportion? American rights doctrine and the problem of balancing" (2011) 60 Emory L.J. 101, 118–28.

easily achieved its public health protection goal without causing harm to the constitutional interest, the Court in fact found that the state had been completely indifferent to the constitutional interests; it had failed to show regard for, or had ascribed no importance to, those constitutional interests.

A hypothetical example may be further illuminating: Consider a bomber who can drop a bomb on either one of the enemy's two military factories. They are identical except for the fact that in the one there are also civilians who would be killed, while in the other, there are no civilians. Suppose the bomber chooses the factory with civilians based on the toss of a coin or because of very trivial gain to him, such as saving a gallon of fuel. In such a case, a least restrictive means test or large–small tradeoff balancing would function as a means for uncovering the complete indifference and lack of regard for the lives of enemy civilians.

On the face of it, these two examples seem not to follow a conventional deontological or intent-based model, since they do not involve a clear intention to violate a constitutional norm. In the first case, the Minnesota legislature had not intended to harm interstate commerce and, similarly, our bomber did not intend to harm civilians. Rather, this harm was caused as a side-effect in the pursuit of another, legitimate, end. We suggest, however, that they both are connected to the underlying precept of the deonotological prohibition on causing intentional harm: the need to respect human autonomy and dignity. The reason why causing intentional harm to people is more objectionable than unintentional harm is related to the fact that it indicates a disregard for their autonomy and self-worth. This is the central theme of Kantian deontology. Intentionally harming another person's interests (at least manipulatively doing so) is equivalent to treating that person as a means only to an end and disrespecting her autonomy and dignity.

Although total indifference to causing harm to another person does not amount to using that person as a means, it does convey an attitude of disrespect to her interests and autonomy similar to that shown by someone who does treat her merely as a means. In other words, the state of mind that attributes no weight or importance to another person's interests would seem to easily facilitate using her as a means only in other instances. What counts in terms of the moral significance of an action is not the outcome of that action but the practical rule – or, in Kantian terms, the *maxim* – by which the action was conducted. If the maxim is to assign no weight to a person's interests, then any action following that maxim should be invalid whether it constitutes no more than disregard for that person's interests or consists also of using her as a means.

Shelly Kagan makes this point quite clearly:

> There is certainly a strong temptation to insist that to intend the harm of another is to fail to accord that individual the respect which is his due … [T]his will again prompt the reply that indifference to the fate of a person seems a sure sign of disrespect (or, at least, the absence of respect).[38]

As in the smoking-out context, balancing could help determine whether a person is acting with total indifference to another person's interests. If a person could easily opt for an alternative that would not cause harm to someone else but refrains from doing so, this would reveal complete indifference to the interests of the other and complete disregard for his or her autonomy and self-worth. As explained by Kagan, this seems as objectionable as using someone as a means.

The maxim – the rule of action of the actor – cannot be identified on the basis of one particular action but, rather, a series of actions. If from that series it emerges that the actor's rule of action is indifference towards human life, it is reasonable to assert that he acts immorally. The very choice of the more restrictive alternative is indicative of indifference and disregard. In fact, in most cases, this would be the only way to determine the existence of indifference, since we have no direct access to the minds of others. In this sense, the choice of the more restrictive means (that are as effective as the means chosen) is almost constitutive of the presence of indifference.

Indifference in experimental philosophy: the Knobe Effect

An interesting phenomenon from experimental philosophy research, known as the Knobe Effect, can help in understanding why indifference towards harm is sometimes analogous to intentional harm. In his well-known study from 2003, Joshua Knobe found asymmetry in how people ascribe intentionality in "help" and "harm" situations.[39] He presented the study participants with the following scenario: the vice-president of a company goes to the chairman of the board and says, "We are thinking of starting a new program. It will help us increase profits, but it will also

---

[38] Shelly Kagan, *The Limits of Morality* (Oxford: Oxford University Press, 1989) 171.

[39] Joshua Knobe, "Intentional action and side effects in ordinary language" (2003) 63 Analysis 190.

cause harm to the environment." The chairman of the board replies, "I don't care at all about harming the environment. I just want to make as much profit as I can. Let's start the new program." The participants were then asked whether they thought the chairman had intentionally caused harm to the environment. Most concluded that he had, indeed, done so. However, when the scenario was turned around so that instead of causing harm, the new program would help the environment, the majority of the participants concluded that the chairman had not intentionally helped the environment. Subsequent studies have shown this asymmetry in response – the Knobe Effect – to be robust and pervasive, although explanations for it vary.[40] In the context of an intent-based constitutional design, the question would be whether we can ascribe intentionality to governmental action that seems based on total indifference to causing constitutional harm.

Under our proposed understanding of the Knobe Effect, it can be explained as an assessment of the respect or disrespect that our actions convey. Intentionally harming a person or an interest conveys a lack of respect for that person or interest. The same disrespect is also present when we do not care about that person or interest. The identity in attitudes is translated in people's minds into an identity in terms of intentionality. In contrast, however, helping a person or interest does not necessarily indicate respect for that person or interest. There is no inconsistency in saying that someone's actions may have happened to help someone or some interest but that they assigned no respect to the person's autonomy or to the interest. The chairman who said "I don't care at all about harming the environment" but ended up helping the environment showed no respect for the environment, just as the bomber who says "I don't care about civilians" but ends up helping civilians is not showing any respect towards them. It is only when helping a person or interest is motivated by the *wish* to help them that we show respect. Richard Holton demonstrated an identical asymmetry in the context of following a norm versus violating a norm.[41] In order to follow a norm, one must be motivated by the norm and not just happen to act in a way that does not violate it (just as for the bomber to show respect for civilians, he would have had to be motivated by the desire not to hurt them and not simply happen to not to hurt them). However, in order to violate a norm,

---

[40] See, e.g., Joshua Knobe, "The concept of intentional action: a case study in the uses of folk psychology" (2006) 130 Philosophical Studies 203.

[41] Richard Holton, "Norms and the Knobe Effect" (2010) 70 Analysis 417.

it suffices not to act according to the norm, and one need not intentionally violate the norm (just as in order to be disregarding of civilian life, it was sufficient that the bomber harm them, despite the existence of an alternative course of action, and he need not have sought to harm them).

Possible objections

It could be argued that there is still a difference between disregard for the other and causing intentional harm to others, since in the latter, and not the former, the actor gains from not respecting the other person's autonomy. When someone lies or steals or kills intentionally, she achieves some goal she has sought and gains something in the process. Someone who is purely indifferent to the harm she is causing, in contrast, does not thus benefit: she is indifferent to any gain from harming the other person and has no interest in achieving anything by this. We propose, however, that there is nonetheless a certain gain to the actor even in cases of indifference. An actor, who is completely unconcerned with the interests of the person affected by his actions, benefits from the fact that she does not need to change even slightly her plans or actions to avoid harm to those interests. In this respect, she is more free to conduct herself in the world. This person in effect "free rides" on a social scheme that makes the interests of others part of everyday behavior, in order to be able to act as she wishes.[42]

Another objection might be that the argument based on disrespect for individual autonomy applies only to cases of rights being infringed, such as in the bomber example, and not in institutional cases, as in instances of protectionism and commerce clause cases. We suggest, however, that the Kantian notion of the categorical imperative is structural rather than substantive. In commerce clause cases, the prohibition on protectionism is grounded on the idea of protectionism amounting to using someone else as a means only. For protectionism exists as a practice only by virtue of the fact that the rest of the players are not protectionist. And indeed, the Minnesota legislature, in *Minnesota* v. *Barber*, was free-riding on the fact that the legislatures in all other states abided by the rules of free trade and thus failed to respect the autonomy of the out-of-state residents.

---

[42] Consider the following example: I do not bother to move to the side to avoid stepping on my friend's watch. I show complete disrespect for my friend's interests. I gain in not needing to adjust my actions to the interests of other people.

A third possible objection is that the impermissibility of the action is confused with the moral evaluation of the actor. After all, were the indifferent bomber to happen to go in the direction of the factory without the civilians being there (for example, were they to have moved without his knowledge), there would be no reason to forbid his action, although it would be based on indifference to human life. This objection, however, if valid, is applicable to all conceptions based on a distinction between intention and impact, whether generally or specifically in constitutional law. It is similar to objecting to the intention-based approach based on the principle that attempts are not punished as harshly as completed acts, despite identical intent. There are some general responses to this objection, and there are some particular responses in the area of constitutional law, where governmental action has an expressive effect and can thus be disallowed on this count alone, even absent any detrimental effect. We have no intention, however, of putting forth a general defense of an intent-based moral conception. Rather, we seek only to show that such a conception begs an analogy between intent and indifference.

A fourth and final objection that could be raised against our account relates to degrees of indifference and questions whether the indifference approach in fact collapses into consequentialism. Suppose the governmental actor assigns only a very trivial weight to the constitutional value. Should this too be regarded as manifesting indifference towards that norm? In other words, is the question of indifference a matter of degree? And, if so, what is the difference between this approach and pure consequentialism, for in consequentialist balancing we ask what weight should be accorded to a certain value and whether the action under review reflects this weight and, therefore, achieves optimal results.

Our response is that in the context of our discussion, we are interested in the state of mind of the actor, not in optimizing the outcomes of the action. The suboptimal end-results are merely indicative of the actor's state of mind and the maxim guiding her actions. This is best exemplified by cases in which the government achieves less than optimal results, but there is no indication of disregard for any of the constitutional values. This outcome would still be of concern under a consequentialist approach, but less pertinent to an approach interested in the state of mind of indifference.

This is well demonstrated by a pair of cases handed down by the Israeli Supreme Court regarding the appropriate representation of women and minorities on public committees. In the one, *Israel Women's*

Network,[43] the Court held that a rigorous standard of care applies with regard to the government's compliance with the procedural requirements for ensuring appropriate representation of women on the boards of directors of government companies. The Court then ruled that this standard had not been met in the case at hand and that the lack of intentionality on the part of the government was no excuse:

> Hence, there is no significance to the argument that the defective decisions were the result of an oversight. On the contrary, if further proof is required of the essentiality of enforcing this law, the alleged lack of awareness of the Ministers to act in accordance with its binding provision provides the necessary proof. Furthermore, the approach underlying the procedure laid down by the Minister of Finance following the passage of the Appointments Law, and the affidavits in reply that were submitted in these petitions merely strengthen the impression that the nature of the obligation imposed on the Ministers under Section 18A(b) has not yet been properly understood.[44]

A second case, *Itach*, also well illustrates the logic of indifference and the notion that the decisionmaker must internalize the constitutional norm.[45] In the wake of the mass demonstrations for social justice in the summer of 2011 in Israel, the government appointed the Trachtenberg Committee for Social and Economic Change. The Committee consisted of fourteen members, none of whom was of Arab descent. The petitioners in *Itach* demanded that an Arab female member be appointed to the Committee. In granting the petition, Justice Rubinstein noted that although the matter of appropriate representation of Arabs is on the government's agenda, "the real problem lies of course in its internalization and realization, in order for it to exist constantly in the state of mind of those who appoint committees."[46]

Justice Rubinstein turned to a biblical passage in making his point:

> Surely, this commandment that I am commanding you today is not too hard for you, nor is it too far away. It is not in heaven, that you should say, "Who will go up to heaven for us, and get it for us so that we may hear it and observe it?" Neither is it beyond the sea, that you should say, "Who will cross to the other side of the sea for us, and get it for us so that we may hear it and observe it?" No, the word is very near to you; it is in your mouth and in your heart for you to observe.[47]

***

---

[43] HCJ 2671/98, *Israel Women's Network* v. *Minister of Work & Welfare*, 52(3) PD 630 (1998) para. 34.
[44] *Ibid.*   [45] HCJ 5980/11, *Itach* v. *Prime Minister* (given August 28, 2011).
[46] *Ibid.* para. 5.   [47] *Ibid.* para. 6.

This chapter may seem to have deviated from the general line taken thus far in this book, in that it is particularly focused on the US context and in being more conceptual than the other chapters. However, we believe this to be crucial for addressing an important possible objection to our characterization of the American constitutional model: that it cannot be entirely explained in terms of intent-based jurisprudence. We have tried to show here that there are, indeed, nuances and complexities in the seemingly dichotomous distinction between an intent-based and impact-based approach to constitutional law, but that a distinction nonetheless exists. Our conclusion was that the intent-based model, while differenti-ated from the impact-based model, has ways of extending its logic into cases that are not strictly cases of bad intent, i.e. cases of indifference.

5

Epistemology

This chapter deals with the way balancing and proportionality are conceived in their respective legal cultures along a spectrum between rules and standards. Different constitutional cultures develop different approaches to rules and standards. These approaches vary in accordance with the fundamental cultural assumptions in the legal system regarding human rationality and epistemic capabilities; rules are usually associated with skepticism about epistemic capabilities and standards with optimism. The variance in these approaches is also impacted by institutional factors such as the size of the judiciary and the cohesiveness and makeup of the national Constitutional Court. Continuing along the path begun in Chapters 2–4, we present and discuss the different approaches to rules and standards that have developed in the USA and Germany and how this has affected the conception of balancing and proportionality in their respective "home cultures."

Rules and standards in the USA

American epistemological skepticism

As described in Chapter 3, American legal culture has been associated from its inception with pluralism and a strong resistance to a state-imposed unitary conception of the good.[1] The historical origins of the USA as a society founded by members of religious minorities that were persecuted by the state in Europe were accompanied by a deep skepticism of Truth and of state interference in individual liberty in the name of that Truth.[2] Although each of these religious groups lay claim to the Truth,

---

[1] Jean Wahl, *The Pluralist Philosophies of England and America* (Fred Rothwell trans., London: The Open Court Co., 1925) 317–18.

[2] Roderick A. Macdonald, "Metaphors of multiplicity: civil society, regimes and legal pluralism," (1998) 15 Ariz. J. Int'l & Comp. L. 69, 71.

the political system as a whole was built on many truths co-existing on pluralism and on maintaining a system of diverging and even conflicting conceptions of the good. This was clearly reflected in the First Amendment's free exercise and establishment clauses, which prohibit the interference with the free exercise of religion and the establishment of religion by the state. In addition, American culture was greatly influenced by English empiricism and liberalism and the English pragmatic approach to politics and law that emphasized negative liberty at the expense of positive liberty and conceptualism. "Pluralism had much in common with pragmatism. Both approaches substituted empiricism, particularism, indeterminacy, and uncertainty for rationalism, universalism, determinacy, and certainty."[3]

Epistemological skepticism is best represented, both generally and in American legal and political culture, by two prominent ideas: the primacy of the notions of "many minds over one mind" and of bottom-up social experiment over top-down social regulation. A common thread in the skeptic school of thought is the belief in the superiority of the knowledge amassed by many minds as opposed to the knowledge of one mind. The roots of this precept can be found in the works of such conservative thinkers as Edmund Burke and Friedrich Hayek. The general lines of the theory are that since human rationality is limited, preference should be given to the aggregation of many minds over the decision of one mind. Edmund Burke famously asserted, "we suspect that th[e] stock [of reason] in each man is small" and that it is better to rely on "the general bank and capital of nations and of ages."[4] This is clearly illustrated by market behavior. Markets are constituted by a very complex web of forces and interests, which are difficult to discern and the outcomes of which are difficult to predict for the lone mind. Therefore, any attempt to regulate the market will be rife with inaccuracies and unexpected consequences; we are thus better off leaving the forces of the market untouched. The aggregate outcome resulting from many minds, each making his or her individual choice, will be superior, under this conception, to the outcome of centralized regulation. Hayek similarly

---

[3] Dalia Tsuk, "The new deal origins of American legal pluralism" (2001) 29 Florida State U.L. Rev. 189, 199 ("A pluralist theory of knowledge insisted on the multiplicity (whether limited or infinite) of knowers in the world and various forms of knowledge or truth, none of which could claim epistemological primacy. In ethics, pluralism implied the existence of a variety of competing ends, among which policymakers had to choose.").

[4] Edmund Burke, "Reflections on the revolution in France" (1790), in Isaac Kramnick (ed.), *The Portable Edmund Burke* (New York: Penguin, 1999) 451–2.

argued that it is difficult to see economic issues from the above. Without receiving true input from below on essential matters and dilemmas, regulators will not know nor understand the reality of the citizens of their community.[5]

An analogous argument can be made regarding judicial decisionmaking, focusing on how the common law evolves from case to case. In this context, the argument in favor of many minds is that law produced by the aggregation of many cases, each dealing with a particular aspect of a given problem through the particular circumstances of the case, is superior to law produced by a single judicial panel or single legislative session. The reasoning is that a single mind is unable to grasp the entire set of possibilities and complexities embedded in the aggregate of decisions on numerous cases. In the political sphere, the idea of many minds being preferable to one mind implies an emphasis on popular democracy versus governance by elites, which is accompanied by a suspicion of top-down politics from the judicial elite.

Also analogous to the many minds argument is the "great laboratory" argument in favor of federalism. This argument is related to the second prominent idea underlying epistemological skepticism, namely, the preference for bottom-up social experiment over top-down social regulation. A top-down regulatory approach is treated dubiously, as being overambitious. There is no way to predict all the possible consequences of adopting any given social policy. Federalism expresses this skepticism by allowing local experimentation and letting states test the efficacy of different social policies before they are adopted on a national scale. Thus, according to this approach social knowledge is built bottom-up, out of the "many minds" of the different states, and the ideas that "work" eventually prevail. James Bryce succinctly noted this about federalism:

> Federalism enables a people to try experiments in legislation and adminis-tration which could not be safely tried in a large centralized country. A comparatively small commonwealth like an American state easily makes and unmakes its laws; mistakes are not serious, for they are soon corrected; other States profit by the experience of a law or a method which has worked well or ill in the State that has tried it.[6]

---

[5] See Fredrick Hayek, *The Constitution of Liberty* (Chicago, IL: University of Chicago Press, 1960). See also Russell Hardin, "Representing ignorance" (2004) 21 Soc. Phil. & Pol. 76, 85–7, describing Hayek's argument against market regulation.

[6] James Bryce, *The American Commonwealth* (3rd edn., London: Macmillan, 1893) 353. See also *New State Ice Co.* v. *Liebmann*, 285 US 262, 311 (1932) (Brandeis, J., dissenting) ("It is one of the happy incidents of the federal system, that a single courageous state may, if its

The many minds principle and preference for bottom-up development are both at the root also of the traditional insistence on separation of powers and perpetual suspicion of concentrated state power in the USA. As described in Chapter 3, most American political institutions are characterized by a large degree of decentralization, including, quite prominently, the federal judicial system. Governmental power should be viewed with suspicion, and power not concentrated, not only to prevent corruption and abuse of power, but also in light of the understanding that no one person, or one institution, can fully grasp and contend with all of the complexities of social relations, as well as given the primacy of bottom-up social experiment as opposed to top-down social regulation and planning. Indeed, one of the central features of free speech in America to this day is the precedence of pluralism in the market of ideas over the imposition of orthodoxies.

Epistemological skepticism and rules and standards

Epistemological skepticism usually points to the adoption of rules but, as we will show here, it may also point to the adoption of standards, understood in a certain way.

Epistemological skepticism and rules

Epistemological skepticism is usually associated with the adoption of rules, both generally and specifically as a mode of constitutional interpretation. The affinity between the two derives from the understanding that it seems like a good idea to bind ourselves in our future decisionmaking because of the possibility of future mistakes. By setting a rule, judges shield themselves from their own subjectivity and fallibility. Acknowledging cognitive biases, for example, is a reason for having rules. Studies that point out such biases in judges often conclude with a recommendation for rules as corrective mechanisms.[7] This is actually what constitutions are for: we fear our fallibility or of being swayed, so we try to create rules in an optimal setting that will bind us in later decisions.[8]

---

citizens choose, serve as a laboratory; and try novel social and economic experiments without risk to the rest of the country.").

[7] Chris Guthrie *et al.*, "Inside the judicial mind" (2001) 86 Cornell L. Rev. 777; Frederick Schauer, "On the supposed jury-dependence of evidence law" (2006) 155 U. Pa. L. Rev.165.

[8] Jon Elster, *Ulysses and the Sirens: Studies in Rationality and Irrationality* (Cambridge: Cambridge Paperback Library, 1979); Stephen Holmes, "Precommitment and the paradox

Justice Holmes was among the most prominent jurists who articulated a worldview that ties rules to epistemological skepticism. Holmes wrote that, sometimes, judges should openly admit that they do not know the legal answer (epistemological skepticism) and that in such cases it might be better to set a rule, even by fiat, so that everyone will be aware of the law and will make their private decisions accordingly.[9] Setting a rule is preferable to letting each individual judge decide according to her own subjective conception of what is right in the given case (epistemological optimism).

Under the now classical critical legal studies analysis, a "rules person" is someone who does not trust the beneficence or rationality of others.[10] He or she thinks that there should be clear rules of the game, where each player promotes his or her own interests within the boundaries of those rules. In addition, rules are important for separation of powers, since they enable a clear demarcation of power between the different branches of government. Rules facilitate this separation of powers and the pluralism-based structure in that they supply a framework for the coexistence of diverging conceptions.

Since rules, rather than standards, seem best suited to epistemo-logical skepticism as an interpretative mode, balancing has taken a relatively marginal role in American constitutional culture. And when it is actually espoused, it is often subjected to criticism and debate.

---

of democracy," in Jon Elster and Rune Slagstad (eds.), *Constitutionalism and Democracy* (Cambridge: *Cambridge University Press*, 1988) 195; Cass Sunstein, *What Constitutions Do* (Oxford: Oxford University Press, 2001) 96–101.

[9] In *Olmstead* v. *United States*, 277 US 438, 469 (1928), Justice Holmes acknowledged that a gap existed in the law and then went on to create a rule to fill that gap: "There is no body of precedents by which we are bound, and which confines us to logical deduction from established rules ... [W]e are [therefore] free to choose between two principles of policy." *Ibid.* 469 (Holmes, J., dissenting).

[10] Duncan Kennedy famously equated standards with "altruism" and rules with "individual-ism" and suggested that standards favor distributive and paternalist motives, whereas rules favor efficiency and the status quo. Duncan Kennedy, "Form and substance in private law adjudication" (1976) 89 Harv. L. Rev. 1685, 1737–51, 1753–6. Morton Horowitz argued that rules "promote ... substantive inequality by ... enabl[ing] the shrewd, the calculating, and the wealthy to manipulate its forms to their own advantage." Morton J. Horowitz, "The rule of law: an unqualified human good?" (1977) 86 Yale L.J. 561, 566 (reviewing E. P. Thomson, *Whigs and Hunters*, New York: Random House, 1976). Note that Horowitz may have backtracked from this position in his later work. Carol Rose promotes a similar argument in the realm of property, see Carol Rose, "Crystals and mud in property law" (1988) 40 Stan. L. Rev. 577, 601–4; see also Douglas Baird and Robert Weisberg, "Rules, standards, and the battle of the forms: a reassessment of § 2–207" (1982) 68 Va. L. Rev. 1217.

This conforms to the relatively bounded role of balancing in American law, as discussed in Chapters 2–4.[11]

Epistemological skepticism and standards: balancing and minimalism

Even though rules are generally preferred in a culture of epistemological skepticism, standards and, in particular, balancing should not necessarily be ruled out either in this legal culture. For balancing can be adapted to conform to epistemological skepticism rather than being an exception to it – that is, by shaping the doctrine as promoting, rather than rejecting, epistemological skepticism. Minimalism, the most recent expression of epistemological skepticism in American legal culture, in fact endorses standards and balancing rather than rules.

Judicial minimalism, which was defined and promoted by Cass Sunstein in a series of prominent articles and books, advocates judicial decisions that are minimal in terms of their effects and theoretical aspirations.[12] It is grounded on two leading principles: a preference for narrow, versus broad, reasoning and a preference for shallow, versus deep, reasoning. Both of these principles are directly related to epistemological skepticism. If we assume that the wisdom of one judge is limited, then we will want judicial decisions to be narrow in their reasoning and not to exceed the limits of the given case or apply to a broad set of cases. We will prefer that doctrine evolve through "many minds," as the product of the aggregation of many discrete and narrow judicial decisions. The shallow reasoning principle is also related to epistemological skepticism by being premised on doubt as to the ability to get "the big questions" right or to reach agreement on them as opposed to narrower or technical questions on which agreement can be made.

---

[11] Bounded balancing was discussed in the context of the doctrine's historical origins, cultural embeddedness, and operation within an intent-based constitutional model, in Chapters 2, 3, and 4, respectively.

[12] Cass R. Sunstein, "Incompletely theorized agreements" (1995) 103 Harv. L. Rev. 1733; Cass R. Sunstein, "Foreword: leaving things undecided" (1996) 10 Harv. L. Rev. 6; Cass Sunstein, *One Case at a Time: Judicial Minimalism on the Supreme Court* (Cambridge, MA: Harvard University Press, 1999); Cass R. Sunstein, "Minimalism at war" (2004) Sup. Ct. Rev. 47; Cass R. Sunstein, "Comments from contributors," in Jack M. Balkin (ed.), *What Roe v. Wade Should Have Said* (New York: New York University Press, 2005) 248–50; Cass R. Sunstein, "Beyond judicial minimalism" Harvard Public Law Working Paper No. 08–40, http://papers.ssrn.com/sol3/papers.cfm?abstract_id=1274200. See also Cass R. Sunstein, "Problems with minimalism" (2007) 58 Stan. L. Rev. 1899.

The "big questions" should be left unanswered or else resolved through an aggregation of many discrete cases.

The narrow and shallow reasoning principles seem to point to a preference for standards and balancing over rules. As Sunstein has stated, "[a] preference for minimalism is very close, analytically, to a preference for standards over rules."[13] From the perspective of narrowness, the argument goes, standards are preferable since reasoning based on standards is contingent on the particular circumstances of the case and applies to only the particular case at hand; judicial reasoning that sets a rule, on the other hand, determines the outcome of all future cases that fall within the scope of that rule. From the perspective of shallowness, standards are more favorable than rules, for in concentrating on the particular case, they do not necessitate any grand theory or deep values in order to be implemented. Moreover, standards are primarily concerned with facts and the particular circumstances of the case and thus resort to low-level considerations on which there is general agreement rather than profound theories that will generate disagreement. They facilitate what Sunstein terms "incompletely theorized agreements," which are easier to reach than completely theorized agreements.

Minimalism therefore links balancing, as the ultimate standards-based doctrine, with epistemological skepticism. By opting for a reasoning based on balancing, a court limits its holding in a case to the particular circumstances. It thus refrains from the ambitious attempt to regulate a broad set of cases and to answer big theoretical questions. In addition, by opting for balancing, a court allows the doctrine to be developed through the experience of many minds, evolving bottom-up, through the working of many courts, rather than being imposed top-down, by "one mind" – a single court.

Minimalists, such as Sunstein, we should note, assume that standards necessarily lead to minimalistic decisionmaking, i.e. narrow and shallow. We do not share this assumption. As we will show in the next section, proportionality – the ultimate standard – has been used in German constitutional law in ways that come nowhere near minimalism. Our claim is culturally based. We reframe the claim regarding the relationship between minimalism, epistemological skepticism, and balancing as follows: there is no necessary correlation between proportionality or balancing and epistemological modesty and minimalism.

---

[13] Sunstein, "Problems with minimalism" 1909.

However, a culture, such as the American one, which is based on epistemological skepticism, can shape the use of balancing, so that it is consistent with principles of minimalism. Of course, this, too, is a generalization. There are naturally instances of balancing that do not conform to the minimalist ideal, and, furthermore, different periods in American jurisprudential history have reflected different attitudes – more or less minimalist – towards the use of balancing.[14] But by and large, our claim is that the fact that balancing is situated within a legal and political culture that has strong tendencies towards epistemological skepticism creates strong pressure for it to be justified as being minimalist rather than maximalist.

Illustrative of how balancing is framed by the American legal culture of epistemological scepticism, as espousing minimalism and less judicial control, is the *Graham v. Florida*[15] decision. This case, concerning a juvenile sentenced to life in prison without parole for a non-homicide crime, represents unique Eighth Amendment jurisprudence. Chief Justice Roberts, who concurred in judgment, agreed with the majority opinion that the sentence was disproportionate to the crime; however, he also strongly objected to the categorical approach of the Court's opinion and to the establishment of a new constitutional rule. Roberts criticized the Court for using the *Graham* Case "as a vehicle to proclaim a new constitutional rule – applicable well beyond the particular facts of Graham's case."[16] Such an approach, he claimed, "is unnecessary as it is unwise."[17] Instead, Roberts preferred a case-by-case balancing approach and rejected the Court's opinion that clear lines are necessary for preventing errors in trial judges' sentences. While he conceded that trial judges might never have perfect foresight, he argues that "[o]ur system depends upon sentencing judges applying their reasoned judgment to each case that comes before them."[18] Rather than establishing a clear or consistent path for Courts to follow, he espoused the "highly deferential

---

[14] The periods in which balancing was associated with judicial deference, for example, the Lochner and McCarthy eras, can be seen to reflect a more minimalist attitude towards balancing; those periods in which it was associated with judicial activism, such as its application by liberals on the Court from the late 1970s until recently, can be seen to reflect a less minimalist approach to the use of balancing. Currently there seems to be a tendency to return to a more minimalist use of balancing, as the following discussion on the *Graham* Case will show. See *infra* n. 15 and accompanying text.

[15] *Graham v. Florida*, 560 US 2010.

[16] *Graham v. Florida*, 560 US 10 (Roberts, J., concurring in judgment).

[17] *Ibid.* 10.   [18] *Ibid.* 11.

'narrow proportionality' approach" that, *inter alia*, "emphasized the primacy of the legislature in setting sentences" and "the state-by-state diversity protected by our federal system."[19] To Roberts, such an approach "does not grant [federal] judges blanket authority to second-guess decisions made by legislatures or sentencing courts."[20]

European epistemological optimism

European-based legal and political culture, particularly in Germany, is generally characterized as epistemologically optimistic rather than skeptical. This is reflected in its optimism with regard to the human capacity to discern right from wrong and to achieve moral progress, as well as its less suspicious attitude towards intellectual elites. The judiciary is held to be an institution with the tools for imposing rationality and reasonableness on other public entities, since it is relatively insulated from populism, bias, and irrational motives.

The origins of these views with regard to law in particular can be traced back to the nineteenth-century German legal science movement (*Rechtswissenschaft*). The *Rechtswissenschaft* movement was based on a complex combination of Savigny's rule-based conceptualism (*Begriffsjurisprudenz*) and Jhering's theory of interests-balancing theory (*Interessenjurisprudenz*) and infused with elements of idealism.[21] The belief in pure reason was especially promising and tempting in the context of the legal chaos that prevailed in nineteenth-century Germany. Reason was meta-textual and a cure for the "the accidental, the error, the passion, the irrational" characteristics of positive law.[22] Reason was also associated with a strong belief in human progress.

This tradition of rationalism was characterized also by optimism regarding the jurist's ability to "discover" the law through the exercise of reason and logic.[23] Through the exercise of pure reason, it was posited, almost every case

---

[19] *Ibid.* 2–3.

[20] *Ibid.* 2. See Moshe Cohen-Eliya and Iddo Porat, "Judicial minimalism and the double effect of rules and standards" (2012) 25 Can. J.L. & Juris. 283.

[21] The *Rechtswissenschaft* movement was also described in Chapter 2.

[22] Mathias Reimann, "Nineteenth century German legal science" (1990) Boston College L. Rev. 881 (German legal scholars of the nineteenth century strongly believed that the legal norms that follow from *Rechtswissenschaft* develop "independent from accident and individual arbitrariness").

[23] According to Reimann, *ibid.* 881, Savigny was convinced that even "as merely preliminary knowledge, philosophy is not at all necessary for the jurist." Its speculative or normative potential offered no help in performing the essential task of the legal scientist,

could be solved. Indeed, Jhering decisively asserted that with few exceptions, "we can solve every case."[24] The *Rechtswissenschaft* scholars merged idealism with a belief in legal rationality and objectivity. At the core of Savigny's theory of law lie ideals associated with historicism and romanticism, such as the *Volksgeist* (the spirit of the nation). According to Savigny, law is rooted in the organic whole of the culture and is designed to serve its core values. But the detection of these core values is a scientific enterprise based on logic: it is the "ability of the mind to demonstrate everything that one asserts in an undisputable manner on undeniable grounds."[25]

German legal political culture is also shaped by the rationalism of the civil law. Unlike the common law bottom-up, many-minds approach, the civil law tradition is a top-down, one-mind approach: a group of scholars attempts to identify the core principles of the law and the entire code of law that derives from them and then hands them down to judges and lawyers. The civil law is also characterized by a search for coherency and consistency in a small set of principles that are "discoverable" and can be set with finality through logic.

The following quote by Robert Post sums up some of these themes as they are reflected in the differences between German/European and American conceptions of constitutional law:

> Although [as Bogdandy notes] "most Continental constitutional scholars conceive of constitutional scholarship as a science" few if any American legal scholars, with the possible exception of those specializing in law and economics, would conceive of their work as "science." Since the advent of legal realism, American legal scholars have understood the study of law to be the study of the social practice of law. They have sought to clarify the goals of that practice and to explore how those goals can be most effectively achieved.[26]

Epistemological optimism and standards

Standards are usually associated with optimism with respect to the ability of decisionmakers to arrive at the right decisions. Unlike rules, standards such as balancing do not bind decisionmakers in their future decisions.

---

i.e. the understanding and systematization of positive law. In Jhering's system, everything was logic and nothing experience; this logic was considered to be inherently present in the law, simply waiting to be discovered.

[24] Rudolf Jhering, *Vom Geist des römischen Rechts auf den verschiedenen Stufen seiner Entwicklung* (9th edn., 1907), as cited in Reimann, *ibid.* 881.

[25] See Reimann, "Nineteenth century German legal science" 848.

[26] Robert Post, "Constitutional scholarship in the United States" (2009) 7 Int. J. of Const. L. 416, 422.

Rather, they leave things open and allow judges to balance the entire array of considerations that apply to the case. A standard, furthermore, does not shield against the possible bias or subjectivity of judges, since it does not bind their decisions in any meaningful way. Therefore, a system based on standards is necessarily grounded on confidence in the epistemological abilities and objectivity of judges. In such a system, the bulk of decisionmaking occurs at the adjudication stage, with the application of standards, rather than at the legislative stage, when the state sets the standard.

From the Critical Legal Studies perspective, the standards person, unlike the rules person, is more optimistic as to the human capacity to get things right, as well as to be good. The standards person seeks to provide people with the optimal tools for correcting wrongs, thus helping the weaker groups in society and acting out of empathy for them. In contract law, this distinction is manifested in the difference between rule-based freedom of contract and standard-based good faith. The latter principle can be used by judges to rectify power imbalances between the parties to a contract and to achieve social justice by offering remedy to the weaker side, whereas freedom of contract is usually conceived of as working in favor of the stronger party to the contract.[27]

Proportionality and epistemological optimism

How does epistemological optimism impact the framing and use of proportionality in European-based legal systems? Unlike in a culture of epistemological skepticism, there is no discrepancy between proportionality, as a standard, and the legal and political culture in which it is used. There is, therefore, no need to frame proportionality as minimalist in order to enable its application in the prevailing legal and political culture, for it retains the classical association of standards with epistemological optimism. Put differently, whereas the ramifications of epistemological skepticism for balancing in American legal culture were its framing as a minimalist and pragmatic doctrine, the epistemological optimism of European-based legal systems shaped proportionality as a more maximalist, idealist, and rational doctrine.

David Beatty has described the role of proportionality as promoting reason in contemporary constitutional adjudication across the globe:

---

[27] Duncan Kennedy, "Form and substance in private law adjudication" (1976) 89 Harv. L. Rev. 1685, 1737–51, 1753–6.

[P]roportionality permits disputes about the limits of legitimate law making to be settled on the basis of reason and rational argument. It makes it possible to compare and evaluate interests and ideas, values and facts, that are radically different in a way that is both rational and fair. It allows judgments to be made about ways of thinking that are as incommensurable as reason and faith.[28]

His colleague, Lorraine Weinrib, sets proportionality "within a coherent system of rights that form an objective normative order."[29] She asserts that "[c]onstitutional adjudication remains a juridical exercise tightly constrained by an established legal methodology that reflects the higher or supreme law status of the system of rights-protection. Judges do not apply their preferred personal or potential views or theories of justice."[30]

Unlike balancing in the USA, which reflects the shallow and narrow reasoning principles of minimalism, the European proportionality often features quite the opposite characteristics: depth and breadth of reasoning. To begin with, in European-based constitutional systems, proportionality is often applied to encompass a broad set of cases and thus reflects a broad rather than a narrow type of reasoning. This happens when proportionality sets a norm that is applicable for an entire category of cases to be decided in the future and not only for the case at hand; this would be the case when a proportionality-based decision follows a period in which the relevant norm had been rule-driven.[31] In Israel, for example, judicial review of parliamentary proceedings was, for quite some time, governed by a rule very similar to the British rule that such proceedings are non-justiciable. At a certain point, this rule was replaced by a proportionality-like standard, under which the question of justiciability is to be determined in accordance with the particular circumstances of each case.[32] The standard thus applies to a broad set of cases: all cases pertaining to parliamentary proceedings. Secondly, proportionality has broad application when its effect is spread over time.

---

[28] Beatty, *The Ultimate Rule of Law* 169.

[29] Weinrib, "The postwar paradigm and American exceptionalism" (2006) University of Toronto Faculty of Law, Legal Studies Research Paper No. 899131 93.

[30] Lorraine Weinrib, "The postwar paradigm and American exceptionalism," in Sujit Choudry (ed.), *The Migration of Constitutional Ideas* 84, 98 (Cambridge: Cambridge University Press, 2007).

[31] This aspect of standards perhaps reveals a certain tension between the two main features of minimalism, because the application of a standard can be narrow – that is, limited to the facts of the case – but deep – in that it rests on deep values in making the particular decision.

[32] HCJ 652/81 *MK Sarid v. Knesset Chairman* PD 36(2) 197.

While each individual decision may be narrow, in that it is confined to the particularities of the given case, a court may use proportionality so that, with time, the entire body of decisions aggregates to create a new norm to be deciphered by lower courts and practitioners and function quite similarly to a rule that directs and controls lower courts.[33]

Proportionality also often reflects a deep rather than a shallow type of reasoning. Applying the standard-like, case-by-case proportionality test requires a criterion or reference point for determining the proportionality of the action under deliberation. In European-based legal systems, that reference point is often a deep and general principle of the legal and political culture. For example, when the FGCC applies its proportionality doctrine, the reference point is the optimal promotion of the basic constitutional values, in particular the fundamental value of human dignity, clearly grounding the doctrine in high-level theory.[34] In Canada, where the constitutionality of hate speech is decided by balancing free speech and equality, the very profound standard for proportionality is the core values of the Canadian system, multiculturalism and tolerance.[35] Similarly, in Israel, the reference point for determining proportionality is the "fundamental values of Israel as a Jewish and democratic society."[36]

Balancing, proportionality, and control

The choice of either rules or standards, as we have shown, can be impacted by basic assumptions about human nature and rationality. However, it is also affected by more banal and mundane considerations

---

[33] Paul W. Kahn, "The court, the community and the judicial balance: the jurisprudence of Justice Powell" (1987) 97 Yale L.J. 1 35.

[34] See, e.g., the *Mephisto* Case, 30 BVerfGE, 173 (1971) and the *Microzensus* Case, 27 BVerfGE 1 (1969).

[35] *R. v. Keegstra*, [1990] 3 SCR 697, 755 (Can.) (the reference point for applying the standard-based principle of proportionality in a hate-speech case is the characterization of Canada as a "multicultural society in which the diversity and richness of various cultural groups is a value to be protected and enhanced"). See also *R. v. Butler* [1992] 1 SCR 452, 509 (Can.) (as above with regard to pornography).

[36] Basic Law: Human Dignity and Liberty, Art. 1, 1A,8 1992, SH 150 amended 1994 SH 90. An English translation of the law is available at www.knesset.gov.il/laws/special/eng/basic3_eng. htm; Aharon Barak, *The Judge in a Democracy* (Princeton, NJ: Princeton University Press, 2006) 28–32. See also HCJ 5016/96 *Horev* v. *Minister of Transportation*. ("The general purposes are the values of the State of Israel as a Jewish and democratic state; the specific purposes refer to the specific 'proper purpose' specified by the limitation clause. The principle of proportionality, as provided for in the Basic Law, is another expression of the reasonableness standard according to which we generally interpret any piece of legislation.").

such as the need for efficiency in administering the judicial system. Thus, while a constitutional court might be motivated by general cultural assumptions regarding the preferability of top-down or bottom-up development of law, it must also take into account the need to exert some sort of control over the system and avoid anarchy.

In this section, we show how this consideration – what we call the control consideration – also affects the centrality, or marginality, of balancing and proportionality within their respective legal systems. In particular, it can explain the American legal system's emphasis on rules, rather than standards such as balancing – or, at the very least, why it might be difficult for that system to opt for complete reliance on such standards as proportionality in its constitutional system, while easier for other legal systems, such as in Germany or Israel, to rely much more extensively on such standards. To this end, we present an analytical distinction between two types of judicial control: vertical control and horizontal control.

Vertical and horizontal control

Judicial control over the legal system can be effected on two levels: (1) vertical control of lower court decisions and (2) horizontal control over the supreme court's future decisions. Rules and standards therefore have a dual effect in terms of retaining control, both negative and positive. Rules allow constitutional court judges vertical control over lower courts, since they provide the latter with relatively clear guidelines as to how to decide cases; they also, however, limit the supreme court's horizontal control over its future decisions, in that it will be bound by its own rules as well. This would be true, of course, of any type of managerial decisionmaking body.[37] Standards have the opposite effect: they guarantee

---

[37] The choice between rules and standards as a method of business control is sometimes termed in the management literature "formalization." See Jeffrey D. Jones and John W. Slocum, Jr., "Size, technology, environment, and the structure of organizations" (1977) 2 Academy Mgmt. Rev. 561 (defining organizational formalization as the level of formal administrative rules, policies, and procedures that determine work activities); Susan E. Jackson and Randall S. Schuler, "A meta-analysis and conceptual critique of research on role ambiguity and role conflict in work settings" (1985) 36 Org. Behav. & Hum. Decision Processes 16 (explicit rules and procedures clarify role expectations and reduce role ambiguity); Ronald E. Michaels, William L. Cron, Alan J. Dubinsky, and Erich A. Joachimsthaler, "Influence of formalization on the organizational commitment and work alienation of salespeople and industrial buyers" (1988) 25 J. Marketing Res. 376 ("[C]ontrol of employee behavior does not seem to alienate marketers from their work

that the members of a decisionmaking body will retain control over their future decisions but lose vertical control over lower decisionmaking bodies, since standards do not provide precise directives for their decisions.[38]

Yet this dual effect of rules and standards is contingent on factors that can vary from system to system. We proceed now to explain how this variance is a function of the size of the system, the size of the docket, and the coherency of the decisions made by the decisionmaking body.[39]

or reduce their commitment to the organization ... [F]ormalization influenced organizational commitment indirectly through its effects on role ambiguity and role conflict."); Robert N. Anthony, *The Management Control Function* (Cambridge, MA: Harvard Business School Press, 1970) (assessing more generally management and control).

[38] Our use of the term "control" may be a bit confusing since its meaning changes at the two levels. Control on the vertical level is what I have when I tell others what to do. It is the exertion of control. At the horizontal level, in contrast, control is what I have when no one tells me what to do. It is the retention of control. But when we are concerned with the aggregate possibilities, or power, of a particular body, control is actually a combination of both. It is true that we choose to focus on one aspect for the horizontal level and on another for the vertical level, but we do so because we wish to highlight all the aspects of power, or control, for each option (rules or standards), in the combined sense of "control."

To be more precise, there are two pairs of terms, "exert control/let go" and "retain control/lose control." These terms apply differently in relation to rules and standards. When a supreme court sets rules, it limits the discretion of lower courts (it exerts control over their decisions, and they lose control over their own decisions). At the same time, the supreme court also limits its own discretion (it exerts control over its own future decisions, which leads it to lose control over those decisions). When the court sets standards, it does not limit lower courts' discretion (it lets go of control over their decisions, and they retain control over their own decisions) but, likewise, it does not limit its own decisions either (it lets go of control over its future decisions and thus retains control over those decisions). When we talk about the dual effect, we are referring to only two of the four options in these pairs of terms.

[39] This will not be an exhaustive presentation of all the institutional factors that could affect the choice between rules and standards. Instead, we focus on those factors that are more directly linked to the American and German epistemic cultures. One factor that we do not discuss extensively in the following sections is whether the constitutional court sits in a panel or *en banc*. The US Supreme Court, as well as various American and international appellate courts, hear all cases *en banc*. However, most courts (in the USA and outside the USA as well), especially lower courts, sit in alternating panels of three judges or even just one judge, as sitting *en banc* is very costly. It seems that the temptation to lock-in a policy preference through rules is even stronger in institutions with alternating panels. Even if a judge on a panel can muster a majority for his position, he cannot know how other panels would decide the same issue. It therefore makes sense for him to opt for a rule. The cost of mustering a majority on a panel of three judges is lower than for a panel of nine, for example, while the pay-off from locking-in a policy remains the same. On the strategic use of panels in appellate and constitutional courts, see Frank B. Cross and Emerson H. Tiller, "Judicial partisanship and obedience to legal doctrine: whistleblowing on the

The size of the system and docket: America versus Israel

If a judicial system is large, and especially if it is decentralized, it will be very difficult for a supreme court to exert any sort of control over lower courts using standards alone. The reason for this, as explained already, is that standards – generally speaking – leave discretion in the hands of lower courts and do not give them any clear guidelines. Thus, in a large and decentralized system only a few decisions will be directly reviewed by the supreme court, and it will need rules to maintain control. In such a system, even if the court's judicial ethos is to relinquish control and allow bottom-up development of the law, it might not prefer standards after all, since this could lead to chaos in the legal system and an inability of the supreme court to effectively administer the system and coordinate between the different lower courts.

However, for judicial systems that are small, particularly if they are centralized, opting for standards may have very different ramifications for the supreme court's ability to administer the system. In such a legal system, the court can make certain that it directly supervises enough decisions; it thus has no need for rules to sustain coordination and uniformity among the various courts and can administer the system on a case-by-case basis using standards.

The American judicial system is very large and decentralized. At its apex is the Supreme Court with a very small docket (case load of proceedings), so that it reviews and issues judgment in only a very small fraction of lower court cases.[40] In a system such as this, it is very difficult for the Supreme Court to supervise lower courts through standards. Rules, rather, are the most effective means of controlling lower court

---

Federal Courts of Appeals" (1998) 107 Yale L.J. 2155; Virginia A. Hettinger *et al.*, "Attitudinal and strategic accounts of dissenting behavior on the US Courts of Appeals" (2004) 48 Am. J. Pol. Sci. 123; Stefanie A. Lindquist and Wendy L. Martinek, "Response: psychology, strategy, and behavioral equivalence" (2009) 158 U. Pa. L. Rev. 75, 80; Pauline T. Kim, "Deliberation and strategy on the United States Courts of Appeals: an empirical exploration of panel effects" (2009) 157 U. Pa. L. Rev. 1319.

[40] It is at this point an undisputable fact that the US Supreme Court docket is steadily shrinking. See Adam Liptak, "The case of the plummeting Supreme Court docket" *New York Times*, September 28, 2009, www.nytimes.com/2009/09/29/us/29bar.html. See also David R. Stras."The Supreme Court's declining plenary docket: a membership-based explanation" (2010) 27 Const. Commentary 151. See also Kenneth W. Starr, "The Supreme Court and its shrinking docket: the ghost of William Howard Taft" (2006) 90 Minn. L. Rev. 1363 (in 2004, the Supreme Court issued judgments in only 1 percent of the cases disposed of by Signed Opinion, whereas in 1926, there was a much higher figure of 18.9 percent).

decisions. Therefore, despite the insistence of minimalists such as Sunstein and Roberts that the US Supreme Court should use standards like balancing in order to facilitate the bottom-up development of the law, it seems understandable that the American constitutional system, as a whole, has not embraced this path wholeheartedly and remains relatively rule-bound. In the balance between the vertical and horizontal effects of rules and standards in such a system, rules emerge as preferable.

There are very few judicial systems that are as large and decentralized as the US system. The German system is not as large as the American one, and the FGCC's docket is far heavier than the US Supreme Court docket.[41] Both rules and standards are viable options in such a system; and since the judicial ethos is top-down control, standards can be adopted without posing a risk to vertical control in the system.

The Israeli judicial system illustrates well the interaction between size of system and its docket and the effect of standards. The Israeli system is the exact opposite model of the US system: a small system where the Supreme Court has a heavy docket. Israel's Supreme Court supervises six district courts and thirty-one lower-tiered magistrate courts, which comprise a system of 521 judges.[42] It has no *certiorari* power and all civil and criminal cases heard in the district courts are brought before the Supreme Court on direct appeal.[43] From the perspective of administrative and constitutional law, the system is even more centralized. The Court handles all constitutional cases and many administrative cases, both as first and final instance.[44]

---

[41] Erhard Blankenburg, "Mobilization of the German Federal Constitutional Court," in Ralf Rogowski and Thomas Gawron (eds.), *Constitutional Courts in Comparison: The US Supreme Court and the German Federal Constitutional Court* (Oxford and New York: Berghahn Books, 2002) (examining the scope of individual constitutional complaints in Germany – about 5,000 per year – which account for 95 percent of the Constitutional Court's case load).

[42] As of 2007. For a general overview of the Israeli judicial system, see Itzhak Zamir and Silvian Colombo (eds.), *The Law of Israel: General Surveys* (Jerusalem and Haifa: Harry Sacher and Haifa University, 1995); Amos Shapira and Keren DeWitt-Arar (eds.), *Introduction to the Law of Israel* (The Hague and Boston: Kluwer Law International, 1995). In Israel, there are also several regional labor courts of the first instance and one National Labor Court for appeals from the first instance; decisions from the national labor court can be appealed to the Supreme Court sitting as a High Court of Justice. Additional information is available at http://cpmp.hevra.haifa.ac.il/admin/uploads/files/ Courts_burden_Final_report_5.07.pdf.

[43] It also hears magistrate court criminal and civil cases as a court of third instance, although in these cases it sometimes has discretion not to hear the appeal.

[44] Note that using rules, the Court would lose horizontal control only in those systems where a rule or practice of *stare decisis* binds the Supreme Court. Moreover, the same

This is compounded by a considerable relaxation of entry barriers for administrative and constitutional claims, such as justiciability and standing, leading to an exceptionally heavy docket. Indeed, between 2000 and 2010, Israel's fifteen Supreme Court justices heard a staggering 11,000 cases annually.[45] Given this, it is arguably possible for the Court to directly supervise a sizable number of the total cases in the system and control the decisions of lower courts using standards rather than rules, thereby retaining both vertical and horizontal control, which is precisely what it seems to have done in practice.

The prevailing conception of the Israeli Supreme Court is that, since the early 1980s, it has taken an activist tack and led a major reform of the Israeli judicial system, which has focused on enhancing rights protection and strengthening the regulation of political corruption.[46] The Court was not interested in gradual development from below but, rather, sought a rapid pace of change, which it imposed from above. On the one hand, reform of this type entails that the Supreme Court wield considerable control over lower courts' decisions and state decisions. On the other hand, the Court also needed to leave itself leeway for maneuvering and change, for adjusting the reform, so to speak, as it progressed.

Against this background, the Supreme Court's choice of standards as its preferred method of adjudication is understandable: they facilitate both control over lower court decisions and leeway to deviate from its own decisions. Thus, in conjunction with an increase in its docket size and lowering of procedural entry barriers, one can witness

considerations of size and docket would apply to judicial control over the decisions of administrative bodies as well.

[45] See "The judiciary in Israel: a report for the year 2010" (2011) 15, http://elyon1.court.gov.il/heb/haba/dochot/doc/hofesh_meida2010.pdf (in Hebrew) (these numbers refer to the number of new cases opened in each calendar year). The dramatic increase in the docket size of the Supreme Court is not unique to Israel, but rather is a trend being witnessed in many constitutional democracies across the globe. See Blankenburg, "Mobilization of the German Federal Constitutional Court" (examining the scope of individual constitutional complaints in Germany – about 5,000 per year – which account for 95 percent of the Constitutional Court's case load); Laurence R. Helfer, "Redesigning the European Court of Human Rights: embeddedness as a deep structural principle of the European human rights regime" (2008) 19 Eur. J. Int'l L. 125 (asserting that the ECtHR now faces a docket crisis of massive proportions). Israel is, however, unique in the extent of the increase relative to the small size of its legal system.

[46] For an informative overview, see Menachem Mautner, *Law and the Culture of Israel* (Oxford and New York: Oxford University Press, 2011).

a dramatic rise in the application of standards in Israeli Supreme Court jurisprudence, at the expense of rules.[47]

Supreme Court coherency

Another determinative factor in the choice between rules and standards, in term of the administrability of the system, is the extent of personal coherence between the different members of a system's supreme court and the institutional culture of conformity or dissent and adversarialism among the different judges. The American system, in addition to being large and decentralized, is also characterized by the Supreme Court's relatively adversarial makeup.[48] While this can fluctuate over the years, generally speaking, the US system, whereby Supreme Court justices are appointed by the President for an unlimited term, leads to a Court that is divided along party lines and characterized by a great deal of adversarialism. This makes administrability, uniformity, and control through standards even more difficult. In the face of a divided Court, a justice who would have otherwise chosen standards as a means of control might instead opt for rules. For if she manages to garner a majority for her rule-based opinion, she will lock-in her preferred policy for future decisions and thereby shield herself from the odds of the majority turning against her position in the future.[49] The US Supreme Court's *Citizens United* decision is a good example of such a resort to rules for these reasons.[50]

---

[47] Menachem Mautner, *The Decline of Formalism and the Rise of Values in Israeli Law* (Tel Aviv: Tel Aviv University Press, 1993) (in Hebrew).

[48] See, generally Mark V. Tushnet, *A Court Divided: The Rehnquist Court and the Future of Constitutional Law* (New York: W.W. Norton, 2005); Timothy R. Johnson, Ryan C. Black, and Eve M. Ringsmuth, "Hear me roar: what provokes Supreme Court justices to dissent from the bench?" (2009) 93 Minn. L. Rev. 1560; Lee Epstein, Jeffrey A. Segal, and Harold J. Spaeth, "The norm of consensus on the US Supreme Court" (2001) 45 Am. J. Pol. Sci. 362–3; Lee Epstein, William M. Landes, and Richard Posner, "Why (and when) judges dissent: a theoretical and empirical analysis" (January 20, 2010), University of Chicago Law & Economics, Olin Working Paper No. 510, http://ssrn.com/abstract=1542834; Forrest Maltzman, James F. Spriggs, II, and Paul J. Wahlbeck, *Crafting Law on the Supreme Court: The Collegial Game* (New York: Cambridge University Press, 2000); Paul J. Wahlbeck, James F. Spriggs, II, and Forrest Maltzman, "The politics of dissents and concurrences on the US Supreme Court" (1999) 27 Am. Pol. Q. 488. For the federal lower courts, see Cass R. Sunstein *et al., Are Judges Political? An Empirical Analysis of the Federal Judiciary* (Washington, DC: Brookings Institution Press, 2006).

[49] Of course, a doctrine of *stare decisis* is also necessary for this type of control.

[50] *Citizens United* v. *Federal Election Commission*, 558 US 310 (2010) (corporations are entitled to First Amendment constitutional rights protection). For criticism of the broad nature of the *Citizens United* line of reasoning, see, e.g., Elizabeth Pollman, "Citizens not

The conservative justices succeeded in mustering a majority by swaying Justice Kennedy, who tends to hold the middle ground. In this instance, Justice Roberts, who concurred in judgment, applied a rule rather than a standard and thus managed to lock-in his preferred campaign finance policy. Opting for a standard would have meant jeopardizing this position in future rulings, without the certainty of a conservative majority.[51]

A more coherent high court, in contrast, can facilitate control through standards in the horizontal sense as well. The small and centralized Israeli system is an interesting example of this. In the Israeli system, the Supreme Court has a certain extent of direct control over the appointment of new justices to the Court, as three of the nine members of the judicial selection committee are presiding Supreme Court justices, including the Chief Justice.[52] These three justices in fact wield greater weight than their numbers would suggest, because of their prestige relative to the other committee members and because they tend to vote as a bloc.[53] They are able, therefore, to have considerable influence on the appointment of new justices who follow their line of thinking. This has contributed to the consistent push towards coherency in the Court in conjunction with the general shift to standards and increased docket size. The very influential former Chief Justice of the Supreme Court, Aharon

---

united: the lack of stockholder voluntariness in corporate political speech" (2009) 119 Yale L.J. Online 53, www.yalelawjournal.org/2009/10/15/pollman.html.

[51] On the other hand, one can think of commerce clause jurisprudence as an area of law in which, currently, there are no entrenched camps and no divided court and the jurisprudence is emphatically standard-like. In this way, the Court can proceed on a case-by-case basis and retain horizontal control over its own decisions. In the nineteenth century, the commerce clause was a hotly debated area of constitutional law. Today, it is far less controversial, and the prime doctrine is balancing and standards. See Martin H. Redish and Shane V. Nugent, "The dormant commerce clause and the constitutional balance of federalism" (1987) Duke L.J. 569.

[52] The Israeli system of appointing judges is unique in that political control over the process is very limited. Only four of the nine members of the judicial selection committee are politicians (two ministers and two Knesset (parliament) members, one of whom is usually from the Opposition). Three members are Supreme Court justices (including the President of the Supreme Court), and two representatives of the Israeli Bar Association sit on the committee as well. See Martin Edelman, *Courts, Politics, and Culture in Israel* (Charlottesville, VA and London: University Press of Virginia, 1994) 34–5.

[53] Professor Robert J. Aumann, a game theorist and Israeli recipient of the Nobel Prize, argued at the Israeli Knesset Constitutional Committee hearings that the fact that the three Supreme Court justices vote as a bloc increases their influence from 33 percent (3 out of 9) to 43 percent. See Protocol No. 573 of the Knesset Constitutional Committee (June 17, 2008) (in Hebrew), www.knesset.gov.il/protocols/data/html/huka/2008–06–17. html.

Barak, who led the reform towards adopting standards, relaxing procedural barriers, and expanding the Court's docket, also impacted the move
towards a coherent court and has, on occasion, even expressed his
explicit view on this matter.[54]

In sum, balancing and proportionality, despite their distinctions from
one another, are both prototypical standards. And like other standards,
and unlike rules, they leave a great deal of leeway in how future cases are
decided. This feature impacts whether a judicial system makes balancing
or proportionality central or marginal doctrines, as well as its approach
towards their use – in terms of both epistemological ideology and culture
and from the perspective of the system's particular needs deriving from
its institutional components.

---

[54] The President of the Israeli Supreme Court made a controversial remark against the
nomination of Professor Ruth Gavison as a Supreme Court justice, claiming that she "has
an agenda" which, he seemed to imply, ran counter to the prevailing doctrines of Israeli
constitutional law. See Yuval Yoaz, "Barak says he was misunderstood on Ruth Gavison"
(December 12, 2005) Haaretz, www.haaretz.com/print-edition/features/barak-says-he-
was-misunderstood-on-ruth-gavison-1.176413. Gavison is well known for her fierce
criticism of what she claims to be the hyper-activist Barak Court. See, e.g., Ruth Gavison,
The Constitutional Revolution: A Reality or a Self-fulfilling Prophecy? (Jerusalem: Israel
Democracy Institute, 1998) (in Hebrew). The Gavison nomination fell, in the end,
because of the unanimous objection of all the Supreme Court justices. On the cohesiveness of the Israeli Supreme Court justices, see Yoram Shachar *et al.*, "An anatomy of
discourse and dissent in the Israeli Supreme Court – A Quantitative Analysis" (1997) 20
T.A.U.L. Rev. 763 (in Hebrew). On the relative cohesiveness of the Canadian Supreme
Court, see Cynthia L. Ostberg and Matthew E. Wetstein, *Attitudinal Decision-making in
the Supreme Court of Canada* (Vancouver: UBC Press, 2007).

6

Justification and authority

The analysis in this book has progressed along two parallel trajectories: moving from the specific to the general, in terms of level of abstraction, and from the local to the transnational, or global, in terms of geographic scope. Chapter 5, in its discussion of epistemology, moved up one level of abstraction from the chapters on legal and political culture and historical origins and began the process of expanding the geographical breadth of the review by examining countries outside of Germany, such as Israel. In this chapter, we continue this process and consider proportionality as not only a local doctrine but also as a transnational, or global, phenomenon.

At this juncture, balancing and proportionality begin to take different paths. As described in Chapter 1, proportionality has gained incredible prevalence, almost to the point of global dominance. This raises the question of whether the local German culture, that was the breeding ground for proportionality, transcended national boundaries as well. There are two possible accounts for the spread of proportionality beyond Germany's borders. The one is that proportionality has been adopted by many countries for reasons unrelated to the cultural attributes the doctrine acquired in its German birthplace. There is thus no reason to believe that these attributes migrated out of Germany with proportionality. We call this the "functional" account of the spread of proportionality but find it falls short of the mark. A second possible account describes the widespread adoption of proportionality as part of the emergence of a general global constitutional culture, which we term "the culture of justification" and which is strongly tied to some of the main themes discussed in the chapters on culture and epistemology. While not all of the German cultural attributes that shaped proportionality followed it out of Germany and into the culture of justification, some essential features did. Understanding proportionality therefore helps to clarify the new global legal culture that has evolved and to contrast it with the American legal culture, "the culture of authority," which is the setting for balancing.

A functional accounting for the spread of proportionality

Early legal development

Professor Frederick Schauer has offered an intriguing explanation for the widespread adoption of proportionality across the globe.[1] He stresses that with the exception of the USA, constitutional systems with judicial review are relatively recent creations, mainly the products of post-Second World War developments. As a result, he claims, the constitutional jurisprudence in these systems is still in its developing stage, with only a relatively small body of doctrine and case law. In such early stages of legal development, standard-based doctrines like proportionality are more appropriate than categorical ones, as they allow for doctrine to develop naturally and do not constrain it from the outset. In due course, as the case law increases and distinctions are more fine, the standard-based doctrines, such as proportionality, will be replaced with doctrinal-and rule-based tests.

The use of a flexible, standard-based doctrine such as proportionality can also aid in establishing the legitimacy of new legal systems. Proportionality's inherent flexibility provides judges with the leeway to develop doctrine freely and to decide when to intervene and when not, taking into account a wide range of considerations, including public opinion, potential political backlash, and institutional memory.[2] Similar standard-based doctrines, such as the European margin of appreciation doctrine,[3] helped to cement the reputation of the ECtHR as a sensible and cautious institution and to advance its legitimacy in its formative years.[4]

---

[1] Frederick Schauer, "Freedom of expression adjudication in Europe and the United States: a case study in Comparative Constitutional Architecture," in Georg Nolte (ed.), *European and US Constitutionalism* (Cambridge: Cambridge University Press, 2005) 49; Frederick Schauer, "The exceptional First Amendment," in Michael Ignatieff (ed.), *American Exceptionalism and Human Rights* (Princeton, NJ: Princeton University Press, 2005) 29, 32.

[2] For a similar account of Indian Supreme Court jurisprudence, see Shylashri Shankar: *Scaling Justice: India Supreme Court, Anti-terror Laws, and Social Rights* (Oxford: Oxford University Press, 2009).

[3] *Handyside v. The United Kingdom*; see also Yuval Shany, "Toward a general margin of appreciation doctrine in international law?" (2005)16 Eur. J. Int'l L. 907.

[4] Howard C. Yourow, *The Margin of Appreciation in the Dynamics of the European Human Rights Jurisprudence* (The Hague: Martinus Nijhoff, 1996).

However, there are two difficulties with this account of the spread of proportionality. First, unless one identifies sophistication and development in a legal system with the lack of standards, which would seem circular, it must be conceded that not all the legal systems that adopted proportionality are characterized by underdeveloped constitutional jurisprudence. The FGCC, the Canadian Supreme Court, and the ECtHR, which are only a few of the courts that use proportionality extensively, have all produced substantial and sophisticated jurisprudence.

Second, Schauer's account of the typical development of legal thought does not align with the fact that there are many examples of legal systems whose early stages were characterized by categorization and in which the emergence of standard-based doctrines such as proportionality was a later development. In Israel, for example, in the early years of statehood, the fledgling Supreme Court adopted a categorical approach; only since the 1980s has it made the shift to standards such as reasonableness, balancing, and proportionality.[5] A similar process has occurred in the development of proportionality's subtests. In Germany, for example, emphasis has gradually shifted from the less open-ended and more formalistic suitability and necessity subtests to proportionality in the strict sense, which is more open-ended.[6] Other settings too have been characterized by cycles of change rather than linear progression towards categorization. The USA is one clear example of cyclical fluctuation between standards and categorization. Balancing, for example, first emerged in the late 1930s, waned in the 1960s, and then resurfaced in the late 1970s, only to decline once again in the 1990s.[7] Moreover, if proportionality were in

---

[5] Menachem Mautner, *The Decline of Formalism and the Rise of Values in Israeli Law* (Tel Aviv: Tel Aviv University Press, 1993) (in Hebrew). Similar processes took place in England. See Margit Cohn, "Legal transplant chronicles: the evolution of substantive judicial review of the administration in the United Kingdom" (2010) 58 Am. J. Com. L. (referring to the reasonableness test in English administrative law, as established in *Associated Provincial Picture House Ltd.* v. *Wednesbury*, [1948] 1 KB 223, 229, and arguing that "since 1948, more that 2500 decisions have cited *Associated Provincial Picture House Ltd* v. *Wednesbury* … and used the term 'unreasonable,' but of these, 2160 – more than 85% – were delivered after January 1, 1990 (1545, or 61%, were delivered after January 1, 2000).").

[6] See Grimm, "The protective function of the state," in Georg Nolte (ed.), *European and US Constitutionalism* (Cambridge: Cambridge University Press, 2005) 393, who argues that "[t]he most striking difference between [Canada and Germany] is the high relevance of the third step of the proportionality test in Germany and its more residual function in Canada."

[7] T. Alexander Aleinikoff, "Constitutional law in the age of balancing" (1987) 96 Yale L.J. On the decline in the use of balancing in the early 1990s, see, e.g., Stephen E. Gottlieb,

fact a sign of a legal system's immaturity, we would expect it to be discarded once the system matures. The evidence thus far does not support this theory. Indeed, the widespread global appeal of proportionality cannot be explained as resulting from the early development stage of constitutional jurisprudence in the various legal systems.

Pluralism and conflict management

A more compelling explanation for the popularity of proportionality could be that proportionality is a particularly useful judicial device for mitigating conflicts within divided societies, since it emphasizes facts rather than normative disputes.

As noted in Chapter 1 David Beatty has argued that proportionality does not entail deciding on what is right or wrong, but rather calls for an empirical determination of efficiency and of the measure of harm and benefit to each of the conflicting rights and interests in its own terms.[8] The first two proportionality subtests – suitability and necessity – relate to efficiency in terms of means used, while the third subtest – proportionality in its strict sense – primarily involves an empirical assessment of the harm to the conflicting rights and interests. In other words, proportionality does not require a comparison between two incommensurable values.[9]

This explanation is particularly appealing today, with the diversification of many societies due to mass global migration. Proportionality could be seen as conducive to lowering the stakes of politics in pluralistic and deeply divided societies, offering the seeming advantage of emphasizing facts and questions of degree, rather than principles and categorical distinctions. This allows judges to moderate the rhetorical exaggeration that characterizes the presentation of claims in the political sphere.

"The paradox of balancing significant interests" (1994) 45 Hastings L.J. 825 ("The notion of balancing rights and interests has come under increasing criticism and declining explicit judicial use.").

[8] David Beatty, *The Ultimate Rule of Law* (Oxford: Oxford University Press, 2004) 69. ("On this model of judicial review, it is in the formulation of minor premise, where the facts and details of the government's behavior are scrutinized and probed, that all the hard work is done.")

[9] See also David Luban, "Incommensurable values, rational choice, and moral absolute" (1990) 38 Cleveland St. L. Rev. 65, 75, arguing that most cases involved simple small–large tradeoffs. Robert Alexy argues that balancing can be conducted rationally primarily because it involves assessing facts rather than making value judgments, within the framework of what he terms the "weight formula." Robert Alexy, "Balancing, constitutional review and representation" (2005) 3 Int'L J. Con. L.

An illustrative example of how constitutional courts can lower the political stakes of a clash between rights and interests is the Israeli Supreme Court's *Horev* decision, which revolved around a ban on driving through a religious neighborhood on the Sabbath. In the first paragraph of his opinion, Chief Justice Barak emphasized the extreme tension surrounding the case:

> In Israeli public discourse, Bar-Ilan Street is no longer simply a street. It has become a social concept reflecting a deep-seated political dispute between the Ultra-Orthodox and the secular populations in this country. This debate is not limited to the matter of freedom of movement on Bar-Ilan Street on Friday evenings and on the Sabbath. It is, in essence, a difficult debate involving the relationship between religion and state in Israel, which pierces through to Israel's very character as a Jewish or a democratic state. It is a bitter debate about the character of Jerusalem, which has found its way to the Court's doorstep.[10]

Here, the Court applied the proportionality test to mediate the political tension surrounding this case. After examining the facts, it concluded that:

> [t]he harm caused to the secular members of the public, residing outside the Ultra-Orthodox neighborhoods serviced by Bar-Ilan Street, who seek to exercise their freedom of movement and right to travel from one end of the city to the other, is not excessive … [A]ll that is required of them is a detour, taking no more than two extra minutes.[11]

Thus, the Court turned a dispute that was generally regarded to be a bitter cultural war and a matter of fundamental principle into a simple tradeoff that most reasonable people could accept. Proportionality enabled the transformation of the debate over values into a debate over facts, which is easier to resolve. It functioned as a mechanism to transform, in Sunstein's terms, high-level disagreements into low-level disagreements.[12] Indeed, courts around the world have to increasingly contend with such polarizing and sensitive issues as gay marriage and restrictions on wearing the veil, as well as with disputes such as the controversy surrounding the Danish Muhammad cartoons.[13]

---

[10] HCJ 5016/96 *Horev* v. *Minister of Transportation* (the opening paragraph of Barak, CJ's, judgment). See discussion above in Ch. 1.

[11] *Ibid* para. 19.

[12] Cass R. Sunstein, "Incompletely theorized agreements" (1995) 103 Harv. L. Rev. 1733.

[13] Sune Lægaard, "Normative significance of transnationalism? The case of the Danish Cartoons Controversy" (2010) 3(2) Ethics & Global Politics 101.

Consequently, there is a more pressing need for proportionality to be applied in a way that lowers the political stakes and thereby bolsters the stability of pluralistic societies. Proportionality as a fact-finding mechanism is also conceived as a legitimate exercise of judicial powers, because judges have institutional expertise in fact-finding.[14]

Yet, as discussed in Chapter 1,[15] there are several difficulties with this account. First, proportionality cannot bypass normative determinations and resolve cases solely on points of fact. Since most attempts to do so are generally unsuccessfully, it is also questionable whether proportionality can succeed at lowering the political stakes or be explained in these terms. The *Horev* decision, for example, may seem completely common-sensical when viewed in isolation from the wider context: the burden of a two-minute detour seems to be clearly outweighed by severe harm to religious feelings. But this is a very limited understanding of the circumstances and their consequences. The secular population in Jerusalem feared that Bar-Ilan Street would not be the only street to be closed on the Sabbath for the same reasons and that other freedoms would be eroded. The political reality in Israel is such that whenever the government yields to demands to accommodate the Ultra-Orthodox community in Israel, this is followed only by further demands. If we concede, therefore, that the long-term consequences should be taken into account in the balancing process, there is a strong element of indeterminacy in evaluating facts. This could bring the process closer to policymaking, which is more susceptible to subjective normative assumptions.

Second, facts alone cannot determine which considerations are relevant and legitimate for the particular decision and which should be rejected from the outset. Facts alone do not help to distinguish between a ruling in favor of a detour to prevent offense to religious sentiment and a ruling aimed at preventing offense to sentiments grounded in racism. Even a minor two-minute detour would be unacceptable if imposed, for example, on Black commuters so as not to offend the feelings of White racist residents.

Third, when judges weigh the conflicting rights and interests, they measure not only the extent of harm to each value but also make (at least implicit) judgments regarding the relative importance of each of the conflicting values. Accordingly, a minor infringement of the right to

---

[14] Beatty, *The Ultimate Rule of Law* 163; John H. Ely, *Democracy and Distrust: A Theory of Judicial Review* (Cambridge, MA: Harvard University Press, 1980) 102–3.

[15] *Supra*, pp. 20–1.

physical integrity is clearly not equal, in balance, to a minor infringement of the right to property. Although common rhetoric in the jurisprudence of legal systems that apply proportionality, the statement that "all rights bear equal moral value"[16] is very controversial and even counterintuitive.

Finally, the assumption that standard-based doctrines such as proportionality are the most appropriate mechanisms for lowering the stakes of politics in deeply divided societies is also questionable. As Professor William Eskridge has shown,[17] it is quite conceivable that a set of rule-like doctrines could also work to lower these stakes in pluralistic societies. Building on John Hart Ely's democracy-reinforcing theory of judicial review,[18] Eskridge demonstrates that for highly controversial public issues such as gay marriage and abortion, applying a set of neutral rules could serve as an effective doctrinal mechanism for maintaining social stability – for example, setting categorical bans on demonization, stereotyping, and forced assimilation or reversing the burden of inertia for obsolete statutory policies.

A global community of judges and lingua franca

A third possible explanation for the widespread adoption of proportionality is the need for a common language, a *lingua franca*, that transcends national borders and allows for dialogue and exchange of information between constitutional systems. Proportionality is a good candidate for meeting this need: it is broad enough to accommodate the divergences between legal systems, while at the same time capturing some of the essence of rights adjudication that is common to all. Proportionality can thus be viewed as a value-neutral mechanism for reducing

---

[16] For Germany, see Grimm, "Proportionality in Canadian and German constitutional law jurisprudence" (2007) 57 U. Toronto L.J. 383, 394 ("The [German] Constitutional Court does not recognize a hierarchy among the various fundamental rights."). See also Eckart Klein, "Preferred freedoms – Doktrin und deutsches Verfassungsrecht," in *Grundrecht, soziale Ordnung und Verfassungsgerichtsbarkeit: Festschrift für Ernst Benda Zum 70 Geburstag* (Heidelberg: Müller Jur. Verlag, 1995) 130–9 (rejecting the suggestion that the doctrinal mechanism in the American Preferred Rights doctrine should be applied in German constitutional law). The Canadian approach is similar to the German one; see, e.g., *Dagenais* v. *Canadian Broadcasting Corp.*, [1994] 3 SCR 835 (Can.).

[17] William J. Eskridge, "Pluralism and distrust: how courts can support democracy by lowering the stakes of politics" (2005) 114 Yale L.J. 1279; William N. Eskridge, "Foreword: the marriage cases – reversing the burden of inertia in a pluralist constitutional democracy" (2009) 97 Cal. L. Rev. 1785.

[18] Ely, *Democracy and Distrust*.

communication barriers and costs between legal systems. In the age of legal pluralism when, as Professor Michel Rosenfeld argues, "[n]ation-state legal regimes are ... supplemented by numerous transnational and global orders that defy any workable hierarchy or cogent unity," the doctrine of proportionality serves as an important tool for harmonizing the prevailing plurality of legal regimes by creating a shared language.[19]

Indeed, standards like proportionality have the advantage of flexibility and of being able to accommodate many different values. In particular, proportionality offers an analytical platform that has great appeal as a generic framework for rights adjudication. However, like the "conflict management" account, this explanation also fails to fully explain why proportionality (rather than a more categorical doctrine) was chosen. A common language, after all, could also be categorical. For example, in global capitalism, the *lingua franca* is the *Lex Mercatoria*, which is associated with free trade, strong protection for economic liberties, and some degree of market certainty.[20]

Judicial power

The fourth and final functional explanation for the wide proliferation of proportionality rests on conceptions of institutional power struggles. Across the world, Professor Robert Bork has asserted, courts are grabbing power from elected branches of government and "coercing liberal values" on society.[21] Ran Hirschl, a critical legal scholar, has claimed that hegemonic elites use the emerging new constitutionalism in their countries as a mechanism to entrench their values and power by rechanneling their efforts from the democratic process to the courts.[22] Proportionality, like other standard-based doctrines, serves judges well in this respect,

---

[19] Michel Rosenfeld, "Rethinking constitutional ordering in an era of legal and ideological pluralism" (2008) 6 Int'l J. Con L. 415 (from the abstract).

[20] Keith Highet, "Enigma of the Lex Marcatoria" (1988) 63 Tul. L. Rev. 613 n. 30 and accompanying text (arguing that the categorical rules of the INCOTERMS that apply in international commercial transactions are part of the *Lex Mercatoria*). See also United Nations Convention on Contracts for International Sale of Goods, April 11, 1980 1489 UNTS 3 that contains many rule-like provisions.

[21] Robert Bork, *Coercing Virtues: The Worldwide Rule of Judges* (Washington, DC: American Enterprise Institute, 2003).

[22] Ran Hirschl, *Towards Juristocracy: The Origins and Consequences of the New Constitutionalism* (Cambridge, MA: Harvard University Press, 2004).

since it allows them to cloak their discretionary intervention in the legitimacy of doctrine.

The account from raw judicial power, however, reduces the explanation of the phenomenon of judicial behavior to a matter of power relations, which seems too simplistic. In addition, it seems to miss an important point: that the application of proportionality is generally accepted by both the public and by its representatives as a legitimate exercise of judicial authority.

Culture of justification and culture of authority

For the reasons presented above, the various explanations for proportionality's spread fall short of the mark. Common to all of these accounts is a functional approach to explaining the proportionality phenomenon: proportionality has spread because it is a mechanism that promotes flexibility, political stability, efficiency, judicial legitimacy, or simply judicial power. As we have shown, some of the explanations rest on misconceptions regarding proportionality, while others, though touching on important aspects of proportionality, cannot fully explain the selection of proportionality over any other doctrine.

The discussion in this section will offer an intrinsic, rather than instrumental–functional, explanation for the spread of proportionality. We argue that the other accounts fail to touch on the essence of proportionality as a global doctrine: that it is a requirement for *justification*. When courts apply proportionality in constitutional law, they are asking governments to justify their actions on substantive grounds. The global trend towards proportionality is, therefore, a global trend towards justification, for proportionality responds to a widespread basic intuition: that governments must justify all of their actions. Thus, in order to understand the success of proportionality, it must be placed within the larger movement towards what can be referred to as a constitutional "culture of justification."

The first to coin the term "culture of justification" was the South African scholar Étienne Mureinik, who presented this as an ideal for the new South African Constitution and contrasted it with the culture of authority that characterized the Apartheid regime:

> If the new constitution is a bridge away from a culture of authority, it is clear what it must be a bridge to. It must lead to a culture of justification – a culture in which every exercise of power is expected to be justified; in which the leadership given by government rests on the cogency of the case

offered in defense of its decisions, not the fear inspired by the force at its command. The new order must be a community built on persuasion, not coercion.[23]

While, for Mureinik, the contrast is between a democratic and non-democratic regime, we understand this clash between the two cultures as representing the divergence between the two constitutional models at the center of this book: the American model (with its balancing doctrine) versus the European-based model that developed after the Second World War (with proportionality).[24] Since both models function within the liberal tradition, the culture of authority, as presented here, is distinct from a culture of authoritarianism.[25]

A culture of authority is based on the government's authority to exercise power. The legitimacy and legality of governmental action is derived from the fact that the actor is authorized to act. Thus, public law, under this conception, focuses on delimiting the borders of public action and on ensuring that decisions are made only by those authorized to make them. In a culture of justification, in contrast, the authority to act is relevant only insofar as it serves as a starting point for the constitutional analysis; the existence of authorization to act is a necessary but insufficient condition for legitimacy and legality. Instead, the crucial requirement for legitimate and legal governmental action is that it is justified in terms of its cogency and persuasiveness, that is, its rationality and reasonableness.[26]

---

[23] Étienne Mureinik, "A bridge to where? Introducing the Interim Bill of Rights" (1994) 10 S. Afr. J. Hum. Rts. 31, 32.

[24] For a comparison between these models, see Michael Ignatieff, "Introduction: American exceptionalism and human rights," in Michael Ignatieff (ed.), *American Exceptionalism and Human Rights* (Princeton, NJ: Princeton University Press, 2005) 1; Harold Hongju Koh, "On American exceptionalism" (2003) 55 Stan. L. Rev. 1479, 1483; Frederick Schauer, "Freedom of expression adjudication in Europe and the United States: a case study of comparative constitutional architecture" 49–51.

[25] As will be explained on pp. 113–17, the relatively clear boundaries of authority and the division of labor in a culture of authority in liberal democracies are often horizontal rather than vertical, and in this sense, they reflect a respect for the sovereignty of "authorized" institutions.

[26] Mureinik takes "justification" in a culture of justification to be substantive and not merely formal. Formal justifications, such as reliance on legal precedent or legal authority to decide, are from the realm of the culture of authority. See also David Dyzenhaus, M. Hunt, and M. Taggart, "The principle of legality in administrative law: internationalisation and constitutionalisation" (2001) 1 Oxford U. Commonwealth L.J. 5, 29.

It is important to emphasize from the outset that there is no clear dichotomy between justification and authority and that the two concepts are in fact interrelated: when we justify a decision, we often justify it not only in terms of our reasons for the specific decision but also in terms of why we, rather than someone else, are authorized to make this decision. Justification is therefore not analytically isolated from authority. However, in a culture of authority, justification for action is provided mainly at the stage of assigning authority, and once authority has been assigned, the authorized body needs to offer little justification for its specific decisions. In contrast, in a culture of justification, even after authority has been assigned, the authorized body must still provide justification for all of its decisions.[27]

Below we compare the central features of culture of justification and culture of authority. The impact of the two cultures on balancing and proportionality will be discussed later on.

Division of labor and "black holes"

A culture of authority implies a political division of labor: the existence of distinct institutions for distinct spheres of public life, with each institution best equipped to act in its sphere and accountable for its actions

---

[27] Note also that in the culture of justification there are two ways to understand the requirement for justification. The first would be to ascribe intrinsic value to justification: the mere production of justification would be an intrinsic expression of the values of respect, since justification means that we relate to the other side and enter into a certain dialogue with her. The second understanding would ascribe instrumental value to the justification requirement: as a means of producing the best possible outcome or best policy. Hence, countries with a culture of justification might diverge on their understanding of the requirement for justification. For example, it seems that in Canada more emphasis is placed on justification in an intrinsic sense, whereas German law views justification as a requirement for the optimization of constitutional values (i.e. achieving the best outcomes). For a Canadian dialogical understanding of justification, see the exchange between Peter W. Hogg and Allison A. Bushell, "The charter dialogue between courts and legislatures (or perhaps the charter of rights isn't such a bad thing after all)" (1997) 35 Osgoode Hall L.J. 75; Christopher P. Manfredi and James B. Kelly, "Six degrees of dialogue: a response to Hogg and Bushell" (1999) 37 Osgoode Hall L.J. 513; and, again, Peter W. Hogg and Allison A. Bushell, "Reply to six degrees of dialogue" (1999) 37 Osgoode Hall L.J. 529. On the classic German approach to justification as a requirement for optimization, see Robert Alexy, *A Theory of Constitutional Rights* (Julian Rivers trans., Oxford: Oxford University Press, 2002); Mattias Kumm, "What do you have in virtue of having a constitutional right? On the place and limits of the proportionality requirement," in George Pavlakos (ed.), *Law, Rights and Discourse: The Legal Philosophy of Robert Alexy* (Oxford: Hart Publishing, 2007) 131.

within that sphere.[28] In terms of the role of judicial review, then, its main task is to police the borders of this division of labor and make sure that each institution is operating within its sphere and bounds of authority. An institution is not regularly required to justify its actions when acting within the limits of its authority, but merely to identify the legal source of its authority to act. Within the bounds of its authority, an institution has autonomy to make decisions as it sees fit and is sovereign within its sphere of operation.[29] In a culture of authority, such as in the USA, even in cases of clear mistakes, a court will respect the autonomy of the authorized institution and bow to its special expertise when it identifies areas that are within the scope of the institution's exclusive authority.

This idea is reflected in the many barriers to reviewing cases on the merits, which are more strictly applied in American constitutional law than in European-based systems. These barriers include, first and foremost, the political question doctrine or the concept of justiciability, under which certain questions are non-reviewable by the courts and are plainly within the state's scope of authority because of their political nature.[30] Another barrier is the prohibition on the extraterritoriality application of constitutional law, which has been central in rejecting some of the claims of Guantánamo detainees.[31] Third, there are the standing requirements, which filter out all governmental actions that do not create grounds for a specific claim of a specific harm.[32] For example, even if the government has illegally funded development projects that could harm endangered species, it may not need to justify its action to a court if no specific claimant can show specific harm to himself or herself as a result of the

---

[28] This fits well with the American conception of separation of powers. See Rachel E. Barkow, "Institutional design and the policing of prosecutors: lessons from administrative law" (2009) 61 Stan. L. Rev. 689 (describing the US governmental system as one "whose hallmark is supposed to be the separation of powers").

[29] Describing the response of the American Revolution to the changing face of American society, Richard Pildes argues, "The most important element of this response was the adoption of strategies of differentiation between different spheres of authority – the drawing of boundaries to redefine the nature of authority and carve it up into separate spheres." He continues, "[T]he central problem was organizing and legitimating authority; the central solution was differentiation of authority into different and separate realms." Richard H. Pildes, "Avoiding balancing: the role of exclusionary reasons in constitutional law" (1994) 45 Hastings L.J. 707, 720, 722.

[30] *Baker* v. *Carr*, 369 US 691 (1962).   [31] *Boumediene* v. *Bush*, 553 US 723 (2008).

[32] See, e.g., *Warth* v. *Seldin*, 422 US 490, 498 (1975) (United States); *Inland Revenue Commissioners Appellants* v. *National Federation of Self-Employed and Small Businesses Ltd Respondents*, [1982] AC 617 (Great Britain); *Finlay* v. *Canada (Minister of Finance)*, [1986] 2 SCR 607 (Canada).

action.[33] Another example of the standing requirement would be that even were reserve duty by members of Congress to be deemed unconstitutional, no claim could be brought since there is no claimant who can show concrete harm to him or her.[34] Similar doctrines are ripeness and mootness, which exclude claims that are too early or too late from being heard by the courts. And although the US Supreme Court has developed a complex set of doctrines that sometimes ease the standing requirements, these are the exceptions: the standing doctrine continues to carve out a large body of decisions in which the state is immune from the need to justify its actions before the Court.[35]

The US Supreme Court's reluctance to review the legislative process, viewing the latter as distinctly within the authority of Congress and the President, even in clear cases of procedural mistake. Indeed, a federal court ruling held that even when the President and Congress seem to have "conspired to violate the Constitution by enacting legislation that had not passed both the House and Senate," as in the case of the Deficit Reduction Act of 2005, the court will not intervene.[36]

In contrast to the culture of authority, in a culture of justification, in Mureinik's words, "*every*" governmental action is subject to justification, since justification, rather than authority, is considered the main source of legitimacy for governmental action. Maintaining the boundaries between the different spheres of government is less important if we view justification as the main aim.[37] While certain limits on justification are inevitable and required by such pragmatic considerations as the need to respect the authority of other institutions and the fact that resources are limited,[38]

---

[33] See *Lujan v. Defenders of Wildlife*, 504 US 555 (1992).

[34] *Schlesinger v. Reservists Committee to Stop the War*, 418 US 208 (1974).

[35] The central such doctrine is "facial review," which allows, in certain circumstances, for the review of a law on its face and not according to the specific way it was applied in the particular case. See, e.g., *United States v. Salerno*, 481 US 739, 745 (1987). However, this doctrine has very narrow parameters: "A facial challenge to a legislative Act is, of course, the most difficult challenge to mount successfully, since the challenger must establish that no set of circumstances exists under which the Act would be valid." *Ibid.* 931 (Justice Rehnquist).

[36] *OneSimpleLoan v. US Sec'y of Educ.*, 496 F.3d 197, 208 (2d Cir. 2007), cert. denied sub nom., *OneSimpleLoan v. Spellings*, 128 S. Ct. 1220 (2008).

[37] Alec Stone Sweet, *Governing with Judges: Constitutional Politics in Europe* (Oxford: Oxford University Press, 2000) 32, 40 (arguing that European constitutional courts do not conduct judicial review in the anti-majoritarian sense but rather as political organs).

[38] See, for instance, the margin of appreciation doctrine, which was first developed in Europe.

these restrictions are compromises and unavoidable deviations from the ideal, rather than the end in and of themselves.

The jurist most prominently associated with the removal of barriers to judicial review and perhaps best representing the culture of justification is the former Chief Justice of the Israeli Supreme Court, Aharon Barak. Justice Barak has written extensively both in his academic scholarship and his judicial opinions against what he later termed "black holes" and for the reviewability of all governmental actions.[39] Under his leadership, the Israeli Court practically eliminated all barriers to reviewing constitutional claims on the merits.

One illustrative example of this approach is the Israeli Supreme Court's *Sarid* decision. As opposed to the very limited judicial review of internal legislative procedures in the USA, the Israeli Court, shifting strongly towards a culture of justification, ruled that all such procedures are subject to judicial review.[40] Even the decision of the Speaker of the Israeli Parliament setting the time of a parliamentary hearing can be reviewed for legality and justification. The political question doctrine also has been virtually obliterated from the Israeli Court's jurisprudence.[41] Matters relating to the Jewish character of the Israeli state,[42] and even regarding specific military tactics such as targeted killings[43] or the erection of a separation wall in the Occupied Territories,[44] have been deemed justiciable and reviewable by the Court. Standing requirements have also been effectively eliminated; currently, any individual or non-governmental organization (NGO) can file a claim of illegality regarding a governmental action.[45] For example, nominations to public office are routinely petitioned against to the Supreme Court on grounds of unreasonableness, even though no specific claimant would be able to meet the standing requirements.[46] Similarly challenged are decisions regarding the

---

[39] Barak, *The Judge in a Democracy* (Princeton, NJ: Princeton University Press, 2006) 194, 298 (arguing that there are no "black holes" where there is judicial review).

[40] HCJ 652/81 *MK Sarid v. The Chairman of the Knesset*, 36(2) PD 197. For an overview of the Israeli approach to justiciability see Ariel Bendor, "Are there any limits to justiciability? The jurisprudential and constitutional controversy in light of the American and Israeli experience" (1997) 7 Ind. Int'l & Comp. L. Rev. 311.

[41] HCJ 910/86 *Ressler v. Minister of Defense* PD 42(2) 441.

[42] HCJ 6698/95 *Adel Kaadan et al. v. Israel Land Administration et al.* PD 54 (1) 258.

[43] HCJ 769/02 *Public Committee Against Torture in Israel v. Government of Israel* (published 2006).

[44] HCJ 2056/04 *Beit Sourik Village Council v. The Government of Israel*, 58(5) PD 807.

[45] HCJ 852/85 *Aloni v. Minister of Justice* PD 41(2) 1.

[46] HCJ 6163/92 *Eisenberg v. Minister of Building* PD 47(2) 229.

underenforcement of building restrictions[47] and prosecutorial decisions.[48] The concreteness requirement has been substantially relaxed, so that petitions can be brought even if no specific case is involved or the case has become moot.

Israeli jurisprudence, therefore, is a striking example of the culture of justification. It is characterized by a conscious effort to remove as many hurdles to judicial review as possible, in order to make the government accountable for all of its actions to the Court and requiring it to justify almost all of its actions.

Other European-based legal systems have not been as radical in their embrace of the culture of justification. Yet, generally speaking, the barriers to judicial review are less stringently applied in these systems than in the USA.[49] The standing requirement, for example, has been considerably relaxed in India,[50] Canada,[51] and South Africa.[52] The easing of procedural barriers had an impact on docket size. As we have shown in Chapter 5, while the US Supreme Court docket is shrinking,[53] there has been an exponential growth in the number of petitions filed with the ECtHR,[54] the FGCC,[55] and the Israeli Supreme Court.[56]

---

[47] HCJ 851/06 *Amona v. Minister of Security* (published 2006), http://elyon2.court.gov.il/ files/06/510/008/G03/06008510.G03.htm.

[48] HCJ 935/89 *Ganor v. Attorney-General* PD 44(2) 485.

[49] Micheal C. Dorf, "Abstract and concrete review," in Vikram D. Amar and Mark Tushnet (eds.), *Global Perspectives on Constitutional Law* (Oxford: Oxford University Press, 2009) 3–14.

[50] See, e.g., S.P. *Gupta v. Union of India*, AIR 1982 SC 149; *People's Union for Democratic Rights v. Union of India*, [(1982) 3 SCC 235; *M.C. Mehta v. Union of India*, 1988 SCR (2) 530.

[51] *Thorson v. Canada (Attorney General)*, [1975] 1 SCR 138. More recently, the standing requirement was further relaxed in *Downtown Eastside Sex Workers United Against Violence Society v. Canada (Attorney General)*, 2010 BCCA 439.

[52] Article 38 of the South African Constitution grants broad standing rights to "anyone acting in the public interest." *Ferreira v. Levin NO*, 1995 (2) SA 813 (W).

[53] Adam Liptak, "The case of the plummeting Supreme Court docket" *New York Times*, September 28, 2009. See also David R. Stras, "The Supreme Court's declining plenary docket: a membership-based explanation" (2010) 27 Const. Commentary 151.

[54] Laurence R. Helfer, "Redesigning the European Court of Human Rights: embeddedness as a deep structural principle of the European human rights regime" (2008) 19 Eur. J. Int'l L. 125 (arguing that the ECtHR now faces a docket crisis of massive proportions).

[55] Erhard Blankenburg, "Mobilization of the German Federal Constitutional Court," in Ralf Rogowski and Thomas Gawron (eds.), *Constitutional Courts in Comparison: The US Supreme Court and the German Federal Constitutional Court* (Oxford: Berghahn Books, 2002).

[56] The Israeli Supreme Court is an appellate criminal and civil court. It also serves as the High Court of Justice (HCJ), in which capacity it handles public law petitions. See *supra*, Ch. 5 p. 99, n. 45.

The meaning of rights

The conception of rights in a culture of authority derives from the way in which the political division of labor is conceived. In this legal culture, rights are viewed as demarcating the boundaries of the governmental sphere of action and as imposing restrictions on governmental action and authority.[57] The right to free speech, for example, can, arguably, be understood as representing the principle that the government should not be allowed to intervene in the market of ideas.[58] Similarly, the right not to be discriminated against sets boundaries on political power and political goals.[59] This conception of rights is dominant in American constitutional law, and as a consequence, rights are narrowly construed.

In a culture of justification, in contrast, rights are viewed as values – substantive goods – that reflect the aspiration for progress and rationality. Rights, to use a common philosophical phrasing, are seen in "perfectionist" terms,[60] as positive values to be promoted and respected as much as possible by the government in its actions. In this sense, they are the benchmark for good judicial decisions and the substantive parameters by which such decisions are to be measured.

A most succinct account of this conception of rights was offered by German constitutional scholar Robert Alexy, in defining constitutional rights in German law as "principles":

> [P]rinciples are norms requiring that something be realized to the greatest extent possible, given the factual and legal possibilities at hand. Thus,

---

[57] See Pildes, "Avoiding balancing: the role of exclusionary reasons in constitutional law" 723 ("[R]ights actually serve to mark out the boundary lines between different spheres of political authority.").

[58] This is the way Justice Holmes famously viewed the right to free speech in *Abrams* v. *United States*, 250 US 616 (1919). For similar approaches to free speech in the USA that regard it as primarily concerned with setting the bounds of political intervention in the market of ideas and consequently reject balancing, see Laurent B. Frantz, "The First Amendment in the balance" (1962) 71 Yale L.J. 1424; Jed Rubenfeld, "The First Amendment's purpose" (2001) 53 Stan. L. Rev. 767 (rejecting balancing in First Amendment interpretation).

[59] Mark Kelman views anti-discrimination law as primarily concerned with restricting action based on irrational or animus motives and, thus, as categorical in nature. He distinguishes between core anti-discrimination and claims for accommodation. Mark Kelman, "Market discrimination and groups" (2001) 53 Stan. L. Rev. 833, 834–45.

[60] For a classic elaboration of a perfectionist liberal theory, see Joseph Raz, *The Morality of Freedom* (Oxford: Clarendon Press, 1986).

principles are *optimization* requirements. As such, they are characterized by the fact that they can be satisfied to varying degrees, and that the appropriate degree of satisfaction depends not only on what is factually possible but also on what is legally possible. Rules aside, the legal possibilities are determined essentially by opposing principles. For this reason, principles, each taken alone, always comprise a merely *prima facie* requirement.[61]

Conceiving rights as values has led to an expansion of their scope, and in Germany this has been to radical effect.[62] This broad conception of rights serves supporters of the culture of justification, since it promotes the expansion of the scope of government actions requiring justification.

The role of text and interpretation

The difference in how the culture of authority and culture of justification conceive rights implies also a different conception of the role of the text in constitutional law. In a culture of authority, both the government and the judiciary are institutions whose legitimacy rests on their authority, not justification. The constitutional text that authorizes the courts to review governmental action is, therefore, of vital importance. The clearest manifestation of the significance of the text within this culture is the American originalist interpretation of the Constitution.[63] Originalism is based on an understanding of the division of labor that holds that the Framers were responsible for the substantive constitutional commitments and the courts are responsible only for applying them. Accordingly, the courts' role is to make certain that the government does not exceed its authority and abides by the limitations set by the Framers. The courts should not replace the Framers' intentions with their own opinions in interpreting the Constitution. Moreover, the judiciary, as a branch of government, is also required to remain within the bounds of its authority, which are also set by the constitutional text. The originalist approach therefore

---

[61] Robert Alexy, "The construction of constitutional rights" (2010) 4 L. & Ethics Hum. Rts. 21. (Emphasis added.)

[62] See Chapter 3, pp. 60–3. See also Mattias Kumm, "Who's afraid of the total constitution? Constitutional rights as principles and the constitutionalization of private law" (2006) 7 German L.J. 341.

[63] Legal originalism is the classical formulation of the importance of text for the legitimacy of judicial review. See generally Robert H. Bork, *The Tempting of America* (New York: The Free Press, 1990) 143–53; Antonin Scalia, "Originalism: The lesser evil" (1989) 57 U. Cin. L. Rev. 849, 863–4.

seeks to ensure that both government and the judiciary act solely within their spheres of authority.

In a culture of justification, the judiciary's role is to require the government to justify its actions. Under this conception, the constitutional text is of lesser importance. While the text allows for "outward" legitimacy and secures its public status, it is not an essential condition for the court's authority to review governmental action and demand justification. Rather, this authority derives directly from the court's role and from the idea that government action is not legitimate unless it is justified.[64] Even when the text itself lays out a set of justifications for governmental action, the court will aim at broadening the scope of justification. This has happened in the ECtHR's interpretation of the limitation clauses in the European Convention of Human Rights. The Court has downplayed the importance of specific limitation clauses in determining specific goals and justifications for each of the various rights and has instead interpreted them all under a much broader, general doctrine of justification.[65]

Moreover, the culture of justification is manifested in interpretation approaches that attach little weight to the text, such as purposive interpretation and living tree interpretation. Since in a culture of justification the division of labor is less important, these interpretative approaches are less bothered by the notion of the courts' direct involvement in determining the Constitution's contents.

Finality and the limits of reason

The culture of authority is more skeptical regarding human reason than is the culture of justification, a theme that was discussed in Chapter 5. The culture of authority also places greater emphasis on the need for finality of judicial decisions, expressed famously by Justice Robert Jackson, in declaring, "We are not final because we are infallible; but we are infallible only because we are final."[66] This aphorism captures the

---

[64] See Mattias Kumm, "The idea of Socratic contestation and the right to justification: the point of rights based proportionality review" (2010) 4 L. & Ethics Hum. Rts. 142, 144 ("Within contemporary practice of rights adjudication in liberal democracies arguments relating to legal authorities – legal texts, history, precedence, etc. – have a relatively modest role to play. Instead the operative heart of the great majority of human or constitutional rights cases is the proportionality test.").

[65] Bernard Hovious, "The limitation clauses of the European Convention on Human Rights: a guide for the application of section 1 of the Charter?" (1985) 17 Ottawa L. Rev, 213, 256.

[66] *Brown* v. *Allen*, 344 US 443, 540 (1953).

skepticism regarding human infallibility alongside a sense of humility with regard to judicial capability: there is no guarantee that judges will "get it right" more often than others. Rather, what is emphasized is the value of finality and authority. What is "right" is determined by the person or institution authorized to make the final decision. The aspiration for reason, justification, and getting things right is not abandoned, but a limit is set – the limit of finality and authority. In this respect, the culture of authority can be linked to the epistemic conservatism of Burke and Hayek,[67] who stress the limits of Reason, as well as more recent attempts to defend judicial minimalism on similar epistemic grounds.[68]

These ideas do not align with the principles and values of the culture of justification. By emphasizing the need to justify every decision in terms of reasonableness or correctness, it expresses optimism regarding human and judicial ability to distinguish right from wrong. The judiciary in particular is regarded as an institution in possession of the tools for imposing rationality and reasonableness on other authorities, since it is relatively immune from populism and, therefore, more attuned to principled and analytical reasoning.

Pluralist versus substantive/deliberative democracy

The two legal cultures also embody two differing concepts of democratic political theory. The culture of authority is closely related to a pluralist conception of democracy, whereas the culture of justification is linked to the notion of deliberative or substantive democracy.

Under a pluralistic account of democracy, interest groups struggle to promote their goals and values and for resource allocation. These struggles result in compromises that reflect the power relations between the various groups.[69] What motivates groups and individuals in this political struggle need not be justified by rationality or public interest. Under the pluralistic conception of democracy, then, these interest groups have complete autonomy to decide which goals to pursue in the political sphere, without being subject to any outside intervention or need to justify their actions.

---

[67] Edmond Burke, *Reflections on the Revolution in France* (Oxford: Oxford University Press, 1993) (first published 1791); Fredrick Hayek, *The Constitution of Liberty* (Chicago, IL: University of Chicago Press, 1960).

[68] Adrian Vermeule, *Law and the Limits of Reason* (Oxford: Oxford University Press, 2008).

[69] Robert Dahl, *A Preface to Democratic Theory* (Chicago, IL: Chicago University Press, 1959); David Held, *Models of Democracy* (Stanford, CA: Stanford University Press, 3rd edn., 2006) Ch. 5.

By contrast, under theories of deliberative and substantive democracy, there is a requirement for substantive justification of any claim made in the political arena, from which interest groups are not exempt even with regard to the goals they pursue. Under the deliberative democracy conception, only those goals that can be justified based on public reason are legitimate within the political sphere and can enter the deliberative process out of which law is generated.[70] This means that some requirements of rationality are imposed on all political claims. Under the substantive democracy model, the legitimacy of a political claim is assessed in terms of how they conform to the substantive democratic values of the system that, again, imposes standards of rationality on the claims and requires their justification.

In this context, there is a clear connection between these democratic conceptions to their respective legal cultures and the distinction presented in Chapter 5 between epistemological optimism and epistemological skepticism. The pluralistic democracy conception is grounded in epistemological skepticism, since it rejects the notion of identifying a rational Archimedes Point from which all interests and claims can be assessed and weighed. It therefore leaves the resolution of conflicting claims to the democratic process. Deliberative and substantive democracy theories, in contrast, reflect epistemological optimism about the possibility of a rational or moral baseline that will rule out some claims or can be used to assess and reconcile them.

The historical roots of the culture of justification

Above we outlined some key features of constitutional law that are shared by many European-based systems as well as others. This commonality reflects the emergence of a transnational constitutional culture of justification. This section presents a preliminary account of the global ascent of the culture of justification: what is the historical and ideological

---

[70] Amy Gutmann and Dennis Thompson, *Democracy and Disagreement* (Cambridge, MA: Harvard University Press, 1996); Jürgen Habermas, *Between Facts and Norms* (Cambridge, MA: MIT Press, 1996); James Bohman and William Rehg (eds.), *Deliberative Democracy: Essays on Reason and Politics* (Cambridge, MA: MIT Press, 1997); Jon Elster (ed.), *Deliberative Democracy* (Cambridge: Cambridge University Press, 1998); Stephen Macedo (ed.), *Deliberative Politics* (Oxford: Oxford University Press, 1999); Amy Gutmann and Dennis Thompson, *Why Deliberative Democracy?* (Princeton, NJ: Princeton University Press, 2004).

background to the adoption of this legal culture, and how is it related to German culture, which was the breeding ground for proportionality?

The culture of justification has both transnational cultural and historical roots as well as aspects that are more closely associated with German culture in particular. One cannot fully understand the emergence of the culture of justification in Europe without grasping the traumatic effect of the Second World War on the region. The major lesson drawn by Europe from the Second World War in terms of its political culture[71] was that popular democracy must be treated with great suspicion, in view of the disintegration of the young democracies of the early twentieth century and their transformation into totalitarian regimes with broad popular support.[72] An additional understanding was the deep realization of the perils of nationalism.

The development of the culture of justification, as it first developed in Germany can be understood against the background of these concerns, for it is based on an elitism that is held to be a bulwark against the prejudice and irrationality of unchecked popular democracy.[73] In contrast to the culture of authority, the culture of justification is not content with authority and legitimacy grounded on populism. It is wary of allowing popularly elected bodies to decide for themselves and requires, instead, that they provide justification for their actions to external professional and elitist bodies, such as the courts. Popular power is therefore restricted by such institutions, which do not derive their legitimacy from popular support, but from professionalism, rationality, and coherency.

This sense of the failure of popular democracy also provides a possible explanation for the standard-based, two-stage structure of the human rights regimes with limitation clauses adopted in postwar Europe. Protecting rights from anti-democratic threats, after all, could also be effectuated through categorical rules. However, such rules would constrain courts in their decisions, leaving more authority in the hands of

---

[71] Jed Rubenfeld, "Commentary, *Unilateralism and Constitutionalism*" (2004) 79 N.Y.U.L. Rev. 1971.

[72] According to Hanna Arendt, *The Origins of Totalitarianism* (London: Secker & Warburg, 1951), the totalitarian regimes of Nazism and Stalinism emerged as a result of the entry of irrational elements into politics. This was made possible by the democratization process, which gave political weight to the opinions and preferences of the masses, in a period in which their social atomization made them an easy prey for manipulation by demagogues.

[73] The period after the Second World War witnessed a rise in elitist democratic theories. See, e.g., Joseph Schumpeter, *Capitalism, Socialism and Democracy* (New York: Harper-Collins, 1956).

popularly elected bodies. In contrast, a two-stage structure (the first identifying whether a right has been infringed and the second assessing the justification for such an infringement) that emphasizes the second part of justifying a limitation on rights would shift the focus of the analysis to the courts, since they assess the balance of interests and rights.

The emergence of the culture of justification can also be explained against the background of the anti-national sentiment that prevailed in postwar Europe. This is a generic culture and, thus, anti-local and anti-national. The text is of lesser importance, often considered only the shadow of the general principles of rights that have gained global acceptance.[74]

Moreover, the inclusion of limitation clauses was related, among other things, to the practical need to secure wide international agreement among different countries with diverse traditions regarding international human rights norms – or even agreement on the national constitution within diverse societies.[75] The formulation of two examples of typical limitation clauses illustrates this accommodation of the need for broad consent. The first, Article 9(2) of the European Convention of Human Rights (1950) provides that:

> Freedom to manifest one's religion or beliefs shall be subject only to such limitations as are prescribed by law and are *necessary in a democratic society* in the interests of public safety, for the protection of public order, health or morals, or the protection of the rights and freedoms of others [emphasis added].

Similarly, Section 1 of the Canadian Charter of Rights and Freedom (1982) states that:

---

[74] Lorraine Weinrib, "The postwar paradigm and American exceptionalism," in Sujit Choudhry (ed.), *The Migration of Constitutional Ideas* (Cambridge: Cambridge University Press, 2006) 84, 98 (arguing that the postwar paradigm of constitutionalism "cannot be reduced to a text, to be merely interpreted according to historical intent, understanding, or social values").

[75] For example, in Canada, the introduction to a limitation clause helped to secure the agreement of the provinces to the Canadian Charter of Rights and Freedoms. See Janet Hiebert, "The evolution of the limitation clause in the charter" (1990) 28 Osgoode Hall L.J. 103. See also Professor Lorraine Weinrib, "The postwar paradigm and American exceptionalism" 92, who puts this concept of rights into the context of global diversity: "While constitutional principles inform the scope and strength of rights claims they do not function as concrete rules that mechanically dictate uniform results for similar questions whenever or wherever they arise. Given the considerable diversity in the historical, cultural, and social contexts in which these principles must flourish, different legal systems will produce different results."

> The Canadian Charter of Rights and Freedoms guarantees the rights and
> freedoms set out in it subject only to such *reasonable limits prescribed by*
> *law as can be demonstrably justified in a free and democratic society*
> [emphasis added].

In addition to the anti-populism and anti-nationalism trend in postwar
Europe, there are two other, related phenomena, which predated the war
and were strongly tied to the German organic and epistemic constitutional culture:[76] perfectionism and rationalism. Both had a profound
impact on the culture of justification.

Perfectionism reflects an organic and comprehensive conception of
rights and the state, which is quite different from the classic American
approach of state neutrality. As discussed in Chapter 3, Germans do not
regard the state as merely an aggregation of individuals who live in a given
territory and coordinate their activities in aggregation, but rather as a
union of people with a shared system of values that they endeavor to
promote. This organic conception of the state is grounded on a premise of
reciprocal cooperation among all state organs. Rather than operating as
side constraints on government power – which is based on the view that
the government is antagonistic towards the individual – rights under this
approach are conceived of as representing shared values that must be
optimized.

This organic conception of the polity is not restricted to German,
or European, constitutionalism. Canadian Professor Lorraine Weinrib
views it to be an essential component of the postwar paradigm:

> Even though the postwar paradigm reconfigures the disposition of state
> authority to the primacy of constitutional principles, the judiciary is not
> to treat rights as absolute negation of otherwise plenary state authority.
> Nor is there a simple transfer to the courts of the political power or
> prerogatives withheld from elected representatives. Rather, the legitimate
> and complementary institutional strengths of legislatures, the executive,
> and the courts *operate co-operatively within the overarching framework of*
> *the objective normative order.*[77]

Also of significant impact in shaping the culture of justification was
rationalism, which is related to the traditional German appeal to rationality and its conception of law as a science. As we discussed earlier, the
culture of justification, in which proportionality plays a central role,

---

[76] See Chapter 3 for the organic German constitutional culture, and Chapter 5 for the
German epistemic legal culture.
[77] Weinrib, "The postwar paradigm and American exceptionalism" 92 (emphasis added).

features both the non-categorical, standard-based aspects of rights as well as the rationality and objectivity characterizing rights adjudication. The latter two features – rationality and objectivity – have contributed significantly to the unique character of this culture, distinguishing proportionality from the more relaxed and pragmatic notions of balancing. Thus, European courts, particularly the FGCC, in addressing the concept of rights limitation, take the perspective of the European legal tradition of objectivity and rationality.

The impact of legal culture on balancing and proportionality

The distinction between the culture of justification and culture of authority is manifested on two fronts: the first is the degree to which their doctrines – proportionality and balancing, respectively – are inherent and intrinsic to the legal system or, alternatively instrumental, incidental, or even antithetical to that system. The second distinction is in the context of the meaning that balancing and proportionality bear within their respective legal cultures.

With respect to the first distinction, proportionality is an indispensable – inherent – part of the culture of justification. In a culture of justification, every action must be justified in terms of reasonableness, which means that it must be the result of a proper balance between conflicting considerations and reflect appropriate means–ends rationality. In addition, the broad conception of rights in the culture of justification makes proportionality an inevitable and crucial mechanism. For the more expansive the conception of rights, the greater the likelihood that rights will at some point come into conflict with each other or with interests and a need to balance between them will arise in order to reach the most reasonable solution. In other words, the broader the substantive values and goals that rights are taken to represent, the more likely that the judicial system will apply proportionality. In addition, proportionality is inherent in a substantive and deliberative conception of democracy. As put by Mattias Kumm, "Proportionality based judicial review institutionalizes a right to justification that is connected to a particular conception of legitimate legal authority: That law's claim to legitimate authority is plausible only if the law is demonstratively justifiable to those burdened by it in terms that free and equals can accept."[78]

---

[78] Mattias Kumm, "The idea of Socratic contestation: the point of rights based proportionality review" (2010) L. Ethics Hum. Rts 114 (from the abstract). Furthermore, Kumm

The culture of authority, in contrast, is hostile to the concept of balancing, which relegates the doctrine to only a marginal role in the legal culture. The notion of "black holes" in judicial jurisprudence is antithetical to the conception of a judiciary that engages in balancing, since such "holes" represent autonomous zones that are not subject to judicial balancing. Moreover, the conception of rights in a culture of authority as marking the boundaries between different spheres of authority is also antithetical to balancing, since the judicial process implied by this conception is one of categorization: determining whether a given action falls within the authorized sphere of action. For example, if the right to free speech is taken to mean that regulating speech content is outside the boundaries of the government's authority, then the court's role is to determine whether a certain governmental action involves regulating speech, rather than balancing the interest in free speech against other government public interests. From the perspective of the role of the constitutional text, conceiving it to be crucial for legitimacy limits the use of balancing far more than an approach that allows the court interpretative latitude and the weighing of considerations and values that are not explicitly articulated in the text.

The different conceptions of democracy associated with the two legal cultures also have implication for the use of balancing and proportionality. A deliberative conception of democracy deeply rooted in the idea that deliberation is possible, even between strongly divergent points of view, assumes that a common denominator can always be found – the possibility of commensurability. Under this conception, balancing that entails commensurability can be applied to reconcile the conflicting views in society. In contrast, the pluralistic conception of democracy is far more atomistic and conflictual, viewing the position of each group in society as a "discrete island," impenetrable to the reason of the positions of other groups in society. There is no overarching viewpoint or value by which all positions can be assessed – there is no possibility of commensurability – and therefore the conflict between them must be resolved though the democratic process rather than through reason.

views proportionality as a method of Socratic contestation of governmental action. See also Cass Sunstein, "Interest groups in American public law" (1985) 38 Stan L. Rev. 29 (courts should apply a rationality review in order to foster deliberation and public interest in the legislative process). For an attempt to understand American constitutionalism as reflecting a requirement for justification, see Ronald C. Den Otter, *Judicial Review in an Age of Moral Pluralism* (Cambridge: Cambridge University Press, 2009).

Thus, balancing, under such an approach, is marginalized since commensurability is implausible.

The discussion thus far has shown proportionality to be a central and inherent doctrine in the culture of justification, while balancing remained antithetical and, accordingly, marginalized in the culture of authority. But another implication of the distinction between the two cultures relates to the use and functions of balancing and proportionality. In a culture of justification, rights are viewed as principles that must be optimized. Hence, Robert Alexy argues for a deduction of proportionality from the conception of rights as principles – i.e. as claims from optimization:

> The nature of principles implies the principle of proportionality and vice versa. That the nature of principles implies the principle of proportionality means that the principle of proportionality with its three subprinciples of suitability, necessity (use of the least intrusive means), and proportionality on its narrow sense (that is, the balancing requirement) *logically follows from the nature of principles*; it can be deduced from them.[79]

The culture of justification thus operates within a conception of optimization, which is broad and maximalist in its aspiration and the scope of its arguments. This, in turn, affects the use of proportionality and shapes it as a maximalist doctrine. The culture of authority, in contrast, has molded balancing as a minimalist concept. The clearest manifestation of this minimalist character within the American culture of authority is the idea of deferential balancing: the notion that balancing should be left solely to the political branches. Espoused by Justice Frankfurter in the 1950s and 1960s, this conception was rebutted by Justice Black, who took the opposing stance.[80] Both justices were operating in a culture of authority, but arrived at different conclusions. Justice Black held that the Constitution set forth a clear directive regarding free speech and that the courts should not supersede the authority of the Framers who set this

---

[79] Alexy, *A Theory of Constitutional Rights*, 66 (emphasis added).

[80] The debate between the two justices has spanned several court decisions, including *American Communications Ass'n v. Douds*, 339 US 382 (1950); *Dennis v. United States*, 341 US 494 (1951); *Barenblatt v. United States*, 360 US 109 (1959); *Konigsberg v. State Bar*, 366 US 36 (1961); *Communist Party of the United States v. Subversive Activities Control Bd.*, 367 US 1 (1961). Several books were written about this debate, including Wallace Mendelson, *Justices Black and Frankfurter, Conflict in the Court* (Chicago, IL: University of Chicago Press, 1961) and James Simon, *The Antagonists: Hugo Black, Felix Frankfurter and Civil Liberties in Modern America* (New York: Simon & Schuster, 1989).

directive. Frankfurter agreed that the courts should be deferential, but to the legislature, not the Framers. This view was based on his conception of the right to free speech as open-ended and not determined by the text, thus allowing for balancing. However, the Supreme Court, according to Frankfurter's minimalist conception, can intervene only when it must, such as when the text leaves the court no choice but to set aside legislative action. In the event that the text leaves matters open to interpretation, the Court must refrain from intervening and replacing the legislative balancing process with its own balance.

The administratization of constitutional law

We wish to end this chapter by focusing on the place of the constitutional text in the culture of justification. Whereas in the USA, which is characterized by the culture of authority, the text is of paramount importance, an interesting phenomenon has emerged in systems based on the culture of justification. The understanding that proportionality is an intrinsic feature of this legal culture exposes a special relationship between constitutional law and administrative law in these systems. Some scholars speak of the "constitutionalization" of administrative law, i.e. the process by which substantive conceptions of justice, often associated with human rights, gradually filter into administrative law.[81] Yet there is a flipside to this coin: the notion that the conceptual shift to a culture of justification represents what could be understood as an "administratization" of constitutional law. This phenomenon is characterized by four main features.

First, the focus on justification is particularly characteristic of administrative law. As Jerry Marshaw put it, "the discourse of *whyness* and of giving-reasons is more important in administrative law than anywhere else in American law."[82] The insistence on giving reasons and

---

[81] See, e.g., David Dyzenhaus (ed.), *The Unity of Public Law* (Oxford: Hart Publishing, 2004); Dyzenhaus *et al.*, "The principle of legality in administrative law: internationalisation and constitutionalisation" 29; Thomas Poole, "Between the devil and the deep blue sea: administrative law in an age of rights" LSE Law, Society and Economy Working Papers No. 9/2008, http://eprints.lse.ac.uk/24604/1/WPS2008-09_Poole.pdf. Similar processes occur in other areas of the law, such as private law, especially in Europe, where open-textured doctrines of private law have emerged as the vehicle by which constitutional rights penetrate the private law sphere.

[82] Jerry L. Marshaw, "Small things like reasons are put in a jar: reason and legitimacy in the administrative state" (2001) 70 Fordham L. Rev. 17, 18 (emphasis added); Jodi Short, "Justification and the administrative state: a sociology of reason-giving." Paper presented at the annual meeting of the Law and Society Association, Grand Hyatt, Denver,

justification is central to the core purposes of administrative law, which is to ensure governmental efficiency and to avoid arbitrariness.[83] The influence of the culture of justification on constitutional law, therefore, is mirrored by the influence of an administrative law mindset on constitutional law.

Second, when constitutional courts assess the justifications provided by governments, they employ concepts like reasonableness and proportionality. Both of these originated in administrative law: proportionality in nineteenth-century Prussian administrative law and reasonableness in English administrative law. Thus, when these concepts permeated into constitutional law in the second half of the twentieth century, they brought along with them some of the features of administrative law.

Third, the requirement for "whyness," reason, and justification in administrative law always operated within certain institutional boundaries. As noted earlier, ideally, the culture of justification would always have governmental authorities provide justification for their actions and the judicial authorities will always assess that justification on the basis of reason. However, there are some pragmatic considerations that constrain the scope of judicial review, for example, the courts' deference to government due to the European margin of appreciation doctrine.[84] The need

---

Colorado, May 25, 2009 ("[R]eason-giving is central to US administrative law and practice. Courts and legislatures require agencies to support their actions with reasons. And administrative law scholars have theorized that the practice of reason-giving is central to constraining and legitimating administrative agencies.").

[83] The core purpose of avoiding arbitrariness is well captured in the Administrative Procedure Act of 1969, Sec. 10(e), 5 USC Sec. 706(2)(A) (1994), where it is noted that the classic administrative ground for review is when the administrative agency acted in a way that was "arbitrary [and] capricious." Schultz Bressman, "Beyond accountability: arbitrariness and legitimacy in the administrative state" (2003) 78 N.Y.U.L. Rev. 461; Stephen Breyer, *Breaking the Vicious Circle: Toward Effective Risk Regulation* (Cambridge, MA: Harvard University Press, 1993); Martin Shapiro, "The giving reasons requirement" (1992) U. Chi. L. Forum 179, 180 (giving reasons requirements are a form of internal improvement for administrators).

[84] Dyzenhaus *et al.*, "The principle of legality in administrative law: internationalisation and constitutionalisation" 5 ("[The giving reasons] requirement imports deference into the judicial evaluation of the decision, since the judge is no longer concerned with establishing a match or mismatch between what she would have decided and what was decided ... This combination makes decision-makers accountable to fundamental values, without squeezing out the space for exercise of their discretion"). See also Lorraine Weinrib, "The Supreme Court of Canada and Section 1 of the Charter" (1988) 10 Sup. Ct. Rev. 92 ("Even though the postwar paradigm reconfigures the disposition of state authority to the primacy of constitutional principles, the judiciary is not to treat rights as absolute negation of

for deference has become increasingly prominent with the radical expansion of the scope of rights and the emergence of positive rights (for example, socio-economic rights) and even the concept of collective rights. Cass Sunstein has described what he calls the "administrative law" reasoning of the South African Supreme Court in its *Grootboom* decision,[85] which pertained to the social and economic right to housing:

> Hence the *Grootboom* Court's approach is most closely connected to a subset of administrative law principles, involving judicial review of inaction by the government agencies. In cases of this kind, everyone knows that the agency faces a resource constraint and that in the face of a limited budget, any reasonable priority-setting will be valid and perhaps even free from judicial review. At the same time, there is a duty of reasonableness in "priority setting," and an agency decision that rejects a statutory judgment, or that does not take statutory goals sufficiently seriously, will be held invalid. This is what the South African Court rules in *Grootboom*.[86]

Fourth and finally, constitutional courts that operate within a culture of justification generally fill a supervisory role and are anti-textual. As noted earlier, the text is less important in a culture of justification than in a culture of authority, since it is not constitutive of the court's authority to impose a justification requirement on the government. In this respect, there is considerable similarity between constitutional judges functioning within a culture of justification and administrative law judges. Administrative law is a relatively new area that developed in the nineteenth century both in Europe and the USA in reaction to the rapid industrialization processes and the emergence of the regulatory state.[87] As

otherwise plenary state authority. Nor is there a simple transfer to the courts of the political power or prerogatives withheld from elected representatives. Rather, the legitimate and complementary institutional strengths of legislatures, the executive, and the courts operate co-operatively within the overarching framework of the objective normative order."); See also Shapiro, 'The giving reasons requirement', 193 ("[J]udicially enforced demand that the rulemaker prove that it has made the very best decision possible within its range of discretion. An administrator who must choose the "best" rule, of course, has no discretion.").

[85] *Government of the Republic of South Africa and Others* v. *Grootboom and Others*, 2000 (11) BCLR 1169 (CC) (Ruling that the South African Government is in breach of its constitutional obligations to provide access to adequate housing and requiring it to reasonably implement a program that provides for those living in intolerable or crisis situations).

[86] Cass R. Sunstein, *Designing Democracy* (Oxford: Oxford University Press, 2001) 235.

[87] Stephen Breyer, *Administrative Law and Regulatory Policy* (London: Little Brown, 2006) 16.

opposed to US constitutional law, which is codified in a text that needs to be interpreted, administrative law did not originate in a statutory text.[88] Rather, it evolved as a set of common law principles for the purpose of supervising the regulatory state, ensuring its efficacy, and preventing arbitrariness.[89] The emphasis currently placed on justification by constitutional judges throughout the world draws them away from the text and from interpretation. Although the texts of new constitutions direct judges to assess whether the limitations are "justified in a democratic society," this in effect amounts to textual authorization to disregard the text and, therefore, to engage in the assessment of justifications and not in interpretation.

In this chapter we rejected several functional explanations for the wide spread of proportionality, offering instead an intrinsic one: it is an inherent component in the rising global constitutional culture of justification. We suggested two preliminary historical explanations for the ascent of this culture. One is its connection to the rise of the human rights ideology that developed after the Second World War, in response to the perils of nationalism and populism. The other is rooted in the optimistic belief in rationality and reason that can be traced back to the nineteenth-century German legal science movement. We ended our review by suggesting that the rapid shift towards proportionality can be understood as a move towards an administrative model of constitutional law. We set American balancing, in contrast, within a culture that that tends to stand in opposition to the principles underlying the doctrine: the culture of authority. This legal culture is hostile to balancing and has thus assigned it a relatively marginal role or else molded it as a minimalist and deferential concept.

---

[88] *Ibid.* 16 ("[A]dministrative law grew out of common law, and the common law has a large and continuing influence on American administrative law.").

[89] We do not mean to suggest that American and European administrative law lacks statutory text. The 1946 US Administrative Procedures Act set the following standard for administrative review: the regulation must not be "arbitrary and capricious, an abuse of discretion, or otherwise not in accordance with the law." 5 USC § 706(a)(2). But given the vagueness of this text, when judges apply it, they do not really interpret the text and instead resort to other sources of legal reasoning.

7

The effects of proportionality

In this last chapter of the book, we address the following question: what happens to the local legal system when proportionality reaches its gates and is embraced as a doctrine? We began our book with the question of whether the USA should adopt proportionality instead of balancing, and what impact this would have on American constitutional law. This chapter addresses possible answers to this question, discussing the possible effects of adopting proportionality on the adopting system and looking at the actual impact this had on two legal systems. As was the case with the discussion in Chapter 6, this chapter breaks the symmetry between balancing and proportionality to focus solely on the one doctrine that has made the transition as a global doctrine: proportionality.

According to one view, adopting proportionality will have no substantial effect on the local legal system. As Bernhard Schlink recently stated:

> Another way of viewing this is to say that the principle of proportionality doesn't have a standardizing effect on different constitutional cultures, but rather that it is a standard that constitutional cultures share and that they become more and more aware of over time. It is part of a deep structure of constitutional grammar that forms the basis of all different constitutional languages and cultures. It comes to the surface sooner or later – everywhere and even here.[1]

According to this argument, the basic structure of proportionality is already embedded in all legal systems, so that the formal adoption of proportionality will not alter the existing constitutional design.[2] Similarly, it can be argued that each legal system will infuse into the general

---

[1] Bernhard Schlink, "Proportionality in constitutional law: why everywhere but here?" (2012) 22 Duke J. Comp. & Int'l L. 291, 302.

[2] This argument resembles arguments put forth by universalists, as mentioned in the Introduction, according to which superficial barriers of doctrine should be removed and all constitutional systems should adopt proportionality.

structure of proportionality its own distinct characteristics and set of tests, so that, again, adopting proportionality will not have any substantial effect on these legal systems.[3]

Indeed, proportionality's impact might vary from legal system to legal system, yet adopting the doctrine most certainly has some effect on the adopting legal system, possibly substantial. We discuss here three such possible effects. First, we show that adopting proportionality gives the legal system an entry card into the global community of judges. This community shapes the way judges think and write, with the potential to create a "race to the top" in rights protection, which can result in an expansion of the notion of rights in the adopting systems. The second effect, to which the bulk of this chapter is devoted and represents one of the main themes of the book, is that adopting proportionality may bring with it a certain amount of cultural baggage from Germany, something that we demonstrate with examples from the Canadian and Israeli cases. Third, proportionality has the potential to marginalize local doctrines within the adopting legal system. We discuss this effect in the final part of the chapter.

"Race to the top"

The first effect of the migration of proportionality is that it offers the adopting legal system entry into the "global community of judges" that has emerged over the past few decades. Anne-Marie Slaughter has described the way in which constitutional judges across the world are increasingly conceiving themselves as engaging in a shared practice and in transjudicial communication.[4] She showed how these judges participate in international conferences, meet with one another, and correspond with each other through their judicial decisions. Today, many courts make deliberate efforts to communicate their decisions to courts in other

---

[3] Such an argument is implied in Justice Breyer's claim that the proportionality approach already exists in American constitutional law. *District of Columbia* v. *Heller*, 554 US 690 (Breyer, J. dissenting) ("Contrary to the majority's unsupported suggestion that this sort of 'proportionality' approach is unprecedented, the Court has applied it in various constitutional contexts, including election-law cases, speech cases, and due process cases."). See also Alec Stone Sweet and Jud Mathews, "All things in proportion? American rights doctrine and the problem of balancing" (2011) 60 Emory L.J.; David S. Law, "Generic constitutional law" (2005) 89 Minn. L. Rev. 652, 693–95.

[4] Anne-Marie Slaughter, "A typology of transjudicial communication" (1994) 29 U. Rich. L. Rev. 99; Anne-Marie Slaughter, "Judicial globalization" (2000) 40 Va. J. Int'l L. 1103.

legal systems and expand their global influence, facilitated by techno-
logical developments that make transmission easy and quick. The FGCC,
for example, issues English press releases on its official website and
provides links to their counterpart courts in other countries.[5] The
Supreme Court of Canada sends automated messages to subscribers,
giving them a week's notice of impending decisions, along with brief
summaries of the relevant history of cases.[6] Similarly, the Israeli Supreme
Court translates and uploads central decisions onto its website, sometimes only a short time after they have been published in Hebrew.[7]

Proportionality has become a kind of key to the door of this international club, since much of the communication between the judges
flows by way of the conceptual mechanisms that proportionality provides. Thus, proportionality has become a *lingua franca* in this community, allowing its members to communicate and compare decisions and
solutions to constitutional issues. A system that adopts proportionality
can, therefore, more easily participate in this community and contribute
to it.

Joining this global constitutional community also has substantive
effects, in that it expands the conception of rights within the legal system.
A new – global – reference point is set for judges in making their
decisions. Judges write their decisions not only for their local constituents
but also for the global community's judges, who now read and relate to
these decisions more easily than before. This could generate what David
Law has called a "race to the top" with regard to rights protection.[8]
Analyzing empirical data, Law found that countries and constitutional
courts around the world examine one another's jurisprudence and compete over which system is the more "advanced" or expansive in terms of
protecting rights. While Law grounded his finding on an economic
rationale,[9] common knowledge seems to confirm it as well: seldom would

---

[5] An English translation of German case law is available at www.bundesverfassungsgericht.
de/links.html.

[6] James Allan, Grant Huscroft, and Nessa Lynch, "The citation of overseas authority in
rights litigation in New Zealand" (2007) 11 Otago L. Rev. 433, 444.

[7] Some Israeli Supreme Courts cases are available in English at http://elyon1.court.gov.il/
verdictssearch/EnglishVerdictsSearch.aspx.

[8] David S. Law, "Globalization and the future of constitutional rights" (2008) 102 NW.
U. L. Rev. 1277.

[9] Law argues, "As capital and skilled labor become increasingly mobile, countries will face a
growing incentive to compete for both by offering bundles of human and economic rights
that are attractive to investors and elite workers." *Ibid.* 1282.

a court pride itself on being the least protective of rights, and it would be more likely to find a court lamenting the fact that its legal system "lags behind" or has yet to "catch up" to other systems.

Similarly, a New Zealand survey found that the reference to foreign law in interpreting the New Zealand Bill of Rights Act has been substantially biased in favor of expanding, rather than diminishing, the conception of rights.[10] Although there is ample foreign case law that narrows the scope of rights and offers different ways of balancing rights and public interests, the New Zealand judges tend to cite mostly case law that balances in favor of rights protection and to disregard legal systems with a more diminished scope of rights protection. The use of foreign law in the New Zealand case, then, had a "ratcheting up" effect on the scope of rights, at the expense of other considerations.

In the Israeli context, Binyamin Blum has neatly shown how the Israeli Supreme Court strove to portray its ruling on evidentiary law as adopting the most "advanced" standard in the global market – the exclusionary rule – thereby participating, as it were, in the "race to the top" in rights protection in this branch of law.[11] This was despite the fact that the ruling did not in fact diverge dramatically from previous precedents, and its portrayal as adopting the exclusionary rule caused much subsequent confusion in lower court jurisprudence.

The German baggage of proportionality

A distinction can be made between the migration of two types of constitutional ideas: the migration of constitutional substance and the migration of constitutional methodology.[12] A considerable amount of attention has been devoted to *migration of substance* in the debates over migration of constitutional ideas.[13] This has been the case, for example, with the

---

[10] Allan, Huscroft, and Lynch, "The citation of overseas authority in rights litigation in New Zealand" 441.

[11] Binyamin Blum, "Doctrines without borders: The 'New' Israeli exclusionary rule and the dangers of legal transplantation" (2008) 60 Stan. L. Rev. 2131, 2169–70.

[12] See Stephen Gardbaum, "The myth and the reality of American constitutional exceptionalism" (2008) 107 Michigan L. Rev. 391, 395, 419; Frederick Schauer, "The exceptional First Amendment," in Michael Ignatieff (ed.), *American Exceptionalism and Human Rights* (Princeton, NJ: Princeton University Press, 2005) 29, 30.

[13] There is a body of literature in the USA that relates to the migration of substantive constitutional ideas, often termed "the foreign law debate." Proponents of the reference to foreign law on substantive issues assert its invaluable contribution of the vital perspectives and experiences of other countries. They also hint at the inherent benefits of making US

heated debate in US constitutional law over the adoption of foreign substantive legal doctrines, such as those concerning the death penalty,[14] gay rights,[15] gun control,[16] and notions of federalism.[17] Any attempt to introduce foreign substantive ideas into highly contentious areas of constitutional law has attracted considerable criticism and has been labeled as anti-democratic and a usurpation of judicial power.[18] Less focus has been placed on the effects of the migration of constitutional *methodologies*, such as proportionality, due to the assumption that substantive ideas do not attach to them.

Methodology, however, can in fact be just as effective, if not more so, in transmitting substantive ideas as can their direct migration. As

jurisprudence more in tune with the global constitutional community. See Anne-Marie Slaughter, "A global community of courts" (2003) 44 Harv. Int'l L.J. 191, 201–2; Jeremy Waldron, "Foreign law and the modern ius gentium" (2005) 119 Harv. L. Rev. 129 (advocating a cosmopolitical position that supports reliance on foreign law); Vicki C. Jackson, "Comment, constitutional comparisons: convergence, resistance, engagement" (2005) 119 Harv. L. Rev. 109, 111 ("considering foreign and international law within a framework of learning by engagement – assuming neither convergence nor disagreement – is a legitimate interpretive tool that offers modest benefits (and fewer risks than current debate suggests) to the processes of constitutional adjudication"); Sujit Choudhry, "Globalization in search of justification: toward a theory of comparative constitutional interpretation" (1999) 74 Ind. L.J. 819, 835 (advocating engagement in comparativism through "dialogical" interpretation).

[14] *Roper* v. *Simmons* 543 US 624.   [15] *Lawrence* v. *Texas*, 539 US 558.

[16] *District of Columbia* v. *Heller*, 554 US 570.

[17] *Printz* v. *United States*, 521 US 898 (1997).

[18] See Posner, "No thanks, we already have our own laws" (July–August 2004) Legal Aff. 40, 41 (pointing to the "problem with according even limited precedential weight to foreign or international decisions [which lies in] the promiscuous opportunities that are opened up"); Charles Fried, "Scholars and judges: reason and power" (2000) 23 Harv. J.L. & Pub. Pol'y 807, 819 (arguing against Breyer's introduction of foreign law in *Printz* and claiming that "[t]he dispute is particularly striking because it would be one of the few instances of a deliberate attempt by a Justice to expand the canon of authoritative materials from which constitutional common law reasoning might go forward"); Jed Rubenfeld, "Commentary, *Unilateralism and Constitutionalism*" (2004) 79 N.Y.U.L. Rev. 1971, 1999 ("it is critical for constitutional law to be made and interpreted not by international experts, but by national political actors and judges"); Kenneth Anderson, "Squaring the circle? Reconciling sovereignty and global governance through global government networks" (2005) 118 Harv. L. Rev. 1255, 1307 ("[C]onstitutions are unique insofar as they are the constitutive document of a political community. As such, the issue is not so much the content of doctrine but instead its governance – the fact that it comes out of the constitutional and constitutive processes of a particular community."); Robert H. Bork, "Travesty time, again: in its death-penalty decision, the Supreme Court hits a new low" (March 28, 2005) Nat'l Rev. 17, 18, http://findarticles.com/p/articles/mi_m1282/is_5_57/ai_n13490953/pg_1?tag=artBody;col1 (criticizing the Court's reference to foreign law, which "in tacit coordination with foreign courts, is moving toward a global bill of rights").

described in previous chapters, proportionality, in particular, has distinct cultural and ideological associations. It is deeply rooted in the conception of an organic relationship between the judicial and political branches, and certain premises about the nature of rights, which have accompanied it in its spread across the globe. Even if regarded as strictly a mechanism of coherence, proportionality still has substantive effects. For it brings the possibility of one central method being used across different areas of constitutional law and applied in the adjudication of different rights. In contrast to the American conception of a constitutional tool box, from which a different tool for different rights and contexts can be chosen as needed, proportionality reflects the more European conception of *one* tool that is applicable to all contexts and, consequently, lends a coherent logical structure to the system that adopts it.

This change, albeit originating in methodology, can thus have substantive effects. First, the notion of the aspiration for coherency and logical structure to a legal system is itself a substantive European idea, related to its culture of epistemological optimism.[19] Second, adopting proportionality can facilitate the smooth transmission of ideas into all areas of the legal system since they stream in through one methodological channel. Finally, a shared central methodology, especially one as basic and broad as proportionality, can serve to bridge between different legal systems and thus facilitate more useful comparisons of solutions to constitutional questions and easy simpler borrowing of solutions between systems. Issues that may appear to be very different when adjudicated using different methodological tools, emerge as similar when viewed through the lens of a shared methodology.

We now progress to the substantive effects of the migration of proportionality as a methodology, in the specific cases of Canadian and Israeli constitutional jurisprudence. There are two principal reasons for focusing our review on these two jurisdictions. First, since its entry into Canada and Israel, proportionality has become the most dominant doctrine in the constitutional law of those two countries, with a sophisticated body of case law interpreting it. Second, it has been a number of decades since proportionality was introduced into Canadian and Israeli jurisprudence. This provides a sufficient time-perspective to assess the substantive effects of the doctrine's adoption on their constitutional jurisprudence. We will show how the incorporation of proportionality into the constitutional law of Canada and Israel coincided

---

[19] See Chapter 5.

with a shift towards a more European approach to rights adjudication in general, with an emphasis on value rhetoric, in particular.

Canada

Canada serves as a telling example of how the migration of a methodology can lead to the incorporation of substantive aspects into the adopting legal system. Parallel to the introduction of proportionality into Canadian constitutional law, Continental – in particular German – legal principles and ideas also found their way into the Canadian legal system. While this does not establish a causal connection between the migration of the proportionality and these doctrines, this phenomenon might nonetheless be an indication of proportionality's potential to create a common language that facilitates global migration of legal substance. Although Canadian constitutional law has always diverged in many respects from the American system,[20] it is still regarded as a common law system with stronger ties to the Anglo-American legal tradition than to the Continental tradition.[21] However, in several Canadian

---

[20] While the American Constitution speaks of "life, liberty and the pursuit of happiness," principles that are commonly tied to Lockean libertarian ideas, the Canadian constitution speaks of "peace, order and good government," principles rooted in a more communitarian conception of the polity and which assume good faith on the part of the government rather than being wary of it. See Rand Dyck, *Canadian Politics: Critical Approaches* (Scarborough: Nelson Thomson Learning, 3rd edn., 2000). Also notable is the following statement made by Alberta's former Premier on the reasons why Canada should not adopt a constitutional Bill of Rights: "Canada has always operated under the principles of responsible government and the sovereignty of the people as expressed through their legislators who are accountable to the people." Janet Hiebert, "The evolution of the limitation clause" (1990) 28 Osgoode Hall L.J. 103, 110. Some commentators speak specifically in terms of the symbiotic ties between the judiciary and the state in Canada. See, e.g., Jamie Cameron, "The original conception of section 1 and its demise: a comment on *Irwin Toy Ltd.* v. *Attorney General of Quebec*" (1989) 35 McGill L.J. 252, 262; Ruth Colker, "Section 1, contextuality, and the anti-disadvantage principle" (1992) 42 U. Toronto L.J. 77, 84–5, 100–5; Robin M. Elliot, "The Supreme Court of Canada and section 1: the erosion of the common front" (1987) 12 Queen's L.J. 277, 281; Frank Iacobucci, "The evolution of constitutional rights and corresponding duties: the Leon Ladner Lecture" (1992) U.B.C.L. Rev. 1, 16.

[21] For an account of the influence of liberal Dworkinian ideas on the 1982 Canadian Charter of Rights and Freedoms, see Peter Hogg, *Constitutional Law of Canada* (Toronto: Carswell, 3rd edn., 1992 and Supp. 2007) 821–2; see also David Beatty, *Constitutional Law in Theory and Practice* (Toronto: University of Toronto Press, 1995) 63, 108–9, 127; Lorraine Weinrib, "The Supreme Court of Canada and Section 1 of the Charter" (1998) 10 Sup. Ct. L. Rev. 469, 512.

Supreme Court decisions from the last two decades, there has been very clear evidence of a European-type of reasoning and of what was termed in Chapter 3 intrinsic proportionality, both of which were new to the Court's jurisprudence.

In 1986, four years after the adoption of the Canadian Charter of Rights and Freedoms, the Canadian Supreme Court embraced the European doctrine of proportionality by interpreting Section 1 of the Charter as including it,[22] and in the years to come, proportionality analysis became almost synonymous with constitutional analysis in Canada.[23] Concurrently, several Supreme Court decisions applying proportionality showed a clear Continental influence in their reasoning. In the *Keegstra* case,[24] for example, which dealt with hate speech, the Court – following what seemed to be classic "organic" legal reasoning – ruled that the limitations clause has a dual function that links the guarantee of rights and freedoms to their limitations.[25] *Per* the Court, both rights and their limitations stem from the same set of values, which is embedded in the phrase "free and democratic society."[26] The role of the Court is, hence, to weigh competing legitimate interests and find the appropriate balance that best realizes these underlying values. In particular, the Court considered which of the

---

[22] Section 1 of the Canadian Charter of Rights and Freedoms, which is often referred to as the "limitations clause," sets the terms for the justifiable restriction of rights: "The Canadian Charter of Rights and Freedoms guarantees the rights and freedoms set out in it subject only to such reasonable limits prescribed by law as can be demonstrably justified in a free and democratic society." Part I of the Constitution Act, 1982, being Schedule B to the Canada Act 1982, Ch. 11 (UK). This clause was interpreted in *R. v. Oakes*, [1986] 1 SCR 103, to include the following proportionality test, which is very similar to the German test:

First, the measures adopted must be carefully designed to achieve the objective in question. They must not be arbitrary, unfair or based on irrational considerations. In short, they must be rationally connected to the objective. Second, the means, even if rationally connected to the objective in this first sense, should impair "as little as possible" the right or freedom in question. Third, there must be a proportionality between the effects of the measures which are responsible for limiting the Charter right or freedom, and the objective which has been identified as of "sufficient importance."

Ibid. 136–7 (citation omitted).

[23] See generally Sujit Choudhry, "So what is the real legacy of Oakes? Two decades of proportionality analysis under the Canadian Charter's section 1" (2006) 34 Sup. Ct. L. Rev. 501.

[24] *R. v. Keegstra*, [1990] 3 SCR 697, 735–36 (Can.).   [25] *Ibid.* para. 44.

[26] *Ibid.* ("What seems to me to be of significance in this dual function is the commonality that links the guarantee of rights and freedoms to their limitation. This commonality lies in the phrase 'free and democratic society'.")

values are most closely connected to the paramount value of Canadian multiculturalism, similar to the human dignity perspective in German constitutional law. The Canadian Court stated that "Canada possesses a multicultural society in which the diversity and richness of various cultural groups is a value to be protected and enhanced." Furthermore, it held, "multiculturalism cannot be preserved let alone enhanced if free rein is given to the promotion of hatred against identifiable cultural groups."[27] It is important to note that the dissenting opinion criticized the majority for watering down the distinction between rights and interests, arguing that the Court was depicting "a conflict between philosophies and not between rights."[28]

A second case that illustrates even more clearly the migration of constitutional organic ideas is the *Quebec Secession* case, which dealt with the terms by which Quebec can secede from the Canadian Federation.[29] In this decision, the Supreme Court employed particularly expansive language that echoed the underlying values rhetoric typically used in invoking the German and Continental organic conception of the state.[30] The Constitution, declared the Canadian Court, "is more than a written text, rather it embraces a constitutional order consisting of unwritten principles."[31] Balancing between these principles ensures that "no single principle can be defined in isolation from the others, nor does any one principle trump or exclude the operation of any other."[32] Under this approach, therefore, judicial reasoning is not about exclusionary reasons but, rather, about moderation and compromise between competing valid principles. In this case in particular, the outcome of the balancing analysis was grounded on the values of moderation and compromise associated with intrinsic balancing proportionality. The Court imposed a positive duty on both sides to negotiate in good faith the terms of secession.[33] This decision also

---

[27] *Ibid.* 757–8.   [28] *Ibid.* 833 (McLachlin, J., dissenting).

[29] See *Reference re Secession of Que.*, [1998] 2 SCR 217 (Can.).

[30] Jean-François Gaudreault-Desbiens, "Underlying principles and the migration of reasoning templates: a trans-systemic reading of the Quebec Secession Reference," in Sujit Choudhry (ed.), *The Migration of Constitutional Ideas* (Cambridge: Cambridge University Press, 2006) 178, 189–207.

[31] *Reference re Secession of Que.* 2 SCR 292.   [32] *Ibid.* 248.

[33] The Court ruled that "no negotiations could be effective if their ultimate outcome, secession, is cast as an absolute legal entitlement based upon an obligation to give effect to that act of secession in the Constitution. Such a foregone conclusion would actually undermine the obligation to negotiate and render it hollow." *Ibid.* 267.

served to promote dialogue between the judiciary and elected state organs, with both bearing joint constitutional responsibility.[34]

The Canadian example is far from conclusive proof that the introduction of proportionality language into US constitutional jurisprudence would similarly result in the subsequent adoption of the organic conception of the state. Canada may have been far more receptive to Continental ideas from the outset, as compared to the USA. However, the Canadian case does seem to offer some indication that proportionality facilitates the infiltration of Continental constitutional ideas into a common law judicial system. At the very least, the adoption of proportionality seems to coincide with the entry of a more Continental organic-based approach.

Israel

Developments in Israeli constitutional law also illustrate the potential impact that adopting proportionality can have on a legal system's constitutional culture. Only in the 1990s did Israel adopt proportionality, and, as in Canada, this coincided with a shift towards a more European approach to rights adjudication.

The state of Israel was established in 1948 following thirty years of British colonial rule, which left a deep mark on Israeli legal culture. Israeli public law, in particular, was heavily influenced in its formative years by English public law. One reason for this was that Israel had no formal Constitution and thus essentially instituted a parliamentary sovereignty system similar to the British system; a second factor was that several early Israeli Supreme Court justices received their legal training in England. Israeli public law was also shaped, from an early stage, by American constitutional jurisprudence due, in great part, to the prominence of Supreme Court Chief Justice Shimon Agranat, who had immigrated to Israel from the USA and studied law there.[35] In the seminal 1953 *Kol*

---

[34] See Sujit Choudhry and Robert Howse, "Constitutional theory and the Quebec Secession Reference" (2000) 13 Can. J.L. & Juris. 143, 160, who argue that the Canadian Court has in fact adopted a model of joint constitutional responsibility. Under this theory, in extraordinary cases in which the Court lacks the institutional competency or legitimacy to translate abstract constitutional ideals into judicially enforceable standards, "it is for the political organs of the Constitution to frame their own interpretation of those norms and to assess their own compliance with them." *Ibid* 160.

[35] Pnina Lahav, *Judgment in Jerusalem: Chief Justice Simon Agranat and the Zionist Century* (Berkeley, CA: University of California Press, 1997). See also Pnina Lahav, "American influence on Israel's jurisprudence of free speech" (1981) 9 Hastings Const. L.Q. 21.

Ha'am[36] decision, for example, in which the Court established for the first time the right to free speech in Israeli public law, Agranat, writing for the Court, relied heavily on First Amendment jurisprudence and incorporated key concepts of American constitutional law into Israeli law, including the balancing test for free speech.

Second- and third-generation Supreme Court justices were also heavily influenced by Anglo-American public law. Pnina Lahav has described the profound impact of American legal culture on former Supreme Court Chief Justice Aharon Barak and how this, in turn, shaped his impact on Israeli legal culture. Barak, a brilliant academic prior to serving on the Court, did his postdoctoral studies at Harvard Law School. In the academic context, for example, this experience led him to first introduce the Socratic tradition into Israeli legal studies and the idea of a student-run law review; the more substantive aspect, however, was that his scholarly work and judicial opinions relied heavily on American free speech jurisprudence and constitutional law.[37] Other justices, such as Justice Zamir, were well versed in English public law, which to a lesser extent continued to shape Supreme Court jurisprudence.

Until the 1990s, therefore, Israeli public law was heavily influenced by English and American public law, and European public law was almost non-existent as a source of influence.[38] With the entry of proportionality into Israeli public law, there was a concurrent increase in the reference to European and European-related public law in Supreme Court jurisprudence. The major impetus behind the adoption of proportionality was the 1992 enactment of two basic laws: Basic Law: Human Dignity and

---

[36] HCJ 73/53 7 *Kol Ha'am* v. *Minister of Interior* PD 871. In this case, the Minister of Interior used his authority to suspend the publication of a newspaper on the grounds that it had published an op-ed directed against the Israeli government. The main issue deliberated by the Court was the Minister's claim that he could rightfully suspend the newspaper's publication if it seemed "likely to endanger the public peace." The Court rejected the Minister's contention that even a small likelihood would suffice. It held that in a democracy, the government can restrict freedom of speech only if it can show that there is a "near certain" probability that the continued publication of the newspaper will harm the public peace. Since this decision, the "near certainty" test has been the mandatory test for adjudicating conflicts between freedom of political speech and the state interest in public peace and national security.

[37] Pnina Lahav, "American moment[s]: when, how, and why did Israeli law faculties come to resemble elite US law schools?" (2009) 10 Theoretical Inq. in L. 653, 657–77.

[38] For a rare example of reference to German constitutional jurisprudence on banning political parties, see Justice Zussman's opinion in HCJ 1/65 *Yardor* v. *Chairman of the Central Election Committee* PD 19(III) 365.

Freedom, and Basic Law: Freedom of Occupation. These laws were interpreted by the Supreme Court as being constitutional in nature, and both included a limitations clause that restricted any infringement of constitutional rights "to an extent no greater than is required."[39] In *United Mizrachi Bank*, the Court interpreted this clause as setting a requirement of proportionality,[40] relying on German and Canadian jurisprudence, in which proportionality was already the reigning constitutional doctrine.[41] This exemplifies the tendency of constitutional courts to turn to European and European-related sources when interpreting proportionality for the first time and developing its meaning and scope. In the process, bridges are built between the legal cultures, which then become a conduit for the flow of information and input and facilitate European influence on local constitutional culture.[42]

Substantively, the increased interest in European and European-related systems was reflected as in Canada in the Supreme Court's increased use of value-laden judicial rhetoric and application of European and German modes of legal reasoning, which replaced, at times, American methods of reasoning. Very illustrative of this is the Court's decision in *Szenes*.[43] This case revolved around the petition of the family of a famous Jewish heroine from the Second World War, Hannah Szenes, to delete a fictitious scene from a television broadcast that they claimed would tarnish her memory.[44] The judgment, written by Chief Justice

---

[39] Section 8 of Basic Law: Human Dignity and Freedom; Section 4 of Basic Law: Freedom of Occupation.

[40] CA 6821/93 *United Mizrachi Bank* v. *Migdal Cooperative Village* PD 49(4) 221. It should be noted, however, that the Israeli Supreme Court introduced the principle of proportionality into its administrative law jurisprudence somewhat earlier. See, e.g., HCJ 5510/92 *Turkeman* v. *Minister of Def.* PD 48(1) 217, 219; HCJ 987/94 *Euronet Golden Lines (1992) Ltd* v. *Minister of Communication* PD 48(5) 412,435; HCJ 3477/95 *Ben-Atiya* v. *Minister of Educ., Culture & Sports* PD 49(5) 1.

[41] The Court relied on the seminal *Pharmacy* Case, which was the first to introduce proportionality into German constitutional law, see 7 BverfGE 377 (1958). It also relied on the first cases to introduce proportionality into Canadian constitutional law, see *R.* v. *Oakes*, [1986] 1 SCR 103; *R.* v. *Big M. Drug Mart. Ltd*, [1985] 1 SCR 295; *Jones* v. *The Queen*, [1986] 2 SCR 284.

[42] See *infra*, pp. 109–10.

[43] HCJ 6126/94 *Szenes* v. *The Broadcasting Authority* PD 53(3) 817. An English translation of this case is available at www.concernedhistorians.org/content_files/file/le/131.pdf.

[44] Szenes volunteered to be a part of a group parachuting behind the Nazi line in 1944 and was caught by the Hungarian police. Despite being cruelly tortured, she refused to disclose any information to her interrogators and was eventually executed for treason. Szenes' family members, who petitioned the Israeli Supreme Court, claimed that the scriptwriters of the teleplay, *The Kastner Trial*, to be broadcast on national television,

Barak, though sensitive to the claims of the petitioners, ended up protecting the scriptwriter's freedom of speech. Although the outcome reflects the American tendency to prefer free speech over human dignity, the reasoning is decidedly European. Using strong value rhetoric, Barak ruled that an attempt to censor speech in the way requested by the petitioners would be contrary to "the values of the State of Israel as a Jewish and democratic state."[45] Moreover, he analyzed the right to free speech and the right to good reputation as both emanating from the same fundamental constitutional value of human dignity.[46]

The legal reasoning in *Szenes* very much resembles the German constitutional court's approach in *Mephisto*.[47] In the latter case, the German court weighed whether human dignity, the supreme underlying value of the German Constitution, would be more severely harmed by an infringement of the right to free speech or by an infringement of the right to good reputation. The Israeli and German cases differed only in terms of outcome of the balancing process: the German court found the right to good reputation to be closer to the core of human dignity than free speech, whereas the Israeli court gave preference to speech over reputation in the circumstances of the case.[48]

Another Israeli Supreme Court justice, Mishael Cheshin, indicated a similar valued-based approach in his dissent in another case. In

---

falsely portrayed her as someone who had betrayed her comrades and given the Hungarian police information regarding their location.

[45] HCJ 6126/94 *Szenes* v. *The Broadcasting Authority* para. 9 of Barak, CJ's, opinion.

[46] *Ibid.* para. 12, 20 of Barak, CJ's, opinion.

[47] 30 BVerfGE 30, 173 (1971). See Chapter 3 for a detailed discussion of this case. In its *Szenes* v. *The Broadcasting Authority* decision, the Israeli Supreme Court relied on the *Mephisto* Case. See para. 28 of Barak, CJ's, opinion.

[48] Barak was aware of the different balancing outcomes in the two cases and explained it as follows:

I am aware that, under similar circumstances, the German Constitutional Court recognized the possibility of restricting freedom of expression. Even so, this ruling – itself the subject of controversy – related to private law relationships and had no application to public law. The case dealt with the right of an actor's relatives to request an injunction against the publication of a book that, in their opinion, defamed their relative, the deceased. It does not address the duty of a public authority to prevent the work's publication for reasons of public interest. *Mephisto* involved a conflict between two rights – the freedom of expression and artistic creativity as opposed to human dignity. The remedy requested was within the realm of private law. In the petition at bar, the right of freedom of expression and artistic creation conflicts with the public interest (human dignity). Accordingly, the balance in the two cases may be different (citations omitted).

HCJ 6126/94 *Szenes* v. *The Broadcasting Authority* para. 28 (citations omitted).

Movement for Quality Government in Israel v. Knesset,[49] which pertained
to the constitutionality of exempting Ultra-Orthodox Jews from mandatory
military service, Cheshin stated that the values of Israel as a Jewish and
democratic state "are norms that provide the infrastructure for the existence
of the state of Israel";[50] the exemption, he asserted, constitutes a violation of
these underlying values. Cheshin went so far to acknowledge the Court's
authority to nullify laws that infringe the basic values of the state, even if
they do not constitute a specific violation of any of the basic laws.

It is important to note that value rhetoric was present in Israeli
jurisprudence even prior to the adoption of proportionality in the early
1990s.[51] However, the above examples are illustrative of the increased
intensity with which such rhetoric has been used since then and its
increasing resemblance to the European forms of value rhetoric.

Canada and Israel: foreign law citation

The rise in interest in European and European-related public law in
Israel is also reflected in studies examining the citation practices of the
Israeli Supreme Court. Up until 1994, the almost exclusive sources of
non-Israeli citations in Supreme Court jurisprudence were English or
Commonwealth cases and American case-law, each accounting for about
50 percent of the foreign law citations.[52] Citations of Continental and
international sources were very rare.[53] A very different picture emerged,
however, in a recent study conducted by Suzie Navot, which surveyed
foreign law citations in Supreme Court constitutional case law solely
from the period in which proportionality became more dominant – i.e.
between 1994 and 2002. Indeed, the Navot study found a dramatic
increase in the citation of Canadian and German cases, which previously
had been virtually non-existent in Supreme Court case-law: 18 percent of

---

[49] HCJ 6427/02 *Movement* for *Quality Government in Israel* v. *Knesset* PD 61(1) 619 (2006).
[50] *Ibid.* para. 11 of Cheshin, J.'s, dissenting opinion.
[51] See Menachem Mautner, *The Decline of Formalism and the Rise of Values in Israeli Law*
(Tel Aviv: Tel Aviv University Press, 1993) (in Hebrew).
[52] Miron Gross, Ron Haris, and Yoram Schachar, "References patterns of the Supreme
Court in Israel – quantitative analysis" (1996) 26 27 Hebrew U.L. Rev. 115 119 (in
Hebrew).
[53] But see Eli Salzberger and Fania Oz-Salzberger, "The German heritage of the Israeli
Supreme Court" (1998) 21 Tel Aviv U.L. Rev. 259 (in Hebrew) (arguing that the influence
of Continental law, especially German law, on Israeli law is profound but hidden, due to
the anti-German sentiments following the Holocaust).

the citations were to Canadian sources and 7 percent to German sources. The remaining foreign law citations were from American and English jurisprudence, with a shift in the proportion of American citations at the expense of English ones.[54]

Data regarding the use of foreign law after 2002 have yet to be gathered. However, a prominent decision given by the Supreme Court in *Adalah*[55] could offer some indication about how this trend has continued and even intensified. The case, which dealt with the controversial issue of whether residents of the Palestinian Authority who marry Israeli citizens can move to Israel and become residents and then eventually citizens, certainly lends itself to comparative review of immigration and residency policies in other countries. What is interesting for our purposes, however, is the impressive extent to which foreign law was cited in the decision: out of the 243 cases cited, 60 are foreign law cases, amounting to 25 percent of the citations. The breakdown for the different sources according to country of origin is also interesting and seems to correspond with the Navot study finding of a lower proportion of English case law referencing. The wide range of legal systems from which the citations are taken is also remarkable: 30 cases from the USA; 9 from Canada; 8 from the ECtHR; 6 from England; 3 from Germany; 3 from South Africa; 1 from Ireland; and 1 from Australia.

In both Canada and Israel, the increasing resort to foreign law in general, and European law, in particular, has coincided with the incorporation of proportionality into the legal system. It should be noted, however, that such processes are not necessarily linear and a decline in the influence and use of foreign law can also be expected at some point. In fact, just such a decrease in the use of foreign sources was identified in studies conducted in Canada and Israel.[56] This phenomenon can be explained by the fact that following a major development in the legal system, such as the adoption of proportionality or of new basic

---

[54] Suzie Navot, "The use of foreign precedents by constitutional judges" 8 (manuscript on file with the author).

[55] HCJ 7052/03 *Adalah* v. *Minister of Interior* (given 2006).

[56] For Canada, see Peter McCormick, "The Supreme Court of Canada and American citations 1945–1994: a statistical overview" (1997) 8 Sup. Ct. L. Rev. 527, 533; Daniel M. London, "Cites unseen: The Canadian Supreme Court and comparative constitutionalism," paper presented at the Annual Conference of the American Political Science Association Philadelphia, August 31, 2006. For Israel, see Navot, "The use of foreign precedents by constitutional judges."

constitutional laws, the court has to build a new corpus of case-law interpreting the provisions and setting standards for their application. This process could entail turning to foreign case law for insight, guidance, and specific instances. This is particularly the case regarding proportionality, which is an imported, rather than local, doctrine and for which there is a very rich body of comparative jurisprudence to draw on. Once the local corpus has been established, however, the court might begin to rely on local sources and cite fewer foreign sources.

Yet such a drop in the frequency of foreign source citations does not necessarily mark a similar decline in the impact of foreign law on the system. Rather, foreign doctrines and concepts continue to linger in the system when the local major cases that referenced and were shaped by foreign case law are subsequently cited themselves. Thus, what at this later stage may seem to be a local legal development actually has its origins in foreign or global sources, with the latter now an integral part of the local system. The impact of external legal sources, then, should be measured not only in terms of frequency of their citation but also by the extent to which the local system has been transformed by foreign influences.

Common law baggage? Some objections

A possible counterclaim to the depiction of proportionality as having a "German effect" is that proportionality in fact molds the adopting legal system into a standard-based model that resolves cases on an ad hoc basis. This resembles more the common law constitutional model than the European civil law model, which is more textually oriented. In fact, Bernhard Schlink recently put forth just such a proposition regarding the effect of proportionality:

> Constitutional cultures with a doctrinal tradition [which apply proportionality] will progressively be transformed in the direction of a culture of case law. The often-praised asset of proportionality analysis is its flexibility; from case to case, facts may be assessed differently and rights and interests weighed and balanced differently. The case-specific configuration of facts, interests and rights becomes more important and more significant than the doctrine that surrounds the case.[57]

---

[57] Schlink, "Proportionality in constitutional law: why everywhere but here?"

This tension between these two seemingly oppositional effects can be explained and resolved. For it is necessary to distinguish between German, or European, constitutional culture and German, or European, private law culture. Many of the attributes of civil law, including the emphasis on text and legal formalism, are more prominent in private law than in constitutional law.[58] European constitutional law is conceived of as separate and distinct from the other branches of law and, moreover, is even viewed by some not as law at all but an extension of politics.[59] In America, too, there seems to be divergence between constitutional law interpretation and private law interpretation. In the past few decades, American constitutional law has been portrayed as rule-based and doctrinal, at least as compared to American private law, which has always been characterized by case-by-case and "cost-benefit" analysis through the use of standards. Robert Post has argued, along similar lines, that the law-and-economics cost-benefit analysis typical of American private law is not applicable to American constitutional law, which is rule-based and stresses deontological constraints rather than open-ended balancing.[60] The dichotomy between common law and civil law, which can account for differences in the private law of the German/ European legal systems, is not directly related to divergences in their constitutional law.

In addition, even though German constitutional law seems to be grounded on a case-by-case, standard-based approach, it must be understood as operating within an epistemological framework that differs from that of the common law. As we showed in Chapter 5, the German and European standard-based constitutionalism is rooted in epistemological optimism and a strong belief in human rationality, as opposed to the epistemological skepticism that underlies the common law case-by-case approach. A standard-based and case-by-case approach can also operate within a top–bottom legal order, as is the case in Israel, where the

---

[58] Martijn W. Hesselink, "The new European legal culture," in Martijn W. Hesselink (ed.), *The New European Private Law: Essays on the Future of Private Law in Europe* (Alphen aan den Rijn: Kluwer Law International, 2002) 11, 20 (describing the traditional formalist features of European private law and its appeal to political neutrality).

[59] Alec Stone Sweet, *Governing with Judges: Constitutional Politics in Europe* (Oxford: Oxford University Press, 2000) 32, 40.

[60] Robert Post, "Constitutional law scholarship in the United States" (2009) 7 Int'l J. Const. L. 416, 421–2 (while the "scientific" law and economics scholarship has had a profound impact on American legal culture, it exerted only minimal influence on constitutional scholarship).

Supreme Court supervises lower court decisions and retains both vertical and horizontal control of the case law.[61]

Proportionality's doctrinal imperialism

The generic and universal nature of proportionality can lead also to the effect that we term "doctrinal imperialism." Indeed, as a logical, coherent, and systematic doctrine, proportionality has compelling appeal and can take the place of local doctrines that have evolved over many years and were shaped and reshaped by their particular environment. These local doctrines are sometimes more idiosyncratic and less structured than proportionality and have a hard time competing with the latter's logical appeal. In fact, this attractiveness as a doctrine may also lead to the spread of proportionality into other areas of law, such as private law and even criminal law, breaking down the boundaries between the different legal branches.

This outcome can certainly be viewed as a positive development: proportionality brings order and coherence into legal systems that were evolved in an idiosyncratic or haphazard way, as well as enhancing coherency between different areas of the law. But there may also be negative effects. The danger of proportionality's imperialism lies in the possible loss of the richness and nuances of the local doctrines and of their compatibility to their local environment, like a universally adaptable bird that migrates beyond its natural environment and drives out the local species in its new environment.[62] This creates a loss in terms of the richness of the local system in favor of functionality and adaptability. Moreover, proportionality may also blur important differences and distinctions between different areas of law when it travels beyond the boundaries of constitutional law in the same legal system.

---

[61] See Chapter 5, pp. 94–102.

[62] Such species are often termed "invasive species." See, e.g., D.F. Sax, S.D. Gaines, and J.H. Brown, "Species invasions exceed extinctions on islands worldwide: a comparative study of plants and birds" (2002) 160 (6) Am. Naturalist 766–83. Invasive species are characterized, among other things, by fast growth, rapid reproduction, high dispersal ability, ecological competence (tolerance of a wide range of environmental conditions), and generalism (the ability to live off of a wide range of food types). See J.D. Williams and G.K. Meffe, "'Nonindigenous Species' status and trends of the nation's biological resource" (Reston, VA: United States Department of the Interior, Geological Survey: 1998) 1.

Israeli constitutional law exemplifies these "imperialistic" effects of proportionality, with respect to both its impact on local constitutional doctrines as well as the effect of its infiltration into other areas of law. Before proportionality was incorporated into Israeli constitutional law, central to judicial review were a set of balancing tests that had each been adapted to certain contexts and certain types of conflicts between rights and interests. For example, any clash between political speech and public order was assigned a balancing test requiring a "near probability" of harming public order in order for this interest to prevail over the right to free speech.[63] When political speech would clash with the state interest in maintaining impartial legal proceedings (*sub judice*), the balancing test required only a "reasonable likelihood" (as opposed to "near certainty") of harm to the interest in impartial legal proceedings.[64]

Over time, the Israeli Supreme Court added to the probability threshold tests the consideration of the magnitude of the harm in question. Thus, in a conflict between freedom of speech and national security or public order, the Court required nothing less than "near certainty" that, without the state's intended restriction on human rights, severe harm would be caused to the state interest.[65] In clashes between human rights and religious feelings, the Court applied an even stricter test, requiring "near certainty" that absent the restriction to human rights, the harm to religious feelings would be "severe, grave and serious."[66]

Yet once proportionality entered Israeli law, the established balancing tests and the probability tests became marginalized.[67] Israeli judges began to apply the three subtests of proportionality as the main doctrine of constitutional review. They either ignored completely the old balancing tests or were unsure as to how to integrate them into the new proportionality test.[68] In the Israeli context, proportionality also had the

---

[63] HCJ 73/53 *Kol Ha'am* v. *Minister of Interior*.

[64] HCJ 696/81 *Azulai* v. *State of Israel* PD 37(2) 565. A similar test of "reasonable likelihood" is applicable in cases of a conflict between the right to run for public office and the state interest in its continued existence as a Jewish and democratic state. See EA 2/84 *Neiman* v. *Chairman of the Central Elections Committee for the Eleventh Knesset* PD 39(2) 225.

[65] HCJ 680/88 *Shnitzer* v. *The Military Censor* PD 42(4).

[66] HCJ 5016/96 *Horev* v. *The Minister of Transportation* para. 68.

[67] See Moshe Cohen-Eliya and Gila Stopler, "Probability thresholds as deontological constraints in global constitutionalism" (2011) 49 Columbia J. Transnat'l L. 75, 100.

[68] In Israeli constitutional case law there are at least three approaches to the probability test within the framework of proportionality analysis. See HCJ 971/06 *Stein* v. *Karadi* (given 2006) (probability should be examined when assessing the importance of the state interest);

imperialistic effect of entering different areas of law, beyond constitutional law. Once the doctrine had entered constitutional jurisprudence, it very quickly moved into other areas of law, including labor law,[69] private law,[70] and civil procedure.[71] It would not be an exaggeration to say that Israeli judges routinely resort to proportionality as a central doctrinal mechanism in adjudication in almost all areas of law.[72]

We have thus far pointed to three possible implications for a legal system when it adopts proportionality. First is that it gains entry into the global community of proportionality, which creates an incentive for judges to "race to the top" in rights protection. This, in turn, results in an expansion of the scope of rights protection. Second, the Canadian and Israeli cases demonstrate that incorporating the proportionality doctrine may be accompanied by a certain extent of legal culture imported from Germany. Finally, proportionality seems to have also a "doctrinal imperialist" effect in that it tends to marginalize and supplant local doctrines in the adopting legal system.

HCJ 2665/98 *Nachum* v. *Israel Police* PD 52(2) 454, 459 (probability should be examined when assessing whether the means used are the least restrictive possible); HCJ 4541/94 *Miller* v. *Minister of Defense* PD 49(4) 94 (probability should be examined when assessing whether the means are proportional in the strict sense).

[69] For an overview, see Guy Davidov, "The principle of proportionality in labor law" (2008) 31 *Iyuney Mishpat* 5 (in Hebrew).

[70] The infiltration of proportionality into Israeli private law was possible, in part, due to the tendency to apply constitutional rights in the private law sphere. See Aharon Barak, "Constitutional human rights and private law," in Daniel Friedmann and Daphna Barak-Erez (eds.), *Human Rights in Private Law* (Oxford: Hart Publishing, 2001) 13; CivApp 1445/04 *Bizman Investments Ltd* v. *Moshe Helia* (given November 13, 2008) (proportionality in contract law); and CivCase (KS) 7830/00 *Barachov* v. *Alishi* (published by Nevo July 14, 2002) (proportionality in tort law).

[71] CivApp 2617/00 *Tnuva* v. *The Licensing Authority* (given June 30, 2005); P/CivApp 6424/98 *Simon* v. *The Liquidator Dgani Amiram Ltd* (proportionality in providing temporary relief – injunction preventing departure from the country).

[72] For the best manifestation of the role of proportionality in general, and in Israeli law in particular, see Aharon Barak, *Proportionality in Law* (Jerusalem: Nevo, 2010) (in Hebrew).

~

Conclusion

This is a book about doctrines in context. Specifically, it is about two crucially important doctrines in constitutional law, proportionality and balancing, and the ways in which history, culture, and philosophy have shaped them. It is a book on taking analytical similarities with a grain of salt and looking beyond them to the baggage borne by doctrines as cultural and historical constructs. It is also about the two currently most influential constitutional cultures, the American and German/European legal cultures, and how we can understand them through the balancing and proportionality doctrines.

Yet while the book focuses on two particular doctrines and two particular legal cultures, it is also about global constitutional law. It has told the tale of the spread of proportionality and the legal culture that it represents – the culture of justification – across national borders and of the emergence of universal and generic constitutional law with proportionality as its *lingua franca*.

Indeed, proportionality is depicted not only as a local doctrine that evolved on its particular historical and cultural background. Rather it is described also as a global doctrine that travels easily and swiftly from legal system to legal system, despite divergences in constitutional culture, reflecting a generic structure to constitutional law across the globe.

In this conclusion, we sum up both the local dimensions and aspects of proportionality and balancing as well as the universal nature of proportionality, and try to account for the way the book resolves the seeming tension between the universal and local dimensions. We wrap up by showing that these two dimensions in effect mirror the losses and gains from the global convergence over proportionality.

Starting out from the most localized level, historic origins, the book showed how nineteenth-century Prussian administrative law and then, later on, German administrative and constitutional law, molded the conception of the application of proportionality as a doctrine in the completely opposite direction taken by early twentieth century US constitutional law in shaping the use of balancing. In Prussia, proportionality stepped into the vacuum created by the absence of constitutional protection for rights, and introduced into administrative law an element of rights-protection through the notion of the rule of law (*Rechtsstaatsprinzip*). In the USA, balancing, albeit a similar doctrinal mechanism, had quite the opposite effect. Given the lack of a limitations clause in the Bill of Rights, balancing enabled a necessary pragmatic aspect of rights restriction in view of circumstances of conflicting interests. The particular historical context of the introduction of each doctrine into its respective "founding" legal system shaped the conception of these doctrines which, to some extent, still characterize them: proportionality as pro-rights and balancing as pragmatic and limiting rights.

It was political culture that shaped the meaning of the respective constructions of rights in Germany and the USA. In postwar Germany, the state was accorded a crucial role in infusing a new ideology based on human rights and human dignity into German society. The combination of this ideology with the organic conception of the state that predated the Second World War led rights promotion to be understood in postwar German political culture as a venture to be shared by the state and its citizens, rather than a nexus of irresolvable tension between the two, as in American political culture. What is more, rights are viewed as values in German culture, with positive contents that should be promoted in both the private and public spheres, not merely, or primarily, as limitations on or boundaries to state power, as in the American cultural context. This layer of the political culture explains the centrality and the intrinsic value accorded proportionality in German constitutional law, as a mechanism that inherently facilitates the joint goal of shaping and optimizing German society's values, and the relative marginalization of balancing in American constitutional law, as a pragmatic exception to the construction of rights as categorical limitations on state power.

As we saw, the divergence between the German and American legal cultures can also be explained by the tendency in US jurisprudence to emphasize intent in reviewing the constitutionality of state actions, whereas the German system emphasizes consequences. This reflects disparate deontological and teleological philosophical underpinnings to the constitutional law in the two systems. This depiction of the American constitutional design could raise questions about the role of balancing, which is mainly consequentialist but, in fact, we showed that there are a number of intent-related functions to balancing. In particular, it can be applied to uncover illegitimate governmental or legislative intent or, even, indifference towards constitutional harm that, we argued, should be treated the same as bad intent in certain circumstances, when it reflects a total disregard for the constitutional value.

Progressing further on the generality axis, we looked at the different conceptions of human rationality and epistemic capabilities manifested in the German and American traditions of legal thought. Rooted in the Continental tradition, German legal thought represents an aspiration for logical coherence, structure, and systematization as well as the optimistic belief in the ability of human rationality to realize those aspirations. American legal thought, in contrast, which is based on the common law tradition, reflects the ideal of case-by-case progression, without any systematic scheme, and of bottom-up incremental accretion of knowledge from the experience of many cases. It reflects a more skeptical view of human rationality, of the need to overcome the shortcomings of "one mind" through the accumulated wisdom of "many minds." The doctrine of proportionality should be understood as characteristic of the traditional German emphasis on logical clarity and coherence; it is conceived of as internally well structured and logical, while serving as an external template that injects coherency into both the constitutional system and into the legal system in its entirety. Indeed, German legal culture has constructed proportionality as a logical and almost scientific doctrine. In contrast, American conceptions of balancing construct it as a pragmatic, relatively unstructured, tool, yet reflecting the need to accommodate different social interests. This approach to balancing, moreover, reflects the minimalist conception of the judiciary in American legal culture, under which the courts should engage in low-level, localized disputes and refrain from broad legal reasoning and any pursuit of general rules and coherency.

Unlike the doctrine of balancing, which has remained largely confined to US constitutional law, German proportionality has attained a global status, migrating to almost all constitutional systems around the world. We maintain that the swift and expansive ascent of proportionality as a dominant doctrine of constitutional law across the globe is best explained as a phenomenon of cultural development, rather than merely a matter of doctrinal or functional adequacy: proportionality has spread since it is intrinsic to what we identified as the emerging global culture of justification. Central to our notion of this culture is the global embracing of a set of constitutional concepts that are based on the notion that the state must justify all of its actions, without exception. Proportionality provided a central doctrinal anchor for this culture. In contrast to this global trend, American constitutional law has steadfastly resisted adopting this set of concepts, remaining a culture of authority in which balancing is either marginally used or else reflects a relatively deferential approach to the state's interests.

This book has presented proportionality, therefore, as both a local phenomenon and as a universal and generic phenomenon. How can this tension be resolved? The answer is two-fold. First, as we showed in Chapter 7, despite losing some of its local attributes as it traveled, proportionality continues to be accompanied by a certain amount of ideological baggage. The adoption of proportionality in countries such as Canada and Israel brought with it the incorporation of some of the hallmark traits of German constitutional law, in particular the emphasis on values and the organic conception of the state. Second, there is no contradiction in understanding proportionality to be both particular and universal at the same time. Proportionality is particular since it developed in a specific time and place. But the particular culture in which it evolved, German legal culture, stressed such ideals as coherency, systematization, and logical structure, all of which are in effect universal rather than particular. The doctrine of proportionality was grounded in these principles – manifested, for example, in the logical structure of its three subtests. As a consequence, proportionality is also non-particular, universal, and easily adapted to different legal systems. In this respect, we can recall again the analogy to a species of birds that has evolved in a particular environment, where the characteristics of this environment developed in the species certain features that make it adaptable to all types of environments.[1] Like proportionality, this species of birds is, consequently, both particular and universal at the same time.

The universal and generic nature of proportionality holds both promise and risk. There is the promise of coherence and simplicity and of the benefits of participating in a global dialogue and global project. But, in Einstein's words, "everything should be made as simple as possible, but not simpler."[2] Indeed, in Chapter 7 we alluded to such a risk posed by proportionality when it is incorporated into new legal systems that, as a result, local doctrines will lose their nuance and richness and become less adapted to their own environment. To return to our zoological analogy,

---

[1] See *supra*, p. 150, n. 62.

[2] Albert Einstein, *The Ultimate Quotable Einstein* (collected and ed. A. Calaprice, Princeton, NJ: Princeton University Press, 2011) 475.

proportionality can be compared to the universally adaptable bird that migrates and pushes out local species wherever it lands. In this case, too, functionality and adaptability come at a cost in terms of the richness of the local environment.

Finally, the two polar ends of the axes in this book's discussion, the local and the universal, represent also two focal points in our assessment of the dilemma of whether legal systems should adopt proportionality, most particularly, American constitutional law. The gains of such a move derive from proportionality's universal aspect: US jurisprudence would have a far greater and more effective impact in the global community of constitutional law were it to embrace proportionality. Over the last decade, significant concern has been expressed by American legal scholars over the growing irrelevance and waning influence of American constitutional law in the jurisprudence of other legal systems.[3] What used to be a major site for the export of American culture and values has lost much of its appeal for other constitutional systems, while other constitutional models have supplanted it as a source of influence and emulation.[4] In a recent empirical study, David Law found that, today, legal systems, in drafting their constitutions, are considerably more influenced by the European and Canadian models than by the American constitutional design.[5] Although adopting proportionality would, of course, not alter the actual text of the American Constitution, it could bring it closer to other constitutional systems in terms of interpretation and constitutional design.

---

[3] Liptak, "US court is now guiding fewer nations" (quoting Princeton Professor Anne-Marie Slaughter: "[O]ne of our great exports used to be constitutional law. We are losing one of the greatest bully pulpits we have ever had."). See also Anthony Lester, "The overseas trade in the American Bill of Rights" (1988) 88 Colum. L. Rev. 537, 561; Claire L'Heureux-Dubé, "The importance of dialogue: globalization and the international impact of the Rehnquist Court" (1998) 34 Tulsa L.J. 15, 37; Melissa Waters, "Mediating norms and identity: the role of transnational judicial dialogue in creating and enforcing international law" (2005) 93 Geo. L.J. 487, 493 n. 26.

[4] Melissa Waters, "Mediating norms and identity: the role of transnational judicial dialogue in creating and enforcing international law" (arguing that instead of looking to US constitutional law, courts are "increasingly looking to judicial decisions from Europe, Australia, Africa, and Canada" ibid. 493 n. 26). See also Diarmuid F. O'Scannlain, "What role should foreign practice and precedent play in the interpretation of domestic law?" (2005) 80 Notre Dame L. Rev. 1893, 1897, quoting Australia High Court Justice Michael Kirby, who stated that the USA is in danger "of becoming something of a legal backwater," in Michael Kirby, "Think globally" (2001) 4 Green Bag 2d 287, 291 (2001).

[5] David Law, "The declining influence of the United States constitution" (2012) 87 N.Y.U.L. Rev. 762.

Yet one of the central points of this book is that there is a price to adopting proportionality: its impact on the integrity of the adopting legal culture. This point is at times overlooked not only by universalists, but also by particularists, who stress autonomy, sovereignty, and authority. The main objections traditionally made to applying foreign law doctrines in US constitutional law have been based on these normative ideals, as well as the notion that this would undermine American legal sovereignty and make the USA subject to the laws of other countries. Our point about the cultural baggage of the foreign doctrine is sometimes overlooked. The purpose of this book has been to stress the implications of the cultural background of migrating legal doctrines for the integrity of the local legal cultures into which they are incorporated.

We leave the task of weighing the advantages and disadvantages of adopting proportionality to others. If this book has provided a more solid starting-point for such a work, we will be content.

INDEX

administrative law
'administrative law' reasoning by
courts, 130–131
'administratization' of constitutional
law, 8, 129–132
case handling, 98
common law origins, 90–91
contractual freedom and public
policy, 38–39
origins of proportionality, 5–6,
10–11, 24–32
Agranat, Shimon
use of US jurisprudence, 142–143
Albania
adoption of proportionality, 12
Alexy, Robert
concept of rights, 118–119
on proportionality, 51, 128
American constitutional law
adoption of proportionality: gains,
157; objections, 158; resistance
to, 4
balancing *see* balancing
common law legal tradition, 155
concept of rights, 118
concept of state, 54–58
culture of authority *see* balancing
disconnection with European
constitutional law, 3
epistemological skepticism and
see balancing
exceptionalism, 4
German law contrasted
see balancing, proportionality
compared
global influence, 1, 4

institutional division of
responsibilities, 113–115
intent-based model *see* intent-based
constitutional model
interpretative approaches, 119–120
Langdellianism *see* Langdell,
Christopher Columbus
libertarian emphasis, 52–54
Lochner decision *see* *Lochner*
decision
pluralist concept of democracy,
121–122
Progressive movement and anti-
Langdellianism, 34–35
rule-based constitutionalism, 149
uniqueness, 1
American judicial system
finality of judicial decisions, 120–121
German system contrasted, 98
Israeli system contrasted, 97–100
Supreme Court adversarialism, 100–101
Supreme Court remit (docket size),
97–100, 117
American private law
case-by-case, standard-based
approach, 149
origins of balancing in critique of, 33
American public law
case citation in foreign law, 146–147
anti-formalism
anti-Langdellianism, 34–37
anti-Lochnerism, 38–41
balancing as, 32–43
conclusions as to, 43
McCarthy Era, 41–43
see also formalism